WITHDRAWN BY THE
UNIVERSITY OF MICHIGAN

The Lega Nord and Contemporary Politics in Italy

EUROPE IN TRANSITION: THE NYU EUROPEAN STUDIES SERIES

The Marshall Plan: Fifty Years After
Edited by Martin Schain

Europe at the Polls: The European Elections of 1999
Edited by Pascal Perrineau, Gérard Grunberg, and Colette Ysmal

Unions, Immigration, and Internationalization: New Challenges and Changing Coalitions in the United States and France
By Leah Haus

Shadows over Europe: The Development and Impact of the Extreme Right in Western Europe
Edited by Martin Schain, Aristide Zolberg, and Patrick Hossay

German Ideologies since 1945: Studies in the Political Thought and Culture on the Bonn Republic
Edited by Jan-Werner Müller

Defending Europe: The EU, NATO and the Quest for European Autonomy
Edited by Jolyon Howorth and John T. S. Keeler

The Lega Nord and Contemporary Politics in Italy
By Thomas W. Gold

The Lega Nord and Contemporary Politics in Italy

Thomas W. Gold

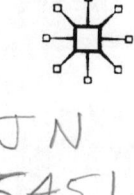

THE LEGA NORD AND CONTEMPORARY POLITICS IN ITALY
© Thomas W. Gold, 2003

All rights reserved. No part of this book may be used or reproduced in any manner whatsoever without written permission except in the case of brief quotations embodied in critical articles or reviews.

First published 2003 by
PALGRAVE MACMILLAN™
175 Fifth Avenue, New York, N.Y. 10010 and
Houndmills, Basingstoke, Hampshire, England RG21 6XS
Companies and representatives throughout the world

PALGRAVE MACMILLAN is the global academic imprint of the Palgrave Macmillan division of St. Martin's Press, LLC and of Palgrave Macmillan Ltd. Macmillan® is a registered trademark in the United States, United Kingdom and other countries. Palgrave is a registered trademark in the European Union and other countries.

ISBN 0–312–29631–2 (hardback)

Library of Congress Cataloging-in-Publication Data
Gold, Thomas W.
  The Lega nord and contemporary politics in Italy/by Thomas W. Gold
    p. cm.—(Europe in transition)
  Includes bibliographical references (p.).
    1. Italy—Politics and government—20th century. 2. Regionalism—Italy—History—20th century. 3. Lega nord. I. Title. II. Europe in transition (New York, N.Y.)

JN5451.G55 2003
324.245'084—dc21   2002032250

A catalogue record for this book is available from the British Library.

Design by Newgen Imaging Systems (P) Ltd., Chennai, India.

First edition: April, 2003
10 9 8 7 6 5 4 3 2 1

Printed in the United States of America.

For Rohan

Contents

List of Tables	ix
List of Figures	x
Acknowledgments	xi
Abbreviations	xiii
Map 1 Italy (Provinces)	xiv
Map 2 Italy (Regions)	xv

Chapter 1   Overview — 1
1. Introduction — 1
2. The Lega Nord within a European Context — 4
3. The Focus of the Book — 7
4. Regional Divisions in Italy: A Question of Culture? — 10
5. Outline of the Book — 11

Chapter 2   The Origins of the Centralized State in Italy — 13
1. Centralization and Expansion during the Risorgimento — 13
2. The Northern Bias of Unification — 22
3. Voices and Movements against Centralization — 25
4. Developments during the Liberal and Fascist Periods — 30
5. Conclusion — 35

Chapter 3   Centralization in the Postwar Period — 37
1. Federalist Ideas and Secessionist Pressures after the War — 37
2. The Postwar Divide between the North and South — 40
3. The Regions and Cold War Politics — 42
4. Regional Reform of the 1970s and Its Failure — 49
5. Conclusion — 52

Chapter 4   The Christian Democrats and the North–South Divide — 55
1. The Shift of the Christian Democrats in the 1960s and 1970s — 55
2. The Southernization of the Christian Democrats — 61

3	Clientelism and the Southern Question	64
4	Trends in the North's Economy	67
5	From the Southern Question to the Northern Question	70
6	The Northern Question and Local Politics	74
7	Conclusion	78

Chapter 5 The Rise of the Lega in the North — 79
1 The Liga Veneta — 79
2 The Lega Lombarda — 81
3 The Regional Nativism of the Lega — 83
4 The Lega Nord — 85
5 *Mani Pulite* and the Demise of the Postwar Party System — 89
6 The Shift to the Practical Politics of Federalism — 92
7 Victory in Milan — 95
8 Conclusion — 97

Chapter 6 The Lega and Federalist Reform in the Late 1990s — 99
1 The Lega as a Party of Government — 99
2 Padania and the Return of Ethno-Regionalism — 103
3 Marches and a Referendum for Secession — 106
4 A More Extremist Party — 108
5 Growing Restlessness in the Northeast — 112
6 The Bicameral Committee for Reform — 114
7 Devolutionary Reforms of the Late 1990s — 116
8 Constitutional Changes — 120

Chapter 7 Conclusions — 123
1 The State and Regionalist Politics in the North — 123
2 The Recent Decline of the Lega — 125
3 The Lega as a Party against Globalization — 127
4 Globalization and the Populist Right in Europe — 129

Appendices — 131
A.1 Electoral results of Italian parties (1948–1992) — 131
A.2 Electoral results of Italian parties (1994–2001) — 132
A.3 Party cartels — 133
A.4 Electoral results of the Lega parties in central and northern Italy, 1983–2001 — 134

Notes — 135

References — 153

Index — 165

List of Tables

2.1	Regional distribution of ministers in Italy, 1859–1900	24
4.1	Disability pensions in relation to all pensions, 1999	58
4.2	Regional per-capita GDP	66
4.3	Industrial districts by region, 1991	69
5.1	Abrogative referendum on party financing, 1993	91
6.1	Survey question: On independence of the North	105
6.2	Survey question: On independence of the North, divided by area	106
6.3	Those who intended to vote for the Lega, 1991/1994/1996	110
6.4	Social basis of support for the Lega, 1996	112
6.5	Tax receipts and contributions per level of government	119

List of Figures

4.1	The southernization of the DC electorate	63
4.2	Percent of taxes paid to the Public Administration per geographic area	72

Acknowledgments

A number of organizations and individuals have helped me in some way or form in the preparation of this book. Initial research in the summer of 1993 was funded by a short-term grant from the Research Institute for the Study of Man in New York. During this trip to Milan, I gained a great deal of insight into the then newly evolving Italian political context from my discussions with Laura Balbo, Luigi Graziano, Paolo Natale, and Renato Mannheimer.

The bulk of my research was conducted in two phases in the spring of 1996 and the academic year 1996–1997. Both trips were funded generously, the first in part by a grant from the MacArthur program on Global Change and Liberalism at the New School for Social Research and the second by a Fulbright fellowship.

Numerous experts in both phases of research helped me tremendously in finding resources, materials, and informants. Vittorio Moioli at AASTER in Milan provided me with crucial contacts as well as information on the Lega Nord in the province of Bergamo. The people working in the different offices of the Lega furnished me with numerous party documents, materials, and information, and gave me a rare inside look at the party. Moreover, the Department of Political Science at the University of Bologna also generously provided office space and access to computer facilities, assets that facilitated my research a great deal. I would also like to thank Massimiliano Giamprini, Giuseppe Bortolussi, Paolo Zabeo, Luigi Santambrogio, Stefano Bartolini, Piero Ignazi, Silvia d'Alonzo, Umberto Bortolin, Paride Principi, and many others, for their assistance and hospitality while I was in Italy.

In addition, I am most grateful to those who read and commented on major parts of the manuscript. Many of the original ideas for the book were first explored during my graduate work at the New School for Social Research in New York, where students, professors, and my dissertation committee—Ari Zolberg, David Plotke, and Charles Tilly—encouraged me to hone my ideas and explore new angles. I would particularly like to thank Ari for his support, encouragement, and guidance over the years. In addition, Marco Giugni read through the entire manuscript and provided a thorough, constructive critique and also gave me a place to stay while conducting research in Italy. I would also like to express my appreciation for the cooperation and advice of Martin Schain and the editors at Palgrave whose comments helped me tighten the book's argument. Needless to say, responsibility of the final version rests with the author.

Finally, I am greatly indebted to my family who saw me through the writing of this book. My wife Shyama read and reread earlier drafts and listened to me patiently as I hashed out ideas before putting them on paper. My son Rohan provided me with the reminder that there was a life outside of the computer screen. I dedicate this book to him.

Abbreviations

AC	Azione Cattolica (Catholic Action)
ALIA	Associazione Liberi Imprenditori Autonomisti (Association of Free Entrepreneurs for Autonomy)
AN	Alleanza Nazionale (National Alliance)
CGIA	Confederazione Generale Italiana Artigiana (General Confederation of Artisans)
CGIL	Confederazione Generale Italiana del Lavoro (General Confederation of Labor)
CISL	Confederazione Italiana Sindacati Lavoratori (Confederation of Workers' Unions)
Coldiretti	Confederazione Nazionale Coltivatori Diretti (National Confederation of Small Farmers)
Confcommercio	Confederazione Generale Italiana del Commercio (General Confederation of Trade, Tourism, Services, and SMEs)
Confindustria	Confederazione Generale dell'Industria Italiana (General Confederation of Italian Industry)
DC	Democrazia Cristiana (Christian Democratic party)
DS	Democratici di Sinistra (Democratic Left)
FI	Forza Italia ("Go Italy")
LIFE	Liberi Imprenditori Federalisti Europei (Free Entrepreneurs for a Federalist Europe)
MSI	Movimento Sociale Italiano (Italian Social Movement)
PCI	Partito Comunista Italiano (Communist party)
PDS	Partito Democratico della Sinistra (Democratic party of the Left)
PIU	Padani Imprenditori Uniti (United Entrepreneurs of Padania)
PPI	Partito Popolare Italiano (Popular party)
PSI	Partito Socialista Italiano (Socialist party)
RC	Rifondazione Comunista (Refounded Communists)
SME	Small-medium enterprises
UIL	Unione Italiana del Lavoro (Italian Workers' Union)

Map 1   Italy (Provinces)

Map 2 Italy (Regions)

CHAPTER 1

Overview

1. Introduction

In early May 1997, a group of eight youths occupied the famous bell tower located in Piazza San Marco, the central square in Venice. Armed with a loaded, Second World War era machine gun and a makeshift "tank" that was constructed from farm equipment and capable of shooting a long flame, the group was able to remain in the tower for a night. The next day, the *Carabinieri* successfully intervened and removed them from the historic monument. The group, which was seeking the secession of the Veneto, the region that surrounds Venice, from the rest of Italy, had hoped to stay in the tower until May 12th, the two hundredth anniversary of the demise of the Republic of Venice. Once they were taken into custody, the members of the group, which called themselves the *Veneta Serenissima Repubblica* (the original name of the Venetian Republic), declared themselves "political prisoners."

This strange and unexpected event made international headlines as the mainstream press both ridiculed[1] the actions of the young men and expressed concern about a return of domestic terrorism by making comparisons to the Red Brigades, the leftist guerrilla group of the 1970s and 1980s. The local attitude in the Veneto, however, was fairly supportive of the "8 of Venice," with many people calling them heroes and asking for their release from prison. A full-scale investigation by the state showed that the group was tied to an extensive network of Venetian separatists, complete with another makeshift tank, propaganda, lists of numerous other members, and an ideological head, Giuseppe Segato, a writer of Venetian history and culture. The group was further linked to a mysterious series of illegal broadcasts on national television that had been calling for the return of the Venetian Republic and warning of a "spectacular action" to mark the anniversary of its fall.

At any other time, the bell tower affair would have been written off as a youthful escapade at the hands of a group of Venetians expressing pride in their local culture. Instead, the actions of the 8 of Venice heated up an ongoing crisis of national unity in Italy that had been brewing for years as a result of the success of the Lega Nord (Northern League). The Lega is a regionalist party that, since the 1980s, has been calling for greater autonomy and even secession for the northern regions of the country. The core of the party's support base rests in Lombardy and the Veneto, two of the wealthiest regions in Italy and of Europe in general.

The Lega grew during the 1990s from a marginal, folkloristic regional movement to a leading political party, holding important ruling positions, including the mayor's seat in Milan (the financial capital of Italy), and numerous regional and communal councils. In 1996, the Lega received considerable international attention after it became the strongest party in the North during national elections and began calling for the independence of the northern regions from the rest of Italy. Despite recent declines at the polls, the Lega remains an influential political force and is currently part of a national coalition of right-wing parties that now holds the reigns of government.

In addition to its focus on regional issues, the Lega has also been one of the most vocal anti-immigrant forces in Italy, that, similar to many other populist Right parties in Europe, has been demanding tighter border controls and more restrictive immigration legislation. The Lega's leader, Umberto Bossi, also shares many of the characteristics of other populist right-wing leaders in Europe, such as his frequent lapses into racist language, similar to that of Jörg Haider in Austria and Jean-Marie Le Pen in France.

The growth of the Lega in the 1990s has been a significant event in Italy for a number of reasons, including the fact that it broke a long-standing pattern of electoral stasis. For much of the postwar period, the Italian party system suffered from considerable immobility as it was monopolized by three major political parties, the Christian Democratic party (DC), the Communist party (PCI), and the Socialist party (PSI).[2] The Lega was one of the first non-traditional political parties to pull enough votes away from these forces—particularly the more center-right DC—to become a serious contender in the North.

Moreover, despite its regional limitations within the North, the Lega has had a major impact on the national political agenda in Italy. Although regionalist movements and parties have always been a part of the political landscape in Italy, they have generally been marginalized within smaller, ethnically specific enclaves, such as the French-speaking Valle d'Aosta—the least populated region in Italy—and the German-speaking Alto-Adige (South Tyrol), where they have fought primarily for linguistic rights. Similarly, separatist forces in the island regions of Sicily and Sardinia have only played brief roles in national politics at different periods in the nineteenth and twentieth centuries.

In contrast the Lega has been a much more influential political force, whose divisive rhetoric of secession and northern autonomy has helped usher in a number of devolutionary reforms in the last few years. The most recent effort has been the revision of the Italian constitution in a federal direction, transferring a considerable degree of power to the subnational levels. The new devolutionary measure, which was not initiated by the Lega but by a leftist coalition that was in power before the current right-wing one, passed a national referendum by a wide margin in October of 2001. Although the success of this new law is still being measured, it reflects a considerable effort on the part of all Italian parties to reform the centralized and cumbersome state structure.

The Lega's divisive rhetoric has also led to a considerable debate in Italy about the strength of national unity. Although there is little fear of the prospect of the country's dissolution, the Lega's call for secession has further politicized the division between the wealthier North and poorer South, a divide that has existed since the establishment of the Kingdom of Italy in the mid-nineteenth century. More recently, this divide has become worse as global trends appear to favor the more dynamic economy of the North, while the South remains a regional economic backwater and one of the poorest areas of Europe. The Lega has also exploited long-standing animosities toward southerners that exist, and have existed for generations, across the North, as well as more concrete concerns about the fiscal burdens of an underdeveloped South that relies heavily on government largess for survival. In doing so, the Lega has put into question the notions of national solidarity and social equality that have kept the country together for a century and a half.[3]

The emergence of the Lega raises a number of questions that this book seeks to answer. In the first place, we need to understand the factors that account for the support of the Lega's regionalist populism. In addition, why has this support been strongest in the wealthiest areas of the country? Moreover, what factors have enabled a new political force like the Lega to break the domination of the traditional postwar political parties? Finally, what has been the impact of the Lega on Italian politics? Before we begin to address these questions, however, we need to place the Lega within a broader, European context to understand the type of movement it represents.

2. The Lega Nord within a European Context

As many observers have pointed out, the Lega is similar to many populist Right parties in Europe, which have surged in support over the past couple of decades.[4] As in many other European countries, immigration started to become an issue in Italy in the late 1980s when it started to receive more people than it sends, a radical shift for a country that had known primarily *emigration*. Since this time, there have been various changes in immigration legislation and efforts to close the country's notoriously porous borders to make it more difficult for people to enter. Similar to parties like the French National Front and the Austrian Freedom Party, the Lega has exploited fears about immigration, using immigrants as scapegoats for other national problems, from unemployment to rising crime. Despite the fact that the number of foreign residents in Italy is still relatively small, around 5 percent of the population, the Lega warns Italians that the current "flood" of immigrants into the country is detrimental to social stability and the economy.

In addition, the Lega uses the same language as the French New Right (*Nouvelle Droite*), which justifies its anti-immigrant position in favor of a "differentialist" view of the world, arguing that differences between cultures and races should be maintained in order to preserve them. For the New Right, the "real" racists are the people who favor integration and multiculturalism, because such processes destroy cultural differences. The New Right uses the language of "anti-racism" (promoting diversity, celebrating different cultures, etc.) to justify a desire to not mix (mixophobia) and retain racial purity.[5] Such an intolerant worldview has been expressed by politicians like Jean-Marie Le Pen, for example, who has stated that he has no issue with Arabs, as long as they stay in North Africa and do not come to France. Umberto Bossi has also stated "the blackest of the black has the same rights as my neighbor, but in his own country."[6] The Lega has also invited members of the French New Right to Italy and has published articles written by their most prominent thinker, Alain de Benoist, in their party newspaper.

The wide appeal of the ideas of the New Right as well as the general rise in populist Right parties represents in part a growing intolerance within Europe as every country becomes increasingly diverse and multicultural. It also shows that European governments have, by and large, failed to effectively integrate immigrants, many of whom continue to live in the margins of society, often working illegally or in low wage positions. The populist Right, however, is not just a product of immigration and racism, but also a changing political context within Western Europe.

Like other populist Right parties, the Lega has also successfully mobilized an increasingly unstable electorate that has become more and more dissatisfied with the centrist, catchall nature of the traditional political parties. The Lega has presented itself as a kind of anti-party party, opposed to the corruption and clientelism that colored many of the traditional Italian parties during the postwar period. Such a position helped the Lega tremendously in the early 1990s when a series of corruption trials uncovered an extensive network of kickbacks into party coffers. The Lega used the issue of corruption to springboard their then status as a new, "clean" force in contrast to the "dirty" tactics of parties like the Christian Democrats (DC) and the Socialists (PSI), which were eventually wiped out as a result of the trials.

The Lega, however, is not just a xenophobic party that has capitalized on the issues of anti-immigration and anti-partyism, but also a regionalist movement that has gathered support on the issues of federalism, secession, and generally greater local autonomy for the North. The Lega's efforts to devolve powers are consistent with current regionalist tendencies in Europe, where the subnational levels of government are becoming more and more politically active everyday. This has been particularly the case for the regions, a level of government between the municipal and the national level, which since the early 1990s have been represented in the European Union (EU) with their own institution, the Committee of the Regions, giving them a greater voice in European affairs. In addition, practically all of the major regions across Europe have opened offices in Brussels in order to lobby European institutions and gain more influence as the Continent becomes more integrated.[7]

Moreover, decentralization has become a leading mantra for policy makers and politicians across the world today. As one observer has noted, we are witnessing a new "paradigm shift" in policy making, from the postwar strategy of centralized planning to federalism and the devolution of power.[8] As a result of this new thinking, there have been a number of efforts toward the decentralization of state powers, such as in the United Kingdom where, after years of calling for greater local control, the Scottish and Welsh have recently gained a degree of autonomy with the establishment of their own regional parliaments. Most European countries have gone through similar devolutionary reforms, in recent decades, that have shifted power toward the subnational levels of government. Even the French state—arguably one of the most centralized among advanced industrialized nation-states—has ceded some of its own power to subnational bodies.

In addition, ethno-regional tensions continue to persist in European countries, leading to the break up of Yugoslavia and Czechoslovakia during the past decade. Such tensions, however, are not limited to parts of the newly democratizing East but can also be found in the West. Thus, for example, extremists continue to fight for separation in places like the Basque region in Spain and Corsica in France. These and other examples defy many of the long-held assumptions that economic development and social mobility within advanced industrialized countries would eventually undermine provincial local attachments and lead to more unified national cultures.

Overall, as globalization makes the world a smaller place, the subnational level is becoming increasingly politicized and mobilized. Although it is much too early to talk about any "end of the nation-state" as many have in recent years, the hegemony of the centralized state is clearly being challenged by current regionalist pressures.[9] Furthermore, while the "Europe of the Regions"—the idea of an EU where regional boundaries have replaced national ones—will not appear anytime in the near future, the issues of decentralization and devolution of power continue to exist as leading political concerns across the Continent.[10]

Moreover, the desire for regional autonomy is no longer viewed as a traditional defense of provincial values, but rather as a necessary democratic process that brings power closer to the people.[11] This is particularly true of newer regionalist movements that focus more on social and economic concerns of the region rather than on cultural and linguistic ones. As a result, there has emerged a new context in which smaller is considered better—smaller (regional) economies and cultures ruled by smaller (regional/local) powers.

The Lega has, moreover, emerged within the wealthy North, resembling a kind of "revolt of the rich" phenomenon that can be found in other parts of the world today. For example, in the early 1990s, the region of Tatarstan, an area rich in oil, bargained for and gained a significant degree of independence from the rest of the Russian federation to essentially become its own republic. Similarly, Slovenia and Croatia—the wealthier and more productive areas of the former Yugoslavia—were the first to separate from the federal republic. Moreover, the split that divided Czechoslovakia into two republics was divided along economic as well as ethnic lines. And although the drive to secede was initiated by the relatively poorer Slovakians, the Czechs soon saw the benefit of discarding what was essentially an economic ball and chain and came around to supporting the split. Finally, within the EU, Catalonia (Spain), Baden-Württemberg (Germany), Lombardy (Italy), and Rhône Alpes (France) came together in the late 1980s to form the Four Motors of Europe, a lobby group that represents these wealthy and economically strong regions. Arguing that they are essentially the "engine" that pulls the Continent economically, these regions have bypassed their national capitals in order to share information across borders on how to best preserve economic prosperity within their own regions.

The current trend toward globalization of the economy provides a greater incentive for wealthier regions to secede or at least bargain for more autonomy. Because globalization stresses economic competition, wealthier regions are more apt to see greater advantage in "going it alone," separating themselves from the burdensome responsibility of supporting poorer, less productive regions. Greater regional autonomy would also enable wealthy regions to use their funds the way they see best for themselves. Thus, for example, a wealthy region would find it more in their interest to use public funds to support infrastructural developments—such as telecommunications and airports—that would facilitate existing competitive industries, rather than having the funds go toward subsidies to prop up poorer regions.

3. The Focus of the Book

The story of the Lega, however, is a complex one, which cannot simply be reduced to the growth of an increasingly xenophobic electorate or a revolt of the rich regions. In order to understand the Lega, we need to go beyond simply identifying larger trends in European politics that have produced populist right-wing parties and regionalist movements. Rather, we need to understand the political and social dynamics that have created the issues from which the Lega has emerged. Specifically, we need to understand what factors account for the growing regionalist cleavage between the North and South of Italy, and how this has especially affected the North. In addition, we need to understand why this cleavage has become so deep over the past couple of decades as to produce a regional populist party like the Lega in northern Italy. This book argues that the regionalist cleavage between the North and South, which has produced the Lega, is itself a product of three interrelated factors: the crisis of the centralized state structure, recent economic changes in the North, and the patronage politics of the postwar political parties.

As numerous observers have pointed out, the Italian state has, until recently, been highly centralized as the central government in Rome plays a dominant role in the administration and organization of the average Italian's life, from taxation to the distribution of welfare benefits and education. In contrast, the subnational levels of government: the regions, provinces, and communes (municipalities) have all been relatively weak, lacking in power and access to resources. In addition to this, there has been a considerable degree of involvement of the state in the economy, from the establishment of state holding companies, to the distribution of state subsidies for industries in underdeveloped areas. Primarily as a result of the state's intervention, Italy ranked lowest of all advanced industrialized countries in terms of its "economic freedom" in the late 1990s.[12]

The Lega represents in many ways a long tradition of movements that have attempted to devolve power from the central state in Italy. During the Risorgimento, the mid-nineteenth century movement to unify the country, there were a few calls for a more decentralized federalist system. Such plans, however, were rejected by the Piedmontese state-makers who feared that any form of decentralization would unravel the nascent country's fragile unity. In fact, because of the regionally diverse nature of the country the Piedmontese decided to adopt their own Napoleonic administrative system, which gave considerable power to the central government. The state would go through little change during the later liberal period of the late nineteenth century, reaching its height of centralization during the fascist period in the form of the corporatist state.

After the Second World War, pressures to decentralize the state led to the establishment of the regions, a level of government between the center and provincial levels in the constitution of 1948. The realization of the regions, however, would be blocked for decades, by the dominant, center-right ruling parties, which feared that a stronger regional level would give more power to the locally rooted Left. Even after a series of reforms eventually led to the activation of the regions in the 1970s, this level of government has proven to be weak over the past thirty years, with few exclusive powers and resources.[13]

The Italian state, however, reached a crisis point in the early 1990s, becoming increasingly bureaucratic and unresponsive to citizen's needs. The state was, moreover, facing a budgetary crisis that prevented the country from meeting the EU's convergence criteria and threatened to keep the country from adopting the Euro with the rest of its partners. In fact, as a result of its high deficit, Italy had to exit from the early monetary union in 1992, a serious loss of face for a country that was one of the founding members of the European Community and one that has always been highly supportive of an integrated Europe.

The centralized state was also becoming an impediment to economic developments in the North. By the mid-1990s, entrepreneurs began talking of a "Northern Question," calling for a reform of the highly bureaucratized state structure and heavy fiscal pressures that, they argued, kept them from competing effectively on an international level. The angriest entrepreneurs were those occupied with small-scale industries, set within many industrial districts.[14] Although small-scale industries have been an integral part of the central and northern Italian economy for generations, the 1970s and 1980s saw a considerable increase in their productivity, shifting the economic engine of the country from the Northwest to the Northeast in recent years. This sector began to call for devolution of state power as they argued that the distant bureaucracy in Rome was incapable of dealing with the rapid shifts and changes taking place in the industrial districts and the global economy in general.

The growth of small-scale industries has also hardened the regional gap between the North and South. While the North has developed an independent middle class of small-scale entrepreneurs, the South has remained dependent on the state. The gap between the North and South, however, is not simply the product of variation in economic development between the two regions but also due to the specific actions on the part of political elites. Since the unification of the country, the ruling parties have used public resources to co-opt the poorer South, a move that has made the region dependent on the largess of the state. These dynamics continued into the postwar period with the actions of the DC, the dominant ruling party until only recently, creating a massive patronage system that turned the poorer South into a vote bank. The actions of the DC left the South largely underdeveloped as it did little to contribute to local industry.

Postwar clientelism, however, also had a major impact on the North, the latter becoming more associated with economic and industrial development and less integrated into the central state structure. Moreover, the DC drew resources from the North to pay for its patronage networks, turning the region into the "tax payer" of the country while the South remained the "tax receiver." This increased the fiscal burden of the North, and further perpetuated the notion of Rome as a predatory state that was undermining and blocking economic development in the North, particularly for smaller industries with little political clout. Thus, rather than being an instrument of national integration, national parties like the DC became a divisive influence on Italian society, widening further the gap between the North and South.[15]

Within this changing economic and political context, the Lega has emerged as a viable political force capitalizing on the increasingly hardened regional cleavage. The Lega has been effective at presenting northern identity as a "community of interests" that is threatened by a series of enemies ranging from southerners and high taxes to the bureaucracy in Rome.[16] The Lega has been helped by the fact that the diffusion of industrial districts has consolidated regional interests in the North within a tight-knit community. In particular, the industrial districts have created a territorially defined community with a "distinct civil society" in the North, particularly in the Northeast where such industries are most common.[17] The people in these areas share similar values pertaining to work ethics and entrepreneurship, as well as mutual concerns about local businesses, such as fiscal burdens and bureaucratic red tape. Part of the Lega's early success depended on its capacity to mobilize this electorate that was seeking a stronger voice for their social and economic concerns in the North.

4. Regional Divisions in Italy: A Question of Culture?

The theoretical framework of this book raises some important questions about the nature of regional divisions within Italy, an issue that has been the focus of observers for generations. In one of the most controversial works on the subject, Robert Putnam attempts to trace the origins of this divide to culture, or the varying developments of civic associations between the North and South.[18] The better performing regional governments in the North, Putnam argues, is a product of a society that is rich in civic associations, a situation that has also provided the necessary groundwork for a more effective local economy. The South, however, has lacked such a civic society with abundant "social capital," and as a result has poorly performing regional governments and a stalled economy. This book demonstrates, however, that existing regional divisions between the North and South are not simply a consequence of cultural differences but rather the result of actions by national political elites, from the Risorgimento till today. In particular, it shows that the clientelist actions of national elites have exacerbated the divide for their own political gain, with a general disregard for its larger impact. Moreover, the clientelist politics of parties like the DC helped to keep the South lagging by encouraging widespread corruption, a factor that has led to a negative business climate, which has undermined the capacity of the region to build an effective economy.

The rise of the Lega Nord itself raises a host of questions about Putnam's analysis of the North of Italy. If the North is such an area of good governance, then why is it rebelling against the political *status quo*?

Moreover, if this is a relatively more civic area of the country, then why has it produced a decidedly uncivic, populist Right party like the Lega Nord? The emergence of a populist movement like the Lega in the North—not the South—suggests that not all is well in the more "civic" parts of the country, and that the problem rests not with culture but the nature of the country's national institutions. As this book will show, the choices by the Piedmontese during the Risorgimento to impose a highly centralized Napoleonic state structure led to the growth of weak local governments, both in the North, Center and South. This move went completely against the polycentric nature of the peninsula, which cried out for a federalist solution that would respect the different political and cultural traditions of the various regions.[19] Despite minor reforms since the Risorgimento, the subnational level has become an ineffective arena of governance in Italy, a situation made worse by the fact that they have traditionally lacked any degree of fiscal autonomy, which robbed local authorities of their own resources. The regions have been the biggest disappointment, becoming, essentially, appendages of the central government. As a result, the weaker local authorities have been unable to respond effectively to emerging economic and social issues across the country.

5. Outline of the Book

Chapters 2 and 3 examine in detail the dynamics of state centralization and the efforts to devolve power to the subnational level. Chapter 2 focuses specifically on the Risorgimento and the later liberal and fascist periods, while chapter 3 examines the postwar period up to the mid-1990s. Chapter 4 diverges from the question of state centralization to address the postwar political and economic factors that have contributed to increasing regional divisions between the North and South. Much like chapter 3, the focus of chapter 4 is on the role of the DC, with a particular emphasis on the party's clientelism and creation of a vote bank in the South. Chapter 4 also addresses the economic changes in the Northeast and its impact on local politics.

Chapter 5 examines the rise of the Lega up to the early 1990s, focusing on its mobilization strategy and its capacity to replace the DC as the leading party in the North. Chapter 6 examines the Lega in the late 1990s at the party's peak when its call for secession from the rest of the country led to a national crisis. Chapter 6 also examines how the Lega began to face increasing competition from other parties as well as from ongoing devolutionary reforms that have threatened to take much of the wind out of the party's sails. Overall, the reforms of the late 1990s have gone a considerable way in making Italy more "federalist." Finally, chapter 7 concludes the book by presenting the most recent view of the Lega and raises some additional questions about globalization and the rise of populist right-wing politics in Europe.

CHAPTER 2

The Origins of the Centralized State in Italy

1. Centralization and Expansion during the Risorgimento

The crisis of the Italian state has its origins in the mid-nineteenth century Risorgimento—the process of unification that brought the different regions of the peninsula together. The northwestern region of Piedmont (Kingdom of Sardinia)[1] united what is now known as Italy through a process of diplomacy, coercion, and war. The first serious attempt at unification took place during the wave of revolutions that occurred across Europe in 1848–1849. At the time, Piedmont supported rebellions in various regions that were under the control of the Austro-Hungarian Empire and other regional power-holders, like the Papacy in central Italy. During this time, for example, the Veneto in northeastern Italy briefly declared its independence from Austria, as did Rome from the Pope.

After these failed attempts, unification would have to wait another decade when Piedmont's victory against Austria allowed it to annex the northwestern region of Lombardy in 1859. Shortly thereafter, Piedmont was able to annex most of the independent central regions, specifically the Duchies of Parma and Modena, as well as the Grand Duchy of Tuscany. This, however, did not involve fighting but rather a series of plebiscites that asked whether or not the different republics wanted to join a larger Kingdom of Italy.

By 1861, the "Thousands" volunteer army under the republican Giuseppe Garibaldi conquered Sicily and the mainland South, then under the rule of the Bourbons. After the South, Piedmont was able to finally annex the Veneto after it fought and won another war against

Austria as an ally of Prussia. At this point, the only piece that remained outside of a whole Italy were the Papal States surrounding Rome, which were being guarded by French troops. Finally, during the Franco-German war in 1870, Italy defeated the French troops on its soil and was thus able to reclaim the capital for its own.[2] The rift that this caused with the Church would remain strong until the reparations made by Mussolini in the early 1920s (see below).

In spite of the success of the Piedmontese state-makers at unifying Italy, the country still remained a divided nation in the mid to late nineteenth century. This led one statesman at the time to remark that they had made Italy, but they had yet to make Italians. Socially, the country was significantly divided by extensive problems of poverty and high illiteracy. Moreover, there was practically no common language as many people communicated in regional and local dialects. It is interesting to point out that even Camillo Cavour, the Piedmontese count who is credited for leading the Risorgimento, used to prefer writing in French. Clearly, this is due to the fact that Piedmont was once part of the French Savoy Dynasty. However, it also demonstrates how even the new elite of the country felt little attachment to an Italian national culture and felt closer to a broader, European one.

In addition, the peninsula lacked adequate roads and railroad systems, cutting off many of the peripheral, rural areas from urban centers. The provincialism of the country was, moreover, made worse by its geography, with the Alps blocking it from the modernizing developments taking place in northern Europe at the time.[3]

Further, the Risorgimento did not provide Italy with a strong national myth that would have rallied the country and its people.[4] Unlike the French revolution, the Risorgimento was not a popular revolution led by common people, but rather a movement led by intellectuals and other elites. Unification was something that was more or less imposed from above and not something that emerged spontaneously from below. It only made matters worse that at the time Italy was hardly a democracy with only a fraction of the population able to vote and have a say in government.

Overall, the Risorgimento, unlike the French revolution, did not intend to radically change the social and economic balance that existed in Italian society at the time. Rather, the unifiers sought and succeeded in pulling the country away from the foreign powers, such as the Austrians and the Bourbons, which had dominated the peninsula for generations. Such an effort did not involve the active participation of the wider population.

Ironically, the only institution that could have played a larger role in unifying the whole country ideologically, the Catholic Church, officially opposed the Risorgimento and the Italian state![5] In protest to the annexation of the former Papal States and the usurpation of his temporal power, the Pope refused to recognize the Italian state and became a voluntary "prisoner" in the Vatican in 1870.[6] The rift between the Vatican and Italy would persist for over 62 years until the Lateran Treaty (Concordat) of 1929 that gave the Church certain concessions and a financial settlement in return for its recognition of the Italian state. Until the Treaty, the Church even prohibited its followers from participating in politics.

Without a national unifying myth or ideology, the new country emerged with a weak national identity. In addition to the Papal States, other regions briefly retained ties to their respective (Bourbon and Hapsburg) *ancien régimes* during the unification process, therefore loyalty to the new Kingdom of Italy was in short supply beyond Piedmont. The top-down process of unification was resented in the ex-states similar to the way "Bavarians and Hanoverians in Germany felt some rancor against the Prussian unifiers."[7] Most of this resentment, however, was felt in areas of the country that had experienced a previous history of independence. In particular, the Veneto, the last northern region to be annexed, was upset about unification as this meant replacing their republican institutions with the autocratic monarchism of the new Kingdom.[8]

The leader of the new Kingdom moreover did very little to smooth over the fact that Piedmont remained the dominant region. For example, the Piedmontese king, Vittorio Emanuelle II, refused to change his title to Emanuelle I, in recognition of the start of a new kingdom. Rather, his choice of Emanuelle II demonstrated a desire to continue with Piedmont's dominance over the rest of the country.

In order to deal with the centrifugal forces that had the potential to divide the country permanently, the Piedmontese state-makers were eager to create an administrative system that would subjugate the different ex-states to a single authority. In their view, the best option was a strong centralized state, as opposed to a more federal situation that would have given significantly more power to the subnational levels of government. The unifiers believed that centralization was the "only way of forging the states and petty principalities that constituted the new country into a nation."[9]

The first step in this direction was the extension of Piedmont's own constitutional charter known as the Statuto Albertino, or the Albertine Statute. As the document was written only in 1848 for King Charles of Piedmont, it contained a number of modern ideas that many of the ex-states lacked in their own, previous constitutions. For example, the Statute applied the principle of the separation of powers between the executive and parliament. However, despite the progressive aspects of the document, the application of this new Statute was done in an authoritarian manner that ruffled more than a few feathers in various regions of the country. In particular, the Statute was applied without making any concessions to local traditions and institutions.[10] Moreover, the Statute, which remained in effect from this period up until the creation of the current constitution of Italy in 1948, also gave the monarch considerably more power than his counterparts in northern Europe, particularly in foreign affairs.[11]

In addition to the authoritarian nature of the new king and the constitution that backed him, there were other actions of the unifiers that further alienated regional powers from the new government. One particular issue was the use of the plebiscites that were held in each annexed region to guarantee loyalty to the new Kingdom. The plebiscites, which were meant to give a degree of popular participation to the unification process, were, according to some, "blatantly rigged." In many cases, the plebiscites received 99 percent in support of annexation, a result that could only be achieved through corrupt voting procedures and counting. Thus, rather than giving a sense of legitimacy to the new Kingdom, the plebiscites merely added to the top-down nature of unification and the dominance of the Piedmontese.[12]

Although the king played a significant role in the unification process, most of the early state-formation efforts can be credited to the conservative Right (Destra) party that dominated Italian politics from 1860 to 1876. Although Cavour, the leader of the Right until his death in 1861, came from a classic liberal tradition, early on in the unification process he and other members of his party acquired an appreciation for the type of centralized rule found in other parts of Europe at the time, such as in France.[13] Their primary concern was maintaining unity in the face of diverging regions and interests, chiefly those in the South that presented them with the particularly troublesome task of modernizing the mostly underdeveloped area of the country. The Right was determined to extend the Piedmontese system into the South and saw administrative centralization as "the indispensable tool for holding on to power and for affirming their position as the national ruling class."[14]

Cavour was able to gain wide support for his centralizing strategy by building an extensive, centrist coalition of moderates, from the center-right to the center-left. On either side, the government majority was flanked by a few opposing "extremist" voices: republicans and federalists on the Left and clerical movements on the Right. Although the threat from either revolutionary or reactionary forces was limited, Cavour was concerned with stability at the time. As a result, he focused on a middle path for unification to prevent it from going too far to the Left or Right, or from fading away completely.

The primary manifestation of this centralization was the extension of a Franco-Piedmontese "Napoleonic" administrative system. On the one hand, the French administrative tradition was natural to Piedmont as the region was a former domain of the French Savoy Dynasty. On the other hand, various aspects of the Napoleonic system could be found in the rest of the country as the whole peninsula had been under French rule from 1796 to 1815.[15] In spite of this legacy, Napoleonic traditions did not have anything close to a good reputation in Italy. In particular, French rule during this period was seen as harsh, associated as it was with a colonial relationship between a distant "mother country" and its "acquired territories." As a result, Piedmont's further extension of the Napoleonic system, unfortunately, only added to the image of unification as a foreign imposition from above.

In Italy, the extension of the prefectoral field administrative system across the peninsula played a crucial role in the Right's efforts to centralize the administrative system and unify the country. In an ideal-typical "Napoleonic" administrative system, a country is divided into a single set of administrative regions or districts. In each of these areas, there is a "single national official" (usually called a prefect) who "represents the whole executive branch and is meant to exercise direct authority over all national field agents in the area, regardless of their departmental and bureau affiliations."[16] In other words, the prefect acts as the eyes and ears for the central level, making sure that their representatives on the ground are carrying out the center's directives and staying the course.

In the prefectoral system, power is *deconcentrated* rather than decentralized, as in a federal system. Deconcentration of power involves the delegation of bureaucratic authority to field administration offices in the local territory. Such a system is employed to extend the central government's control and "reduce the forces of localism and enforce uniformity in decision-making across the country."[17] On the contrary, decentralization occurs when political authority is legislated to subnational levels of government. Thus, where deconcentration merely extends the arm of the central government, decentralization gives more power to the subnational level in the legislative and administrative process. Decentralization is therefore "designed to reflect the unique characteristics, problems and needs of different regions and localities."[18] Deconcentration simply imposes the central government's view.

To use the language of rational choice theory, we can say that the prefectoral system represents the "predatory" aspects of rule as it helps to maximize the personal objectives of national leaders and maintains the power of the state.[19] In this way, the prefect is the ultimate symbol of central state authority; he is used to directly control the territory, particularly for the purposes of maintaining social order and political compliance. Although the institution of the prefect officially represents the Ministry of the Interior, it usually has the additional role of a "generalist" supervisor over other field offices.

The prefectoral system developed and reached its peak in nineteenth-century France. At this time, the prefect was the central state's most important official in the local territory, with veto powers over other ministries as well as over the municipalities within his jurisdiction. In the words of Chaptal in his description of the prefect in his *Corps legislatif*:

> The Prefect ... transmits orders to the Sub-Prefect; this latter, to the Mayors, of towns, boroughs and villages ... in such a way that the chain of command descends without interruption from the Minister to the subject and transmits the law and orders of the Government ... with the rapidity of electric fluid![20]

The prefectoral system started to take shape in Italy in 1859 with the first local government act that set into motion the division of the country into provinces, districts, and communes (municipalities).[21] There are currently 103 provinces in the country, with over 8,000 communes (see map 1). At this point the unifiers did make somewhat of an effort to appeal to local sentiments by changing the names of various state institutions to make them seem less Piedmontese and "more acceptable" to the ex-states where similar institutions had existed under different terms.[22]

In spite of these cosmetic name changes, many of the ex-states did not welcome the new administration and the way it eradicated preexisting administrative traditions. For example, Lombardy had attempted and failed to gain recognition for their distinctive administrative traditions, such as their *convocato degli estimati*, or roughly a "local taxpayers' democracy," which gave a degree of autonomy to peasants to control their own land.[23] Overall, regions like Lombardy and Tuscany, which had benefited from more decentralized structures before unity, did not care much for the highly centralized nature of the new institutions.[24] Moreover, the new administrative system was introduced to the ex-states in a most authoritarian manner through the use of decree laws and without any parliamentary discussion. The actions of Urbano Rattazi, the conservative Minister of the Interior at the time, were seen as a "severe breach in liberal principles" and further perpetuated the notion of the new state as an imposition on local sovereignty.[25]

The act of 1859 also set out the powers of the prefect, giving him a significant number of responsibilities. Article three of the Act states that the prefect[26] "represents the Executive Power throughout the province" and "provides for the publication and for the execution of the laws." Further, as the chief in charge of public order in the province, the prefect "has the right to dispose of the public police forces and to request the intervention of the armed forces." Finally, he exercises authority over communal and provincial administrations.[27] The powers of the prefect would more or less remain stable until the fascist period when his position was strengthened (more on this below).

However, despite the prefect's access to administrative and coercive powers, his position remained weak in many ways and without a clear role in the governing process. For example, the prefect did not have complete control over the other field offices in his provincial jurisdiction, which had their own, direct link with central government ministries. This situation contrasts with the more "integrated" French system, where the prefect had complete authority over all the field offices, whose policies he supervised, directed, and most importantly, coordinated. The prefect in Italy was mainly used as the field representative for the Ministry of the Interior whose main job was to keep public order.[28]

In many ways, the Italian prefect's inherent weaknesses reflected the nature of the new Italian state that was emerging from the Risorgimento. On the one hand, the prefect facilitated Piedmont's need for control over the country's territory and also their practice of using force and coercion to keep power concentrated in their hands and put down local rebellions. In order to keep support for the governing party, the prefect, along with the police force, was used to rig elections using bribery and patronage as well as force. The prefect "harassed" opponents in elections usually by "denying or cutting off state aid, investigating their administration, dissolving councils that they dominated, and appointed commissioners to run the communes or provinces until new elections and a more favorable outcome could be arranged."[29] This practice, in nineteenth-century Italy, was used equally by both the governments of the Right (1860–1876) and later the Left (Sinistra) (1876–1903). It is ironic that during this so-called liberal period, the role of the prefect actually increased;[30] one would have expected the leaders during this period to be less inclined toward authoritarian rule, as well as more favorable to decentralized forms of government.

On the other hand, the Italian prefect lacked the moral authority needed to effectively execute central government policy. The prefect operated without the legitimacy of a widely shared national myth or progressive/modernizing mission. As a result, the prefect may have had the capacity to wield great coercive force, but only at the cost of his legitimacy and that of the state. In this way, the prefect became a symbol of Piedmontese domination and oppression. The Italian prefect thus repeated the mistakes of his Napoleonic predecessors, half a century before, whose harsh rule was imposed without the benefits of national integration and development.[31]

Centralization of power further resulted in the weakening of the subnational level of government as the central state increased its control over the administrative and fiscal activities of the communal and provincial governments. At the time, the communes had little administrative and political power as the mayors were appointed by the central government. The municipal councils were also under the authority of the prefect, who could easily dissolve them if they felt that local government actions posed a serious threat to public order.[32] The provincial level too was a relatively weak and ineffective arena of government, with few responsibilities and resources.

Many of the calls to deal with the issues of the subnational level of government actually fell on deaf ears in the parliament of the new Kingdom. This is evident by the fact that none of the fourteen local government bills that were drafted between 1861 and 1886 reached the floor to be voted on in the Chamber of Deputies, the lower house of parliament.[33]

Of the entire administrative system, the centralization of the fiscal system probably had the most significant impact on the power of local government. At the time, the Kingdom was having great financial difficulties due to the costs they incurred during the Risorgimento. It is estimated that in 1861, the public debt of Italy was equivalent to around 40 percent of the GDP of that year.[34] There was also a significant deficit, which grew during the 1861–1870 period as the Piedmontese increased their expenditures on infrastructure and the military in order to annex new territory. In 1862 the deficit was 446 million lire, four years later, after the war with Austria over the Veneto, it would almost double to 720 million lire.³⁵ In addition, the Kingdom needed to make a number of necessary expenditures on national infrastructure. Due to the poor situation that the country was in at the time, there was a need to develop such entities as a national telegraph system, post offices, bridges, canals, and especially railroads.³⁶

The government responded to its economic problems by raising taxes across the board and cutting expenditures. In addition, they also centralized the fiscal system by unifying a number of different taxes found in the ex-states, from the different *bollo* (fiscal stamp) systems to the mortgage and land taxes.³⁷ The government also centralized the banking system under the *Banca Nazionale* (National Bank) and issued the Lira as the national currency. This last act effectively took much of the financial power out of the hands of the ex-states, which were now forced to give up their own currencies and the autonomy of their own banks.

The Right's increase of taxes did cause a degree of opposition. In particular, the *macinato* (gristmill tax), which had previously been abolished by the governments of the ex-states, was reinstated in 1869. The tax provoked widespread agitation across the country, particularly in the North, where the protests took on an anti-Risorgimento flavor. For example, many opponents of the tax responded with provocations against the Kingdom such as "long live the Austrian government!" "long live the Pope," and "long live religion," and the like.³⁸ Although the revolts against the gristmill tax did not seriously threaten unification, their messages highlighted the tenuous nature of the new state and the weak legitimacy of the Piedmontese rulers.

Many of the new fiscal policies of the central government caused the local debt to rise. Communal and provincial tax revenues, in fact, diminished during this period, going from 31.1 percent of state revenues in 1869 to 30.6 percent in 1876. Although this does not seem like a significant change, it should be noted that expenditures of the local authorities had also *increased* simultaneously. Thus, while the communes were maintaining budget surpluses in 1868, the communal debt rose to about 540 million lire in 1873, concentrated especially in the large urban centers of Florence, Naples, Milan, and Rome.³⁹ In addition, the central government essentially cut back on resources to local governments, saddling them with unforeseen expenses and forcing them to pull back spending on any new programs.⁴⁰

The centralization of the fiscal system, however, was not just a response to the central government's financial problems. In fact, by 1870, despite the costs incurred by the Risorgimento and infrastructural developments, the budget was almost balanced.⁴¹ Rather, the Piedmontese were concerned about giving too much autonomy to the subnational levels of government, particularly in the South. At the time there was a great deal of preoccupation about continual abuses found across the South in terms of tax collection. Such problems included an undue burden placed on the lower classes, as well as corruption of local officials and a generally inefficient accounting system.[42]

2. The Northern Bias of Unification

In spite of its centralized nature, the state that emerged in Italy in the mid-nineteenth century did little to unify the country. On the contrary, the liberal leaders after the Risorgimento did a great deal to divide the country, widening in particular the gap between the North and the South. Specifically, unification benefited much more the interests of the leading region, Piedmont, and the entire North, in general, over the rest of the country.

On the one hand, the Piedmontese acted in a paternalistic manner toward the South. They were the modernizing region that wanted to "bring the benefits of liberalism" to areas that had only experienced "political corruption."[43] Cavour and his successors felt that the only solution to the "Southern Question"—the intractable problem of poverty and unemployment in the southern regions of the country—was a "vigorous action by a strong central government." Such a system, they argued, was necessary to turn around the South, which had suffered from years of Bourbon mismanagement, corruption, and laxity in government.[44]

This view was to a certain degree on target as the previous Bourbon rulers in the South had accomplished very little in the way of social and economic progress. This laxity produced what eventually became the relatively more underdeveloped region on the peninsula. Not only was poverty extensive but so was lawlessness, as evidenced by the growing strength of groups of bandits in Sicily and the mainland South, which would eventually develop into the various crime organizations that exist across the region. The creation of a centralized administrative structure, it was argued at the time, was the only way to eradicate such ills that were essentially keeping the country behind.

On the other hand, unification resulted in greater benefits for the North than for the South. First, the Kingdom's monetary, credit, fiscal, and commercial policies benefited primarily the interests of industrialists who were located mainly in the North.[45] The unification of Italy also resulted in the expansion of markets for northern industrialists who had been operating under more free-market conditions before unification. In contrast, southern textile manufacturers had benefited from 100 percent protection under the Bourbons. By 1860, the Piedmontese rulers had reduced tariffs to 10 percent, putting southern industrialists at a disadvantage and eventually, due to competition from the North, driving many out of business.[46]

As a result of the new government's industrial policies, a modern industrialized society began to take shape in the North. The new class of entrepreneurs that rose to power in the region began to successfully challenge the entrenched power of the old land-owning elite.[47] The North, particularly the Northwest, would eventually become the birthplace of almost all of Italy's great industrial groups that have dominated the country's economy for most of the past century, from FIAT (Piedmont) to Olivetti (Piedmont) and Pirelli (Lombardy). In contrast, the South remained to a great deal in its feudal past. The power of the gentry and large landowners remained strong, as a similar new community of business leaders and entrepreneurs never took hold in this part of the country.[48] This demonstrates, in part, how regional differences in entrepreneurship and economic development in Italy are to a large extent a product of political decision-making, and not simply culture.

In addition to its industrial policies, the hiring practices of the new administrative bureaucracy also benefited the Piedmontese and the North in general. In particular, there was a considerable degree of "Piedmontization" of the prefectoral corps across the country. From 1861 to 1871, 50 percent of the prefects ruling in the 59 different provinces of the Kingdom were born in the North, while only 20 percent came from the Center and 30 percent from the South.[49] By 1882, the state bureaucracy was still made up primarily of Piedmontese, as well as Tuscans who had entered the state machinery mainly during the six-year period between 1864 and 1870 when Florence (the capital of Tuscany) was designated the interim capital before Rome.[50]

The North would further dominate the central government ministries for the rest of the nineteenth century. Most government ministers from 1859 to 1900 came from one of three northern regions (Piedmont, Lombardy, or Liguria). Thus, for example, the entire mainland South, with almost 27 percent of the population (in 1900), had only 41 out of 174 ministers during this period (about 23 percent). On the other hand, Liguria, with only 3 percent of the population, had 14 ministers (about 8 percent).[51] See table 2.1 for a regional distribution of government ministers.

Table 2.1 Regional distribution of ministers in Italy, 1859–1900*

Region	Number of ministers
Piedmont	47
Lombardy	19
Liguria	14
Sicily	14
Continental South	41
Other regions	39
Total	174

* Politicians who held the position of minister at least once between 1859 and 1900.
Source: Luigi Graziano, "Center–Periphery Relations and the Italian Crisis: The Problem of Clientelism," in *Territorial Politics in Industrial Nations*, ed. Sidney Tarrow, Peter Katzenstein, and Luigi Graziano (New York: Prager, 1977), p. 303.

In addition to state employment, the centralization of the fiscal system also benefited the Piedmontese at the expense of the South. Before unification, Piedmont had the most debt of all the regions in the peninsula. This was due in part to Piedmont's efforts in the 1840s to modernize its infrastructure, which left the former kingdom in massive debt. Most of its debt, however, was brought on by the high cost of maintaining its military, which it needed to fight the various campaigns for unification. In contrast, the Kingdom of the Two Sicilies, the Bourbon dominion that ruled Sicily and the mainland southern regions, had the lowest debt of all the regions before the Risorgimento. By centralizing control over fiscal matters, Piedmont was able to transfer the resources from the South to the North to pay for its debt.[52]

The Kingdom's taxing of the poorer South to pay for the higher debt of the North during the first couple of decades after unification, was further exacerbated by the uneven allocation of state resources. Under the Bourbons, southerners experienced a lax fiscal policy in which taxes were low as well as any public expenditure by the government. The Piedmontese essentially followed the second part of this noninterventionist formula without the first. In other words, they taxed the South as heavily as the North but provided few benefits for the former.

In sum, the Risorgimento had set the foundation for the development of a highly centralized administrative state structure, with a distinct bias toward northern interests. The basis of this structure was the prefectoral field administration system and its emphasis on control by the central level over local territory. The Piedmontese centralizers were led primarily by a fear that giving either political or fiscal autonomy to lower levels of government, particularly in the South, would only encourage an unraveling of the unity that had been carefully put together. Faced with the lack of any national unifying myth and hence a weak national feeling of unity, the Piedmontese relied primarily on coercion and military force. The question remains, however, whether the relative apathy toward unification actually developed into any organized opposition or movement against it.

3. Voices and Movements against Centralization

At the time of the Risorgimento, not everyone favored the development of a centralized state. Even before unification there were public figures that called for the creation of a more decentralized kingdom that would incorporate a certain degree of autonomy to the different regions across the peninsula. One of the best-known pro-federalists of this period was Carlo Cattaneo, an active member of the republican movement that eventually led to the first war for independence against Austria in 1848.

Cattaneo expressed the widely shared notion that Italy differed from other national monarchies in Europe because of its city-state tradition. With such a variety of different cultural centers, Italy, in the words of Cattaneo, is "physically and historically federalist."[53] This opinion was shared by another leader of the republican movement of 1848, Giuseppe Ferrari, who argued that Italy's power structure was "polycentric," and that the designation of a single capital would be an "artificial" solution.[54]

The notion of creating a federalist state first emerged during the earlier republican movements of 1848, when Venice and Rome had briefly declared their independence from their foreign rulers, Austria and the Papal States, respectively. At the time, Cattaneo and other republicans imagined the formation of a Swiss-like confederation of the different regions in Italy. Cattaneo not only saw federalism as a system that would counterbalance the power of Piedmont, but he also felt that such a federation would be more democratic, making it "easier for people to understand political issues, to participate in discussions and elections, and to become accustomed to civic responsibilities."[55]

Although Cattaneo and his ideas on federalism had a strong appeal during this period, the notion of creating a federal Italy during the Risorgimento lost out to centralization. This was due mainly to the fact that the failure of the revolts in 1848 to unify the country convinced Cavour and others that they needed a more centrally coordinated movement to combat foreign domination and liberate Italy. As a result, there were only minimal attempts during the Risorgimento at reducing the strong centralizing tendencies of Piedmont.

The first real effort to decentralize power in Italy occurred during the early post-Risorgimento period. At the time, there was an effort to introduce an additional layer of government by the Minister of the Interior, Marco Minghetti, who, under Prime Minister Cavour, called for the formation of a regional system of government. In his plan, Minghetti argued that regional governments (between the provincial and central state levels) were needed not just to decentralize power but to correct the shortcomings of the provinces, which varied considerably in size, posing potential problems for the consolidation of a universal administrative system. The regions were seen as providing a larger, more uniform layer of government that would more effectively provide administrative services.

Although Minghetti's calls for reform were not necessarily an attempt to introduce a full-fledged federalist structure into the system, his proposed plan, however, would have diffused the powers of the state in an additional layer of government. This would have softened the unification process and put a more benign face on Piedmont. For one thing, the regions would have provided an arena in which the different ex-states could have maintained a degree of autonomy to maintain their administrative traditions, such as Lombardy's taxpayers' democracy. Rather than imposing their structure on the ex-states in an authoritarian manner, Piedmont could have used the regions to bargain with regional elites, taking a more gradual approach.

Moreover, if Minghetti had been successful in his reform efforts, the current regional level of government would have been established long before it actually came about in the constitution of 1948 and eventually established in 1970 (discussed in greater detail in chapter 3). As a result, the federalist tendencies in the Italian system, already apparent in the nineteenth century, would have had greater scope and resources from which to grow and would have institutionalized more regional autonomy in the twentieth century.

In spite of Minghetti's efforts at reform, the issue of regionalization was vetoed by the parliament. The establishment of the regions was seen as providing resources for forces against unification. It was argued at the time that "[t]o establish the region would provide the opponents of national unity with a framework for agitation; it would help nurture the cult of the past; it would detract from faith in national unity."[56] Unification was achieved at great odds, the parliament argued, and they were reluctant to grant any concessions that would have given greater power to Bourbons, other legitimists, clericals, or republicans, and in the process jeopardize national unity. Ironically, Minghetti's plan would probably have had the opposite effect, as it was really the centralizing nature of the new state that caused the most rancor and anti-statist sentiments.

Overall, Minghetti had little political support for his ideas. He had only weak support from Cavour, who was concerned that such a radical idea would alienate members of the delicate coalition that he had put together after the Risorgimento. Cavour was especially careful not to upset the members on the center-left whose sympathies lay with the French system of strong control by the central government.[57] Most of the other leaders of the Risorgimento too would not have tolerated a weakening of the chain of command from the center with the establishment of the regions.

Surprisingly, it was not just the new government that opposed the creation of a regional level of government. The communes and provinces, the two existing levels of government, also greeted the new plan for a regional layer of government with great skepticism. The elites in both these areas saw the establishment of the regions as undermining what little autonomy and power they maintained at that time. Moreover, there was a general feeling at the time that the regional boarders chosen by Minghetti were artificial compared to the more solid and "natural" barriers that divided the communes and provinces. Communal and provincial identities have generally been stronger than either regional or national identities in part due to the legacy of the city-states in Italy. Even geographical rivalries in Italy have generally been between dominant cities—like Rome and Milan—rather than between regions. Only regions like the Veneto and Sicily, areas that have more defined histories—at times as independent republics—and specific regional cultures, have been able to maintain a deep-rooted sense of regional identity that supercede local identity.[58] Moreover, smaller municipalities were concerned that the introduction of a regional layer of government would benefit the dominant cities and place them in a marginal position within the regions.[59]

Ironically, the strong attachment to communal identities in Italy inadvertently facilitated greater centralization. For one thing, a significant number of communal and provincial notables supported the nationalist cause. One reason for this support is the fact that the Piedmontese unifiers co-opted a number of potentially hostile local elites into the new machinery of the state. Moreover, local elites acted as "indispensable mediators between the government and civil society," and thus they played a crucial role in bringing the center and periphery together in the process of unification.[60] Finally, local rivalries between cities fueled the notion that a national ruling class would be a more impartial and incorruptible governing body than a more powerful local elite.[61] This was not necessarily an inaccurate impression, considering the widespread cases of fraud and corruption by local elites, particularly in the South.[62]

In fact, there is significant evidence to prove that communal and provincial authorities were not even eager to increase their own power, particularly in reference to taxation. The communes actually *favored* centralization of the fiscal system because it reduced their own responsibilities of extraction among their local population. Communal authorities were more than happy that the central state received most of the blame for taking away peoples' resources for what was essentially considered an illegitimate government. In the event that the communes needed additional resources the local authorities were content to introduce random additional taxes that were tacked onto central state taxes.[63]

The little opposition from the periphery, which did emerge at the time of the Risorgimento, was weak and disorganized. As mentioned before, Lombardy tried to defend its local government traditions to no avail. Anti-Piedmontese sentiment in the Veneto was strong, probably the strongest in the entire North. The region was the last to be annexed and it opposed the bureaucratic centrism of their new rulers, which was moreover less efficient than that of their former Austrian leaders. And more than any other region, the Veneto was able to draw from its long history of the Venetian Republic, which stretches back to the eleventh century.

The Veneto not only has a long history as an independent republic, it is also the one with the most religiously conservative population. Since unification, the Veneto has been known as the most "white" or Catholic region. Church attendance has always been highest here and various Catholic movements, such as Catholic Action, have found the region to be the most fertile area to mobilize support. At the time, representatives from the Veneto argued about the importance of their local traditions and were particularly concerned about civil marriage and other secular policies that the new government would impose on their region.[64]

There was also a degree of rebelliousness in the South that appeared to threaten the unity of the Kingdom. In this area of the country the Risorgimento had taken on a particularly repressive form, much more than in the North. Although the northern regions were not immune to the pressures of the state—they too felt the grip of Piedmont's efforts to centralize administrative and fiscal powers—the situation was worse in the southern regions. In the South, centralization took on a more colonial relationship between the center and the periphery, and brute repression was used more here than in the North to keep people in line.

Garibaldi himself is partly responsible for the rebelliousness that emerged in the South. After his landing in Sicily and his march up to Naples with the "Thousands" volunteer army, Garibaldi sowed the seeds for future revolts by sympathizing with the deplorable social conditions of the southerners. Further, during his tour of duty in the South, Garibaldi made a number of unfulfilled promises to distribute land after the unification of the country. However, after the Risorgimento, Garibaldi—who was more or less a mercenary hired by Cavour—was not able to keep such promises, causing great ire among the peasants.

As a result, from 1860 to 1865 bands of peasant brigands fought a guerrilla war against both their old landlords as well as their new, yet distant government.[65] Although the brigands were mainly fighting for their land, they inadvertently helped anti-Risorgimento forces. Thus, the local Bourbons who opposed the Piedmontese supported the brigands in their efforts to slow down or prevent unification. Moreover, the brigands were also given help by the papal government in Rome, which sent money and new recruits to the peasants fighting against the Piedmontese.[66] The revolts led to such widespread banditry that Cavour eventually sent in almost half of the Piedmontese army (120,000 soldiers) to restore order. Piedmont acted to squash any additional revolts with the passing of the Pica Law, which suspended constitutional liberties in the South and enabled the police to repress anyone suspected of being a brigand. Despite the repression, the brigands became the nucleus of the gangs that would eventually grow into the organized crime groups like the Mafia in Sicily, as well as the *Camorra* and *'Ndrangheta* that exist on the mainland South.

The revolts in the South, however, only threatened the nascent Kingdom indirectly. Denis Mack Smith, the noted historian of Italy, called it a "minor civil war" that "helped to perpetuate the unfortunate impression that Italy might collapse at any moment."[67] Moreover, the brigands were not politically motivated. Rather, they were driven primarily by unemployment and poverty and thus did not act with great separatist intentions. Moreover, the southern peasants disliked their staunchly feudal Bourbon leaders as much, if not more, than their new, "liberal" Piedmontese rulers. The Bourbons had done little to develop the South socially or economically, keeping their subject population blocked off from the agricultural and industrial revolutions that were occurring in northern Europe at the time.[68] Thus, despite their revolts, southern peasants were at times more patriotic toward the Kingdom than their counterparts in the North.[69] As a result of this animosity, it would have been impossible for the Bourbons to muster any support for a feudal backlash against the Piedmontese and their army.

In spite of the revolts in the South, there was little in the form of constructive mobilization during the early post-Risorgimento period that threatened national unity or the sanctity of the centralized state. Many of the protests were not well organized, taking the form of local "brigandage," and as a result were dismissed as social unrest and repressed by the police. The revolts also lacked leadership after Garibaldi ceased stirring up rebellion and eventually took an oath to the Kingdom of Italy.

4. Developments during the Liberal and Fascist Periods

There was little change in the centralized nature of the state in the late nineteenth and early twentieth centuries. After the fall of the rule of the Right party, the Left then became the dominant force from 1876 to 1903. Although the Left had gained support based on a program of decentralization, they did not make a great deal of progress in this area.

The most important reforms of the state system after the Risorgimento occurred under Francesco Crispi, the Left prime minister during the end of the 1880s and during most of the 1890s. Crispi set into place new laws that gave local government more power and a certain degree of autonomy from the central government. Laws in 1889 and 1896 gave the provincial governments more autonomy by making a clearer delineation of powers between the provincial government (the Provincial Administrative Junta) and the prefect. In the process, the prefect was removed as the head of the provincial government and from this point onwards the provincial juntas would elect their own president. The new laws also gave the communal councils the right to choose their mayors, a significant achievement as the capacity to appoint mayors had given the Crown a considerable amount of leverage, which they had used in the past to influence and manipulate local elites.[70]

In spite of these changes, the communes and provinces still lacked funds and power. They had limited resources and many of their duties were frequently transferred to the prefectoral boards, chambers of commerce, or state field offices.[71] And although the communes enjoyed more responsibilities than in the past, the central state was always in the background and could easily interfere in their affairs when needed. Thus, for example, local tax revenues were often appropriated when the central state needed to balance its own budget.[72] Moreover, the prefect still retained a degree of control over the subnational levels of government, including his access to the police and army and his ability to fix elections.

Further, the entrance of the Left into government did little to change regional divisions within the country between the North and South. Although the deputies of the Left came mainly from the South (Crispi was a Sicilian), the party did little in terms of initiating radical reforms that would have improved the region's position vis-à-vis the North. On the contrary, the Left was instrumental in starting the whole process of clientelism in the South, an unofficial policy that has kept the region behind the North ever since. Rather than putting forth a progressive program for reform of the South, the Left simply sought out positions in the government for its supporters. This strategy kept its urban middle-class supporters happy, as they were eager to use the new government machinery to improve their own social mobility.

The Left's strategy of *trasformismo* also had a major impact on Italian politics up to today. *Trasformismo* (transformation) refers to the way the Left transformed itself, under the leadership of Agostino Depretis from 1876 to 1887, from a potentially progressive reformer to a force that sought out a centrist coalition to stay in power. The party accomplished this by co-opting the parliamentary opposition and sought out a program that was palpable to the Right opposition at the time. It is generally believed that Depretis's *trasformismo*, which led to a lack of party cohesion and a blurring of the ruling and opposition, set the basis for the political cynicism and opportunism among many Italian political elites in the postwar period.

Moreover, as the Left was originally a southern-based party, it is interesting to note how this phenomenon also impacted on regional divisions within the country as the Left missed an opportunity to become a proponent of regional interests in the South. In fact, the DS, the dominant Left party in Italy today, is and has been strongest in the central regions of the country, with no real strongholds in the South.

In many ways, the actions of the Left party were instrumental in preventing the development of a more radical regional elite in the South that might have mobilized against northern dominance in the government. The Left's penchant for power and stability led them to repress any incipient revolts in the area and incorporated any indigenous class of reformers into the state structure. If anything, the security of government jobs, particularly in the late nineteenth and early twentieth centuries, smoothed over the need for the local elite to call for greater regional autonomy. In the words of Gramsci, "the social stratum which could have organized the endemic southern discontent, instead became an instrument of northern policy, a kind of auxiliary private police."[73] In other words, the northern-biased governments of the late nineteenth century prevented any further revolts in the South by co-opting the region into the government structure and doling out government largess.

The Impact of Fascism

Overall, the centralizing tendencies of the Italian state would continue throughout the rest of the liberal period in the late nineteenth and into the early twentieth century. Some of this may have been influenced by the nationalist fervor that existed in the peninsula at the time. There were a number of irredentist movements in northern Italy during the later years of the nineteenth century that were focused on returning areas under Austrian control, in particular the Trentino in the South Tryol region of Austria and Trieste on the Croatian border. Both of these territories would eventually fall within Italian borders after considerable struggles in the first part of the twentieth century (discussed in chapter 3). The early 1900s was also a period of colonial experiments for Italy, from Eritrea and Somalia to Libya, where it fought a war in 1911–1912. One of the most influential publications at the time was *L'Idea Nazionale* (the National Idea), which advocated a great deal of state control, militarism, and colonial expansion. Crispi himself was an intensely patriotic leader who in many ways set the mold for Mussolini.

The centralized state, though, reached its ultimate form during the fascist period when Mussolini introduced the corporatist state, which tried to dominate all aspects of life and leave as few independent organizations as possible.[74] A centralized administration was integral to Mussolini's project of creating the new Roman empire, as the state was supreme and its value more important than any other institution in the country, even more important than the Fascist party itself.

In his effort to project the supremacy of the central state, Mussolini enhanced the power and image of the prefect, particularly in terms of the institution's role vis-à-vis the subnational levels of government. The prefect was given the power not only to review the "legality of local government decisions, but also their merits or convenience."[75] In other words, Mussolini entrusted the prefect with the power to actually interpret the laws and not just enforce them. In turn, fascist prefects used their power and renewed privilege in the state system to dismiss communal and provincial councils summarily and purge the staff of local governments if it deemed that such employees were guilty of activities "incompatible with the general political directives of the government."[76]

Despite its emphasis on a strong state, the fascist regime repeated many of the mistakes of its liberal predecessors. Although the state became increasingly centralized and powerful, such a shift did not lead to greater efficiency and capacity of the administration but, rather, simply bloated it, creating a more Byzantine system. During his twenty years of uncontested rule, Mussolini had introduced numerous additional *enti publici* (special agencies). The enti are units of government that are state funded but act with a great deal of autonomy, forming a kind of "parallel administration," including such organizations in Italy like IRI (industrial reconstruction) and INEA (agrarian affairs) as well as the Bank of Italy. During the 18-year period from 1922 to 1940, 260 of these separate enti were created to run everything from state industries to social and welfare services to regulatory bodies. This is more than twice the number that had been introduced during the prior 60-year period from 1861 to 1921, when only 100 were introduced.[77] The sheer number of these agencies fractionalized the state system making it complex and unwieldy. Moreover, their growth further increased the already substantial number of people working within the state sphere and also politicized the administration by sharpening competition over resources and prestige.

Mussolini's influence on the nature of the state system in Italy should not only be seen in terms of his actions, but also his *inaction*, or what he failed to do while in power. Although the fascist dictator made claims of reforming the Italian state, he did little to change an administrative system that, since the nineteenth century, had revolved around numerous laws, circulars, statutes, and directorates.[78] The laws of the administrative system, many of which are still in effect today, are not simply limited to rules that describe the services that agencies offer and how such services will be rendered. Rather, the regulations of the system describe in fine detail the way the administration works, down to its "internal processes."[79] Thus, today there are about 100,000 laws that regulate the Italian administrative system, compared to the roughly 7,325 in France.[80] Such a system does not allow for creativity and reflective management because the regulations bind the civil servants in red tape, making them reluctant and apathetic to take any initiatives that might go out of the bounds of the law. And while he was credited for "getting the trains to run on time," the fascist leader was not known to be effective at curbing corruption and other similar ills during this period.

It is also interesting to note that Italian civil servants are not all trained in a common school that might create a particular *esprit de corps*, such as the INA school in France. Moreover, Italian civil servants are not seen as part of an elite section of society, but rather as beneficiaries of patronage that allow them to work only half days and receive juicy pension benefits, some of which they have access to well before the legal retirement age.

In addition to his impact on the size of the state, Mussolini also had a major impact on the actions of the institution vis-à-vis the South. In particular, the fascist leader continued the previous liberal policy of incorporating southerners into the national administrative structure. By the early twentieth century, southerners began to outnumber northerners within the state, partly as a result of the state's efforts to ease the endemic problem of unemployment in the region. Thus, where the state was once thoroughly "Piedmontized," by the 1930s it was starting to become more "southernized." At the turn of the century, around half of all top managers in the civil service were born in the North, while only a quarter were from the South. This trend started reversing in the late 1920s, so that by the 1950s and 1960s the number of southerners in the civil service increased to well over half of all civil servants.[81] In return, fewer and fewer northerners maintained positions in the state administrative system. A sample of employees from four different ministries in 1979 showed that only 10 percent came from the North.[82] As a result, by the 1960s, state institutions, from the prefecture to the judicial system, would become dominated by southerners; a situation considered impossible 50 years before.

Mussolini's actions in the South could also be seen as part of the same drive of liberal state-makers in the nineteenth century to turn the South around from its underdeveloped condition. For example, Mussolini is also credited for being the first Italian ruler who made a concerted effort to break the power of local elites in the South who prevented positive change, such as the landlords and the Mafia.

Mussolini's intervention in the South, however, should not be seen as any kind of pro-southern leaning on the part of the Fascists. If anything, Mussolini and the Fascist party were more rooted socially in the North where the fascist ideology, and its focus on modernity and industrialization, appealed to a more urban electorate. Moreover, the fascist regime favored northern interests, particularly those of its industrial elite, for whom Mussolini quelled the growing power of the trade unions. In the long run, Mussolini's strategy of using government employment and state subsidies in the South simply forestalled any urgency to make needed social and economic reforms in the region. Mussolini's clientelism in the South brought the region further into the web of the state so much so that the Fascist party or PNF became known locally as the party "*per necessità familiare*," or out of family necessity.

In fact, Mussolini, who was from the central-northern region of Romagna, argued that providing jobs to southerners was essential to preventing a revolt in the South. Southerners, he said, are

> very much to be feared: they possess an instinctive genius for propaganda, which has much effect in places where friendship and kinship ties are of the greatest importance... We must adopt a policy of maximum job availability in the state bureaucracy unless we want to have on our hands an insurrection of hungry—I repeat, hungry—intellectuals, which would be the most difficult of all insurrections to placate. Besides, it is a duty to take care of them.[83]

5. Conclusion

We can, therefore, conclude that Italian politics was left with a two-fold legacy from the Risorgimento up through the fascist period. First, there is the legacy of centralization without integration. The Piedmontese extended their own system of Napoleonic rule over the peninsula, establishing the dominance of the central government over the local levels. The drive to centralize, however, was not fueled by a national unifying myth that rallied the people and set forth a clear mandate for change. Rather, centralization was imposed from above without a great deal of legitimacy. As a result, the state emerged primarily as a repressive and extractive force, rather than being a progressive and effective one. The unifiers failed to create the strong and focused administration that people like Cavour had hoped for. Rather, the result was "the creation of a political system that was unstable, generally unpopular, and frequently inefficient."[84]

In spite of centralization, the opposition to this system was weak and disorganized. From within the leadership at the time, Minghetti tried to soften the situation with the creation of the regional level. This plan, however, failed to spark the interests of unifiers who were more concerned about suppressing any leftover legitimist claims, controlling the clericals, and incorporating the Bourbon South into the Kingdom. The desire for a regional level also had little support from below as communal and provincial elites saw such a change as a threat to their own power base. Although the South revolted, it did so for primarily economic reasons and without a clearly defined political opposition in mind. The revolts, which were driven more by the desire of the peasants to secure their land, were only sporadic and, after Garibaldi abandoned them, without any credible leadership. The rebelliousness of the South was thus easily quelled with government largess and positions within the new government bureaucracy.

The Risorgimento also set the basis for the legacy of the divide between the North and South. Faced with an underdeveloped South, the northern unifiers imposed the centralized state in order to establish some degree of rational-legal authority in the region. The new state, however, did little to improve the conditions of the South and bring it on par with the North but rather kept the region dependent on government largess. Moreover, the political elite at the center—liberal and, later, fascist—preferred instead to tame the region by co-opting local elites into the new state administrative system. By absorbing the local elite into the central state structure, the new rulers during this period deprived the region of a leadership structure that may have acted as a positive influence in economic and social development. In addition, the policy of co-optation also had the impact of "southernizing" the state administrative structure. Although the administrative structure was dominated by northerners during the nineteenth century, by the early twentieth century there were more southerners in key administrative positions.

CHAPTER 3

Centralization in the Postwar Period

1. Federalist Ideas and Secessionist Pressures after the War

In the postwar period, the Italian state would remain centralized despite attempts to introduce a degree of decentralization. At this point, however, we move into a new context in which the role of the Piedmontese, the Right and Left parties, and the Fascists have been replaced by new political parties in a newly democratized party system. The primary force responsible for the continued centralization of the state was the DC, the hegemonic political party that dominated all postwar governments in Italy until its fall in the early 1990s. Before we begin to discuss the role of the DC, however, we need to understand a little about the context of centralization and regional divisions in early postwar Italy.

In 1945, Italy had inherited a highly centralized state structure and a wide regional gap between the North and South. First, the Italian state made a relatively smooth transition from fascism to democracy; most of the administrative machinery and manpower that had been left before the war remained intact. The relatively few purges of personnel that did take place did not reach the higher echelon of the civil service, like the prefects and police chiefs who kept their jobs well into the postwar period. Most important, the Napoleonic state structure of top-down control was left in place as it was before and during the fascist period.

This transition took place in the midst of considerable distaste for the old system among the general populace. The institution of the prefect was identified with the corrupt and oppressive fascist regime and the excesses of Rome during Mussolini's reign. One can see this, for example, in the words of Luigi Einaudi, the country's first President of the

Republic under the new constitution in 1948 and leading intellectual of the time. In his 1944 essay, "*Via il prefetto*" (Away with the Prefect), Einaudi called for an end of the last vestiges of the Napoleonic system and the removal of the prefect, which, he argued, presented a major obstacle to democracy. "The destruction of the Napoleonic superstructure," Einaudi argued, "which the Italians never loved anyway," is the only way to reconstruct a "real and living state."[1]

Einaudi's comments were also written at a time when the issues of decentralization and federalism were growing in Italy after the fall of fascism and the corporatist state. At the time, a few, small movements—many of them linked to the anti-fascist Resistance—emerged, promoting the idea of a federalist state in post-fascist Italy. One of the earliest of these movements was *Giustizia e Libertà* (Justice and Liberty, GL), an anti-fascist political movement started by three Resistance members, Carlo Rosselli, Emilio Lussu, and Alberto Torchiani in Paris at the height of Mussolini's power in 1929. Although the GL's main goal was the destruction of Mussolini's dictatorship, the movement had over the years expressed in the pages of their journal, *Quaderni di Giustizia e Libertà*, the need for the development of federalist institutions in a reconstructed Italy arguing that a "federal system is the only way to prevent the state from 'devouring' society."[2] Further, in their *Schema*, or political program, the GL called for a "democratic republic, organized on the basis of extensive local autonomy."[3]

In Valle d'Aosta, the local resistance movement in 1943 came out with the *Carta di Chivasso*, a document that called for the formation of a federal republic in post-fascist Italy. The *Carta* focused on the problems of linguistic minorities, in particular the French speakers in Valle d'Aosta, arguing that "federalism is the framework best adapted to guarantee individual and collective rights and represents the solution to the problem of small nationalities." Further, referring to French claims on the region, the *Carta* continues by saying that federalism is the only safeguard against irredentism and a peaceful, stable Europe.[4] The Resistance itself provided a model for a federalist Italy as the CLNs, or Committees for National Liberation that were set up in 1943 by all the major anti-fascist parties, were decentralized, divided regionally, and governed on a local level, sometimes even referring to themselves as their own "*Repubblica Partigiana*" (Partisan Republic).[5]

Federalism was also bandied about toward the end of the war, as part of the emerging discussions about reconstruction of the continent. The 1943 document of the European Federalist Movement stated that "national independence, liberty, and socialism are vital and beneficial things only if they have as a premise—and not simply as a consequence—federation; that is a political order which guarantees peace and international justice."[6] Although the movement would fade into obscurity, it influenced leaders like Alcide De Gaspari, the first prime minister of Italy after the war, who pushed for greater European integration. The federalist direction of the EU today remains a central issue among member states.

Similarly, federalism was also on the minds of the American occupation forces in Italy from 1943 to 1945, which called for stronger local governments in one of their documents for reconstruction. The interdivisional committee for Italy argued that a federalist state was the preferred solution in the reorganization of local government in the country.[7] As it was, the Americans (apart from their own bias toward federalist institutions) were influenced by a number of factors, particularly the weak sense of national identity among Italians after the war, as well as more concrete pressures for secession coming from Sicily and other parts of the peninsula.

Secessionist pressures at the end of the war were strongest in Sicily, where they had been growing since the turn of the century. From 1896 to 1906 during the peasant revolt known as the "Fasci Siciliani," a group of Socialists in Palermo, the capital of Sicily, issued a now famous memorandum that demanded "the right of regional autonomy for the island."[8] Sicily would eventually receive a degree of autonomy in the early postwar period (more on this below) when secessionist pressures emerged again during the first democratic national elections in 1946 for the Constituent Assembly. During this election and the following one in 1948 under the new constitution, the *Movimento per L'indipendenza della Sicilia* (Sicilian Independence Movement) ran a list of candidates and received around 171,000 votes, about 9 percent of the vote on the island.

There were also secessionist pressures coming from Sardinia, the other large island of Italy, which lies to the west of the country in the middle of the Tyrrhenian Sea. Regional autonomy had been a staple for the *Partito Sardo d'Azione* (Sardinian Action Party, PSd'A) that had emerged in 1919 and is still in existence, making it one of the oldest political parties in Italy, regional or otherwise. The PSd'A, which was co-founded by Emilio Lussu before he became active in the anti-fascist struggle, had a platform that called for greater autonomy for the island and gained around 10 percent of the island's support during regional elections in 1949.

Secessionist pressures were also strong in the North, within the regions that border France, Austria, and Slovenia. As mentioned above, France had claims on the Valle d'Aosta region and encouraged the region, which has a large French-speaking population, to secede from Italy. One of the most contested regions of the North was the northeastern region of Trentino-Alto Adige, which Italy acquired from Austria as part of the Treaty of St. Germaine after the First World War. The region included Trentino, the mainly Italian region that was the center of focus for turn of the century irredentist and nationalist movements, and Alto Adige, which is ethnically German. By the end of the Second World War, regionalists within Alto Adige were seeking secession, along with the help of irredentists in Austria. It did not help that the regional identity of the Germans in the area was sharpened by the repression of the fascist regime, which had tried to "denationalize" the population of its German roots.[9]

Similar sentiments were also felt in the area around Trieste in the Northeast, which caused a major rift between Italy and Yugoslavia over the border between the two countries. The conflict reached a peak in 1945 when Yugoslavia, seeking to take back land that had been acquired by Italy after the First World War, occupied a "great part" of Venezia Giulia and "subjected the Italian population to a harsh regime" for six weeks.[10] Although the conflict was eventually settled in 1954, the allotment of much of the area to Yugoslavia and the loss of property for Italians who subsequently migrated to Italy continues to be an issue.[11]

2. The Postwar Divide between the North and South

Italy in the mid-1940s was also a country severely divided regionally between the North and South. Much like the late nineteenth century, industrial growth was taking place almost exclusively in the North, with a particular convergence in the northwestern triangle of Milan, Genoa, and Turin. Here, the growth of firms like FIAT in Turin would lead the second "economic miracle," which took place during the 1950s and 1960s, making Italy at the time one of the most industrialized countries in the world.[12] In contrast, the South was still very much an economic backwater as the local economy was based primarily on agriculture and was strongly dependent on government support. Although poverty existed across the peninsula, it was in the South that extreme conditions persisted, such as people living in large shantytowns outside major cities or crowded into small houses that they shared with farm animals.[13]

The North, moreover, benefited economically from this geographic disparity, as the "economic miracle" in the region would make great use of the influx of cheap labor from the South. From 1952 to 1963, of the

5.3 million southerners who changed residences, 1.9 million went to the North, while the rest went either abroad or to the growing urban centers in the South itself. At the time, 40 percent of the expansion of the Italian economy depended on the existence of inexpensive labor coming from the South, while 12 percent was a product of capital formation and another 20 percent was due to economies of scale.[14]

The state's labor laws in the early postwar period indirectly facilitated the exploitation of southern workers, who lacked "permission" to work in the North from 1949 to 1961. The government finally repealed the 1949 law, which had banned employment registration outside of one's own city of birth and prevented southerners from applying for official vacancies at local labor exchanges in the North.[15] The cheaper, "illegal" workers helped northern firms to cut costs and increase profits, which would have been much more difficult if labor rates had been higher.

Southern migrations not only had an impact on the local economy in the North, they also had a major impact on social conditions in the region. During this period there was a massive growth in the population of major northern cities that contributed to serious conditions of overcrowding while also leading to growing intolerance. In some cases, northerners responded to their new neighbors with anti-southern revolts, such as in Turin with the brief rise of the *Movimento Autonomista Regionale Piemontese* (the Regional Autonomist Movement of Piedmont, MARP). MARP ran a campaign to limit the number of southern immigrants into the city in the 1958 local elections and brought attention to the large-scale population shifts from the South to the North. The rise of such a party and other similar regionalist forces at the time, like the Lombardy-based *Movimento Autonomista Padano* (Autonomist Movement of Padania), were one of the first recorded phenomena of anti-southern movements in the North. Moreover, although such movements were brief, they were clear signs that national integration in Italy was still an issue into the middle of the twentieth century.

The divide between the North and South was also exacerbated by the fact that the Resistance was fought only in the Center and the North. In 1943, the South had already been invaded by the Allied command that had landed in Sicily and eventually forced the king to surrender in September. Although Mussolini was then ousted and arrested, he was eventually released by Germany, which promptly put him back in power in the Lombard city of Salò to rule a Nazi–Fascist puppet regime that controlled most of central-northern Italy. From 1943 to 1945, communist, Catholic, and lay partisans fought a bloody guerilla war against the Nazis and Fascists, contributing to the eventual victory of the Allied forces.

As a result of this geographical imbalance in the liberation of the country, however, anti-fascist sentiment has and continues to be felt mostly in the North as it was here that the bloody battles of the Resistance were fought. To this day, for example, the Resistance still plays a strong role in local culture in central and northern Italian towns where partisan fighters are revered for their heroism during the conflict. In contrast, the collective memory of fascism in the South has been more in terms of the clientelistic aspects of the regime rather than its repressive and violent measures, which the partisans felt firsthand. The South in turn has been more favorable in the postwar period to conservative and right-wing appeals by different parties, from monarchists to neo-fascists.[16] Moreover, during the referendum in 1946 that eventually established the country as a republic, the South voted against the national trend, supporting the monarchy that had collaborated with the Fascists.

3. The Regions and Cold War Politics

The debate over decentralization of the state reached a major turning point during the Constituent Assembly of 1946–1947 when the introduction of the regional level emerged as a central issue. The members of the assembly, which eventually wrote up the modern Italian constitution, represented all the major postwar political parties, including the DC, the Communist party (PCI, now known as the Democratic Left or DS), the Socialist party (PSI), the Liberal party (PLI),[17] as well as a number of other minor parties and lists such as the Action party (*Partito d'Azione*).

The question of regional devolution, however, was a hotly contested issue during the assembly and divided the parties into two relatively distinct pro and con camps. On the pro side the most vocal were the DC[18] and the Action party. The DC emerged as the leading proponent for granting a degree of power to the regional level, arguing that the regions should be given a major role in the areas of economic and social policy making.[19]

The DC had been a strong supporter of federalism and decentralization in the early years of the party's existence. The idea of greater local autonomy went hand in hand with the party's early emphasis on empowering local social groups, in particular the family, Church, and community.[20] Further, the emphasis on decentralization had been a central part of the platform of the DC's predecessor, the Popular party, which was founded by Luigi Sturzo in 1919. Sturzo, who had written extensively on the issue of the regions and devolution,[21] made "administrative decentralization" and "local autonomy" central issues of the party's program.[22] In his "Appeal to the Country," an early (1919) party document, Sturzo condemned the centralized state for limiting civic organization and called for the creation of a more decentralized state that essentially respects the family and encourages private initiative.[23]

The Action party was a small but influential force that was part of the Resistance and also included many members of the former pro-federalist *Giustizia e Libertà* movement. The Action party was "committed to establishing a new democracy based on greater local autonomies"[24] and expressed support during the Constituent Assembly for a federal system like the United States. For the Action party, the appeal of the United States was the combination of a "strong executive" with extensive autonomy to subnational units that would limit the power of the executive. The Action party argued that with a "strong executive," "the different parts of the country can govern themselves without falling into anarchy."[25] Further, coming from a socialist tradition, the Action party argued that greater local autonomy would guarantee the "participation of the working people."[26]

Regional reform was also presented as an essential element in the transition of the country from fascism to democracy. Emilio Lussu, who left the PSd'A to become one of the leading members of the Action party, argued that some form of federalism was needed to prevent the country from returning to fascism. Federalism, he argued, represented an "antithesis" to the corruption and "decadence" that comes from a centralized state structure, which gives too much power to the bureaucracy and dominates the periphery.[27] In this way, Lussu echoed the sentiment of the time that the hyper centralization of the fascist regime was not a revolutionary institution as Mussolini had claimed it to be, but rather a continuation of the corrupt, liberal state.

The anti-regional forces were led by the Liberals on the Right, and the Communists and Socialists on the Left. Both sides felt that regional devolution was a threat to national unity, a sentiment that echoed those of the Risorgimento leaders a century earlier. Although the liberal Luigi Einaudi, who wrote *"Via il prefetto,"* was supportive of creating a regional level, he was skeptical about giving it too much power.[28] More "Jacobinist" in their strategy, the Left desired a stronger centralized state from which they could enact aggressive social reform. The devolution of power to a regional level, they argued, would weaken the capacity of the state and, ultimately, lead to competition between regions over public funds. Palmiro Togliatti, the leader of the PCI at the time, asked whether the country wanted a "federal Italy" where "little states fight against one another over the scarce resources of the state?"[29] Both the Liberals and the Left were concerned that the South would be hurt the most from devolution as it would undermine greater national solidarity.[30]

In the end, the anti-regionalist forces lost out to the pro-regionalist side, partly because of the weaker positions of the former. The Liberals emerged from the war with the taint of having collaborated with the Fascists and as a result never went beyond being a minor party in the postwar period. Once the force that was associated with the unification of the country, the Liberals had lost much of their support to the center-right Christian Democrats. Although the Left felt that regional devolution would weaken the state and its capacity to act as an aggressive force for social change, they were tame in their criticism. The Communists, in particular, were concerned that in an era of growing anti-communism, their support of a centralized state would make them seem much too totalitarian.[31]

In addition, there were other contingent factors that moved along the process toward regional devolution, not the least being considerable pressures from the secessionists movements, both from the North and South. In contrast to the nineteenth-century view that such tendencies should be strapped down in the straight jack of centralization, there was a general consensus that the country needed to devolve powers to respect such things as regional ethnic groups. Such sentiments emerged in a period in Europe when centralization and nationalism were intricately tied to the ideas of ethnic cleansing and genocide.

The recognition of the need for subnational levels of power also reflected the diverse nature of the different forces that participated in the Constituent Assembly, from politically active Catholics to communists, from liberals to regionalists. All sides contributed to the creation of a constitution that visibly represents a mixture of different points of view, from the establishment of Catholicism as the state religion to the guarantee of equality and social justice to liberal notions of individual freedom. This collegiality was greatly influenced by the experience of the Resistance, in which Catholics and communists had fought side by side in the struggle to bring down the Nazi–Fascist regime. It also reflected the influence of political leaders from all areas of the country, North to South.

The constitution established the creation of 20 regions (see map 2), which are "constituted as autonomous territorial bodies with their own powers and functions" (Art. 115). The next articles layout the status of the regions, from their legislative powers (Arts. 117 and 118) to their financial and fiscal powers (Arts. 119 and 120), to the institutional bodies that govern them (Art. 121), to the laws that govern regional elections (Art. 122), to the establishment of the regional statutes (Art. 123), to the role and jurisdiction of central authorities in relation to the region (Arts. 124–127).

The establishment of the regional level in the constitution was the most significant step taken toward any form of decentralization since unification of the country in the mid-nineteenth century. Moreover, the move toward a regional state appeared to move Italy away from its more centralized neighbor France, from which the country had inherited its own Napoleonic traditions, and more toward federalist European countries like Germany and Austria. The honeymoon of the regions, however, ended abruptly after they quickly became a victim of postwar Italian politics, which would make them nothing more than a simple designation on paper.

After the writing of the constitution the ruling parties in Rome blocked legislation that was needed for the actual activation of the regional level for the next three decades, until 1970. Ironically, the party that was most responsible for blocking the regions was the DC, which made an abrupt turn right after the Constituent Assembly and became one of the strongest opponents of the regions in 1948.

The DC's reversal on the regions was precipitated primarily by the party's strong anti-communist position and the possibility that the new layer of government would give the Communists—a party strongly rooted in the local level in the central regions of the country—extra resources and a chance to build its support base and gain national power. In the wake of the Truman Doctrine and the closing of the Iron Curtain, the DC put an end to the collegial atmosphere of the Constituent Assembly and emerged as the leading party of anti-communism. One of the most famous posters of the first national elections under the new constitution in 1948 shows a number of Italian women guarding their young children from "communist wolves." The poster further turns the electoral campaign into conflict between "Christ and communism," showing snakes "bearing the poison of 'free love'" and "rearing up to destroy the Italian family with a giant Stalin trampling underfoot the Roman monument to Victor Emanuel II."[32] Similar kinds of scare tactics against the PCI were used in successive DC electoral campaigns, when the latter associated communism with the aggressive methods of the Soviet Union, such as during the invasion of Hungary in 1956 and the Prague Spring in 1968.[33]

The anti-communism of the DC went over well with the electorate during the election as the party polled its best return ever, 48.5 percent of the vote. On the Left, the Popular Front coalition, which included both the PCI and the PSI, gained only 31.0 percent. For the next 45 years, the DC would remain the dominant party in the government, gaining between 35 and 45 percent of the vote nationally and acting as a pivot around which all national governing coalitions would revolve. The PCI was left in the position of permanent opposition, hovering between 25 and 35 percent, excluded from any national governing coalitions for being outside of the "democratic arc" of the governing parties. The DC governed either alone or, as was more often the case, with one or more of the smaller "lay" parties of the Center: the Republican party (PRI), which was formed by ex-members of the Action party after it disbanded in the late 1940s, the Social Democrats (PSDI), the Liberals (PLI), and later the Socialists (PSI). Despite the fact that during the four decades after the war the average government coalition lasted only nine months, the prime minister was always a Christian Democrat. It wasn't until the 1980s that non-Christian Democrats became prime ministers: Giovanni Spadolini (PRI) from 1981 to 1982 and Bettino Craxi (PSI) from 1983 to 1987.

The fear of communism was, moreover, made all the more tangible by pressures from external forces. The United States' intervention in Italian national politics and its expressed support for the DC further helped to boost the party's electoral fortunes and marginalize the Left in the 1950s.[34] Marshall aid funds, for example, were distributed with the intention of drawing voters to the DC, particularly during the elections of 1948. Thus, "[w]henever a new bridge or school or hospital was constructed with American help, there was the indefatigable ambassador [James Dunn] traveling the length of the peninsula to speak in the name of America, the Free World and, by implication, the Christian Democrats."[35]

The introduction of the regional level not only threatened the DC by potentially benefiting the PCI, it also undermined the party's capacity to maintain its power and dominate the political system. Much like past ruling parties in Italy, the DC benefited from the structures of the centralized state, particularly the prefect, which enabled the party to win elections. According to one eyewitness account, the prefect used to plan election campaigns "on behalf of the government parties" along with the provincial DC party secretary. The prefect would, moreover, negotiate "agreements with local notables, based on promises of state aid or threats of deprivation," and would arrange "the necessary campaign alliances." The prefect would finally provide "guidance to the government and its candidates on the suitability of various appeals and the activities of the opposition," and "distribute relief directly or through government supporters."[36]

The introduction of the region did in fact remove many of the powers of the prefect, particularly his capacity to control the actions of provinces, communes, and other local authorities, which were taken over by regionally appointed control committees (*comitati regionale di controllo*).[37] Today, the prefect still exists as the central government representative on the provincial level, but without the kind of power he had in the past.

The DC did everything in its power to prevent decentralization of any of the powers guaranteed to the regions in the constitution. In 1953, the DC passed the Schelba Law, which was named after the Interior Minister, Mario Schelba. Like his nineteenth-century predecessor, Urbano Ratazzi, Schelba was known to favor not only centralization but also authoritarian methods against his opponents, especially the many leftist groups that were demonstrating in the piazzas at the time. The Schelba Law essentially laid down stipulations that, even if the regions did come into existence, they would "constitute only a slight nuisance to the central government."[38] Schelba set limits on regional legislative initiatives and the use of regional referenda (all of which had been granted to the regions in the constitution). The law also gave the government control commissioner—the central government official who heads the control committees—considerably more powers to intervene in the affairs of the regions.[39] Overall, when the DC was not openly critical of the regions, its inaction further prevented the decentralization of any powers.

The DC was not alone in opposing the creation of the regions. The party was indirectly helped by the far-right MSI and the Monarchists who were also in favor of greater centralism to maintain "law and order," particularly in the South where these parties gained the majority of their support. The country's civil servants were also supportive of the DC's actions because of their general skepticism toward the regions and their apprehension that a change in the *status quo* would force them to transfer to less prestigious regional positions.[40]

In reaction to the DC's new quest to prevent decentralization, the Left also switched its position, becoming the regions' greatest supporter in the 1950s and 1960s. The switch was not a hard one for the Left for many reasons. For one thing, the pro-regionalist position of the PCI gave the party an ideal issue on which it could campaign against its nemesis, the DC, by criticizing the ruling party's perpetuation of a centralized and bureaucratized state. The Communists were able to emerge in this period, ironically, as the promoter of democracy, as the party called for the activation of the regions as a way to reduce the growing problems of over-bureaucratization and to bring greater participation to the grassroots. Thus, the Communists quickly shifted from their former stand for centralized planning to the promoter of the regional level as a crucial linkage between local authorities and the state, and as organs of "direct democracy."[41]

The PCI had, moreover, changed as a result of its marginalization on the national level, establishing itself by the late 1960s and early 1970s as a considerable force in local politics, particularly in cities across the central regions known as the Red Belt. In these regions, the PCI demonstrated a great capacity to manage local and regional affairs in an effective way. As a result, the central region of Emilia-Romagna, the heart of the Red Belt, is known to have some of the best-run local governments with considerably more efficient local services than in other parts of the country. The main Emilian cities of Bologna, Reggio Emilia, Modena, and Parma, for example, are the most prosperous, with some of the highest standards of living and the best performing regional governments in the country.[42] Thus, the PCI's embracing of decentralization and good governance enabled the party to move away from its close identification with the issues of the working class and to gain a greater deal of cross-class support. This support, then, translated into overall electoral success as the party went from about 25 percent of the vote in 1963 to around 35 percent of the vote in 1976.

In contrast to the rest of the country, the five regions with secessionist movements (Sicily, Sardinia, Valle d'Aosta, Trentino-Alto Adige, and Friuli-Venezia Giulia) were given regional powers right after the war. These five regions were all given special statuses under Art. 116 of the constitution, stating that they have "particular forms and conditions of autonomy, according to special statutes approved with constitutional laws." The special statutes for the northern regions of Valle d'Aosta, Trentino-Alto Adige, and Friuli-Venezia Giulia focus primarily on issues of culture and/or linguistic rights for the respective French, German, and Slovenian populations in these regions.[43] The special statutes for the island regions of Sicily (which was actually conferred in 1946, before the national constitution) and Sardinia focus primarily on social issues and economic development.[44]

The devolution to the special regions, however, did not take place without conflict, including the scuffle between Italy and Yugoslavia over Trieste after the War, described earlier. The most heated conflict took place in Trentino-Alto Adige where the German-speakers wanted their own region, separate from Italians. The conflict between the two communities raged for years, straining relations between Italy and Austria, with the latter supporting the German population in Alto Adige. After sporadic terrorist bombings by separatists, the government finally split the region, making Trento and Bolzano "autonomous provinces" within the region of Trentino-Alto Adige.

4. Regional Reform of the 1970s and Its Failure

The regional issue reached a major turning point in the late 1960s when the pro-regionalist Left began to make significant electoral gains, putting pressure on the DC to decentralize power to the regions. The DC was pressured, in particular, by their new junior partner on the national level, the PSI, which had made the activation of the regional level a crucial part of its electoral bargain with the DC. The coalition with the PSI was a more stable option than the usual alliance with the other centrist lay parties, each of the latter gained at best from 4 to 6 percent during elections. In contrast, the PSI had been gaining steadily since 1953, doubling its support from 7 to 14 percent in only ten years. The alliance with the PSI also enabled the DC to further secure its position in the latter part of the 1960s by putting an end to any lingering hopes of a return to the Popular Front coalition between the PSI and the PCI. Although the PSI continued to participate in local coalitions with the Communists, it remained a close ally of the DC on the national level, playing an active role in two-thirds of the 30 coalition governments from 1963 to 1992. Except for a brief period in 1987, the PSI was in coalition with the DC for twelve straight years in parliament from 1980 to 1992.

Eventually, the Left, along with a newly politicized interregional front (headed by the central and northern regions of Lombardy and Emilia-Romagna), pushed the senate to pass pending legislation that put the regional level into effect. In 1970, restrictions held over the regions by the Schelba Law of 1953 were eased and the first regional elections were finally conducted. By 1975, the parliament had passed law 382 that guaranteed the powers originally attributed to the regions in the constitution but which at the time were still exercised by the central government. It also gave the remaining administrative functions that were not as yet passed down in 1972 and granted expenditures for the regions in a block and not a piecemeal fashion.

Many observers have remarked on the significant changes that took place during this period in Italy. Robert Putnam, for example, argues that the 1970s was a "tumultuous period of reform," which "broke with Italy's century-long pattern of centralized government," and which "delegated unprecedented power and resources" to the regions.[45] During the period of the reforms, another close observer of Italian politics, Sidney Tarrow, also championed the efforts in Italy as "one of the few attempts to create new representative institutions in the nation-states of the West."[46] Indeed, Italy did appear to be moving away from a strictly centralized state to something in between a unitary and a federal system. Writing around the time of the reform, the historian P.A. Allum referred to Italy as a "unitary system characterized by regional autonomy."[47]

However, in spite of the reforms, the regions themselves have proven to be weak arenas for legislation and administration due to a number of reasons. First, the constitution of 1948 never really gave the regions a great deal of autonomous legislative powers. In particular, the "normal regions" have very few "exclusive powers" that are independent of the national level. Thus, Art. 117 of the constitution states that the regions have legislative powers over a number of areas, such as health care (health and hospital assistance); policing (local, urban, and rural police); economic development (fairs and markets, artisan and professional training and school aid, tourist trade and hotel industry); culture (museums and libraries of local bodies); transportation (tram and motor coach services of regional interest); public works (roads, aqueducts, and public works of regional interest); agriculture and forestry; hunting and fishing. However, the regions can legislate only "within the limits of the fundamental principles established by the laws of the State," and that such legislation cannot run "in contrast with the national interest or with that of other Regions." Thus, the powers over the forementioned areas are mainly "complementary," which can only be exercised within the framework of national laws. In other words, the regions were not given the exclusive power to make legislation on, for example, health care, but rather in conjunction with national laws that delegate specific powers to the regions and limit their scope of action. In this way, the regions have simply become an extension of central government power, and do not constitute a true separate unit of power as do the states in the United States.

The regions with special statutes, however, do have some "exclusive" legislative powers. With some variation between them, special regions have exclusive powers over agriculture and forestry, communal boundaries, public works, hunting and fishing, town planning, civic customs, tourism, artisanship, museums and libraries of regional interest, local and regional roads, regional markets and fairs.[48] These, however, are all fairly minor powers.

Second, and probably most important, the regions have never had much in the way of their own resources until recently, depending primarily on central government transfers for financial resources. Until recent efforts at fiscal federalism (discussed in chapter 6), Italy's tax system was highly centralized compared with other OECD countries, both unitary and federal. In 1993, the tax receipts from all three levels of local government in Italy—regional, provincial, and communal—accounted for only 3.7 percent of total tax revenues, considerably less than the 12 percent average for unitary countries and 31.4 percent for federal countries within this group.[49] To make matters worse, the funds that are transferred to the region are generally earmarked for specific projects, without much leeway for regional governments to be creative. In fact, in 1992, most the regional budget, about 80 percent, went toward health services, while about 16 percent went toward personnel and administration costs and 4 percent went toward other local services.[50]

Much of this centralization occurred around the time of the regional reforms when the ruling DC put into effect a series of reforms that consolidated the control of most taxes under the central government, abolishing many local taxes except for the most minor.[51] The reform was presented as a way to correct the imbalance between the wealthy cities of the North and the poor ones in the South that was growing as a result of the disparity in industrialization. However, the centralization of taxes can also be seen as a way for the DC to undermine the capacity of its more locally rooted political opponent, the PCI.

The lack of fiscal autonomy and the tendency toward a more redistributive—and hence centralized—fiscal system is inscribed in the constitution as well. Article 119 of the constitution, which outlines the financial status of the regions, states that regional fiscal autonomy is "within the forms and limits laid down by the laws of the Republic," which coordinates "this autonomy with the finances of the State," provinces, and communes. The tempered fiscal autonomy is further intended to favor the South as the article continues by stating that the state can by law allocate funds for "specific purposes," "particularly for the development of southern and insular Italy." Thus, although the constitution recognizes the necessity of local autonomy, any form of decentralization has to be done within the context of maintaining national equality.

The lack of fiscal autonomy has done a great deal to undermine the capacity of the regions to emerge as effective organs of governance. As one observer noted, regional officials have few political incentives to be more accountable about regional funds as they do not come from local taxpayers but from the central purse.[52] As a result, the regions are prevented from reaching their full potential to confront local issues. Even the regions with special statutes are limited in their fiscal autonomy. Although they have more power to collect and keep more of their own resources,[53] they too have to "coordinate this autonomy with the finances" of the central state.

Finally, regional reform did little to change established political patterns of the country, failing to make the regions important centers for political mobilization in Italy. A study in the late 1980s demonstrated that almost two decades after the establishment of the regions, the reforms did not have a significant impact on the organization of the major parties at the time, the DC, PCI, and PSI. In general, the parties' communal and even provincial organizations remained dominant compared to the regional structures. Thus, for example, within the DC, regional party secretaries continued to lack full powers in the party's national council, compared to other party leaders.[54]

In many ways, reorganization of the party along regional lines threatened the interests of a number of party elites. Within the DC, regionalization was actually seen as a foreign imposition on established party traditions, taking power away from party factions, along with their clientele, which were based more on the provincial and communal levels.[55] A regionalization of the party structure, moreover, meant that the party would have had to create new, regionally based patronage structures, which would have challenged existing clientelist networks.

5. Conclusion

The DC perpetuated the centralizing tendencies of the state in the postwar period by blocking the regions. Although the regions were finally activated in the early 1970s, they have emerged as ineffective arenas of governance, with few incentives or resources to act more efficiently. The regional reforms have also been criticized for not changing some of the basic patterns of the centralized system that have existed since the nineteenth century. The subnational level of government continues to suffer from a lack of autonomy, just as the central level continues to have a large presence in all areas of policy formation and execution. In addition to this, even the subnational levels are much too interdependent of each other to allow for autonomous decision-making. Apart from a few exceptions, the regions have the power to keep local authorities in check with their control committees, much like the prefect did before.

The communal level too has suffered from a lack of power and autonomy during the postwar period. In spite of the expansion of local government functions since the late 1940s, this shift did not involve "qualitative change in the role of local authorities in service delivery" but rather simply kept them subordinated to the central level.[56] For example, one of the biggest initiatives of the postwar period, the *Cassa per il Mezzogiorno* (fund for the South), as well as those in the areas of construction, town planning, pollution, hospitals, and infant schools forced the expansion of local government functions in the 1950s and 1960s, but did little to increase their autonomy from the central level. Rather than decentralize power to the local level for these projects, the central government simply *deconcentrated* central state power to the local level, increasing the presence of the central government and fueling clientelist networks of the governing parties,[57] an issue that we will discuss in chapter 4.

CHAPTER 4

The Christian Democrats and the North–South Divide

1. The Shift of the Christian Democrats in the 1960s and 1970s

The place of the DC in this story goes beyond the party's perpetuation of the centralizing tendencies of the state, to its role in exacerbating the divide between the North and South, which it accomplished with a crucial shift in its strategy in the early postwar period. In the mid-1950s, the DC was eager to move in a direction that would make it a more independent force in Italian society. In the North, the party wanted to break free from the control of the Church, to which the party was strongly attached in its early years. When it started out, the DC lacked a solid organizational structure of its own and as a result was heavily dependent on its ties to the Church and its numerous Catholic associations. The Catholic movement gave the DC an active organizational base as well as a degree of legitimacy, which would have been nearly impossible for the party to muster on its own in the early postwar period. Thus, for example, 75 percent of the DC's parliamentarians in 1946 were members of Catholic Action.[1] During the same year, Catholic Action had over 2.5 million members, compared to the DC's 1 million.[2]

The Catholic movement was always strongest in the North, particularly the Northeast. Even at the height of its power in 1954, Catholic Action remained a northern-based association, with most of its members located in the Veneto (239,273), Lombardy (219,475) and Piedmont (103,630). The largest representation of the association in the South was in Sicily, which had only 63,846 members.[3] One might assume that the poorer South is more religious, but Church attendance has been by and large higher in the North. For example, in 1973, when a majority of the

DC's voters could still be defined as "religious,"[4] 51 percent in the North said they were "Church-going," compared to only 30 percent in the South and 26 percent in the Center.[5]

The DC's mobilization in the 1940s and 1950s took place within the sphere of Catholic Action and other collateral organizations, such as the Catholic trade union CISL, the association for Catholic workers ACLI, and particularly Coldiretti, the agricultural workers association, which had the "ability to mobilize a massive rural vote" for the party.[6] In addition to these organizations, the Church was active in running schools, hospitals, and local banks. Although these associations existed nationwide, it was in the Northeast that they were the most integrated into the social fabric and provided the DC with a considerable network from which to organize political support. Some, such as Catholic cooperatives, were found only in the Center and North.

The DC's links to these Church-based organizations allowed it to establish a secure territorial hold in the Catholic "sub-culture" in the northeastern part of the country. These areas, known collectively as the "White" zone, include the regions of the Veneto, Friuli-Venezia Giulia, Trentino,[7] and the provinces of Bergamo, Como, and Brescia in Lombardy. Catholic and communist subcultures, which were strong in Italy from the turn of the century until recently, had been the source of electoral stability and predictable voting behavior in the twentieth century. Research conducted in the 1960s by the Cattaneo Institute, a leading political research organization in Italy, demonstrated that:

> [There are] regions—the White area and the Red Belt—in which the political tradition is so deeply rooted that it becomes a family tradition . . . where party preference is handed down from father to son . . . In the areas in which there is a high congruence between family and community in terms of images of society, models of behavior and socialization patterns, the dominant parties benefit from the widely shared notion that the vote for a party is an enduring attitude, one that can be changed only in exceptional circumstances.[8]

Both the DC and the PCI gained their most consistent support in their respective subcultural strongholds. The DC, for example, won over 40 percent of the vote in every postwar election in the White area, where it mobilized support primarily through the Church and the parish structure.

The DC's relationship with the Church, however, was not always a smooth one. One of the reasons for this move toward autonomy was the conflict between the party's leadership and the Vatican hierarchy over the selection of political allies for the party. Moreover, the DC was not content to remain dependent on the resources and manpower of the Church and the Catholic movement, which the party wanted to bypass and create a direct link with the electorate. In particular, the DC was interested in weaning itself from the clutches of Catholic Action—the strongest Catholic social movement—by absorbing many of the movement's activists within the party structure.[9] Despite these power struggles between the DC and the Catholic world, the party's support in the Northeast was solid.

The South, however, was another story as the DC lacked the infrastructure of Catholic institutions and the strong sense of associationalism and political participation that existed in its White subcultures. Rather, in the South, the party's supporters were mainly middle-class notables who were not strongly tied to the party, but simply saw the DC as a stabilizing force that was strong enough to block any radical social or political changes in the region.[10] The notion of the DC as the lesser of evils eventually led to the saying, "hold your nose and vote for the DC."

The shaky nature of the DC's southern base became clear during the national elections in 1953, when many local notables briefly left the DC to protest the party's agrarian reform plan that undermined their power as landlords considerably.[11] During the elections, the party lost 8.5 percent of the national vote, with most of its losses concentrated in the southern regions where local elites had shifted their support to the Monarchists and neo-fascist MSI, two more conservative forces that were the DC's main competitors on the Right. From this time onwards, the DC began a shift in its strategy that would shore up its southern support, making the party more independent of local notables and increase the presence of the party in southern society.

Lacking any strong ideological appeal among the local population, the DC began to increase its support in the South by diverting more and more public funds to the region, eventually creating a solid vote bank, or a simple exchange of votes for resources. From the 1960s onwards, the DC's clientelist networks grew in the South as the party invested increasing amounts of government money for development projects in the South, the single most important being the *Cassa per il Mezzogiorno* (development fund for the South). Thirty years after the *Cassa* was instituted in the 1950s, it had contributed over 20 billion dollars to the region. Although some projects funded by the *Cassa* were successful—for example, it helped the construction of necessary roadways in the region[12]—the moneys were used mostly to benefit the party. In the words of one observer in the early 1960s, the *Cassa* was a "gigantic patronage organization" controlled by the ruling DC that "employs people and awards developmental contracts strictly on the basis of political considerations."[13]

Other state initiatives for industrial and infrastructural development in the South—such as the requirement that state-holding companies direct a large percentage of their capital investment into the region[14]—were also geared toward helping the party's fortunes. For example, the public managers of these firms who got votes for the ruling party would receive funds, regardless of the firm's productivity.[15] In this way, the state's selective industrialization of the *Mezzogiorno* provided funds for southern party bosses as public contracts were used by the DC either to guarantee electoral support or to procure kickbacks to finance the party's coffers. Overall, the people who ran the industries in the South were guided more by their need to satisfy political demands than economic effectiveness.

In the 1960s, the DC's clientelist state ballooned in size with the rise of welfare agencies like INPS (pensions and social security) and INAIL (workers' compensation), benefits that the DC gave to voters and party organizers in return for votes and support.[16] False disability pensions, for example, were a favorite tool used by the DC and its partners in the national government to secure their vote banks in the South. The historian Paul Ginsborg has shown that in 1975 the South, "with 34 per cent of the country's population, received 31 per cent of all pensions, which was about twice the amount it should have received in strict relation to its working population."[17] The problem still exists today as half of all disability pensions are distributed to people residing within the *Mezzogiorno*, while the rest are distributed relatively evenly between the North and Center (see table 4.1).

Table 4.1 Distribution of disability pensions in relation to all pensions (1999) (percent)

Geographic area	Disability pensions	All pensions
North	28.5	47.3
Center	20.2	19.6
South	49.4	29.5
Italy	98.1	96.3
Abroad	1.9	3.0
Not able to be distributed	0.0	0.7
Total	100.0	100.0

Source: Adapted from ISTAT, *I beneficiari delle prestazioni pensionistiche* (December 21, 2000), www.istat.it.

Finally, a considerable amount of patronage also came during the 1960s from the expanding local government sector when the DC consolidated its hold on jobs in the administration in southern cities, from housing and hospitals to municipal authorities. At times, the DC's use of public money in the South went beyond simple pork-barrel politics and involved outright corruption and illegal activities such as when the DC aligned with local Mafia bosses in public construction projects.[18] Similarly, there is still a cloud of suspicion that hangs over the DC about the misuse of disaster relief funds that were earmarked for the reconstruction of the southern town of Irpinia after the earthquake there in 1980, which killed over 2,000 people.

By the 1960s, the DC had consolidated its clientelist links in the South and succeeded in replacing the power of local notables, and effectively became the dominant institution in the region. Local drives by the DC increased membership in the South, where in 1963 there were twice as many members than in the Catholic subculture in the Northeast. Although after the 1960s party membership would drop for the DC, by the mid-1980s there were still more card carrying members in the South than in the North. At that time, 14 out of every 100 DC voters in the mainland South were members of the party, while the same number was only 9.3 in the Northeast. There were even more members on the Islands of Sicily and Sardinia, where for every 100 DC voters there were around 16 party members.

The appeal to party membership in the South was based, moreover, on different issues than in its subculture in the Northeast. In the latter, membership was still associated with the ideological attachment to the party and its identification with the Catholic movement.[19] In the South, membership had little to do with ideological concerns and more with the material benefits that it provided, from jobs to pensions. Thus, much like their fascist predecessors, the alignment to the DC in the South was less ideological or programmatic and more one of convenience and practicality.

Clientelism also became a major currency used by the different factions or *correnti* (currents) *within* the DC to gain power and loyalty. By 1971, there were nine identifiable *correnti*, all headed by a leader within the party. Although in the 1940s the original divisions within the DC were drawn along clear ideological lines—from a progressive social-Catholic Left to a more pro-business conservative Right—by the 1960s they were little more than vague political differences that separated a Left, Center, and Right. Competition over the spoils smoothed over these differences of opinion as factions acted like clans fighting for their share of the public resources. Such conflicts over state resources were not only endemic within the DC, but also between the leading party and its junior partners in the various governing coalitions. Thus, even though the party and its allies were united in their efforts to hold onto the majority in parliament, they were simultaneously conducting "civil wars" with and among themselves over state resources.[20]

In addition, voters in the South were twice as prone as those in other parts of the country to use the "preference vote" for the DC, further demonstrating the region's "instrumental" attachment to the party. Preference votes allow the electorate to choose individual candidates on a party list and therefore became a valuable currency that party leaders—particularly the heads of the different factions within the DC—used to support their standing within the organization. However, because politicians are generally rewarded with preference votes for (substantive) favors they give to friends and family—as opposed to broad ideological positions—the system was an integral part of the DC's patronage networks and facilitated the corrupt use of public funds.

The DC competed for support in the South not only with the parties of the Left, but also the neo-fascist MSI, which had a solid hold in the region. The MSI was started by Fascists who were close to Mussolini during the Republic of Saló period from 1943 to 1945. From its birth in 1947 to the 1990s, the MSI has steadily held onto a core of supporters and became the dominant force on the far Right after eventually absorbing the Monarchists and other similar right-wing movements, such as the L'Uomo Qualunque ("Everday Man") party. Much like the movement of Pierre Poujade, which emerged in France around the same time, L'Uomo Qualunque was an "anti-modernist" party that protested against the rapid social and economic changes taking place in the early postwar period and their impact on southern society. From the 1950s to the early 1990s the MSI consistently held onto an average of around 5 percent of the vote share nationwide, with considerably more support in the South. Much of the MSI's support was in major urban centers like Rome, Naples, and Bari where the neo-fascists played a leading role in local governing coalitions from time to time.

Although much of the MSI's propaganda in the postwar period focused on nationalist themes, the party gained recognition in the South by taking on many issues that were similar to the L'Uomo Qualunque, such as their identification with the southern urban poor who were much less mobile than their co-nationals in the North. The MSI mobilized both the underclass and sections of the middle class who had limited opportunities in large southern cities. In these areas, "unemployment and poverty, completely inadequate public services, and growing needs [fed] unrest and [gave] rise to protests that often [found] expression in a vote for the MSI."[21] The MSI was able to exploit widespread discontent among southerners—particularly educated urban youths who found little opportunity outside of the DC's patronage networks—by presenting itself as an outsider.[22] Thus, while the DC was appealing to its southern electorate on a clientelistic basis, the MSI appealed on a protest vote that criticized the mismanagement of the state and called for more competence in local administration. By the 1970s, the leader of the MSI at the time, Georgio Almirante, defined the party as a "proletarian" movement with a "southern base." Almirante often took on the voice of a regional populist who argued that the marginalization of the South was a product of capitalist exploitation of the North.[23]

Overall, the DC's use of state resources were most effective at limiting the support for the extremist MSI as well as any other movements that emerged as a result of popular discontent toward the state and enduring problems of unemployment and infrastructural decay. Much like their nineteenth-century predecessors, the DC's use of patronage quelled upsurges of popular discontent in the South, such as those in Reggio Calabria in 1970,[24] weakening the autonomous capacities of local leaders, like those in the MSI, who might have waged a battle of the southern periphery against the state.

2. The Southernization of the Christian Democrats

The DC's support in the South became even more important as the years wore on and the party's bonds to the Northeast began to erode rapidly, particularly as the Catholic subculture began to demobilize as a result of secularization and generational change taking place in the country at the time. While in the 1950s, two out of every three Italians regularly attended Church, this figure had dropped to one-third of the population in the 1970s.[25] Moreover, not only was the pool of practicing Catholics—once a secure factor in the party's support base—declining, there was also a subsequent loosening of the "tie between the religious and political spheres,"[26] freeing up religious Catholics to vote for other parties.

The Catholic institutions that were left in the region, however, were undergoing changes and were no longer providing the DC with the consistent "transmission belt" that had once mobilized support from various groups in civil society. By the late 1970s, the labor and working-class organizations, CISL and ACLI, had stopped their traditional policy of always supporting DC candidates or running their own members on DC lists. The distance of the DC to the labor movement became even wider after the large-scale student and labor strikes in 1968 when (in a surge of antiparty sentiment) all of the major trade unions decided to loosen their ties to their respective parties and become a more autonomous force. As a result, CISL became more autonomous of the DC as it improved its ties to the lay UIL, and the communist CGIL, which had also distanced itself from the PCI.

In addition, Catholic Action—which continued to support the party, despite the latter's efforts to undermine its influence—was beginning to falter, dropping considerably in membership, from its high of 3.3 million in the mid-1960s to 1,650,000 in 1970 to 816,000 in 1973.[27] Eventually, the once pivotal Catholic organization would abandon its unconditional support for the party and even withdraw from politics altogether.[28] Although there would be a resurgence of new Catholic inspired associations in the 1980s, their influence in an increasingly secular society did not have the kind of impact that was possible in earlier periods.[29] As a result of these changes in the Northeast subculture, by the 1980s the DC "found itself confronted with a progressive demobilization of the organization of the Catholic world . . . the old 'collateralism' [was] waning throughout the national territory."[30]

The lack of appeal of the DC in the North, which was in part due to the party's own conflicting relationship with the Catholic movement, was becoming evident by the mid-1970s. From 1972 to 1987, the DC's support in the Veneto, the core of the Catholic subculture, dropped from 53.1 to 43.5 percent. During the same period, in Friuli-Venezia Giulia and the "White" provinces of Lombardy, the DC also lost 9.8 and 7.8 percent of the vote, respectively.[31] By the early 1990s, the DC's vote share dropped from an average high of 51 to only 27 percent in its former stronghold.

In contrast to the DC's losses in the North, the party held on to its support in the South from the 1970s to the 1980s. For example, during the decade leading up to 1987, the DC's average vote share dropped from 31.30 to 23.30 percent in the six largest central and northern cities of Milan, Turin, Bologna, Florence, and Venice. However, in the four largest cities in the South (Bari, Naples, Palermo, and Rome), the DC fell by only 2.2 percent and held onto 32.3 percent of the total vote share in the region.[32] Then, from the mid-1980s to 1992 the DC's support in the South actually showed a sharp increase, surpassing its base in the North, growing to 40 percent, up four points from its average during the thirty-year period from the 1940s to the 1970s (see figure 4.1). Thus, even

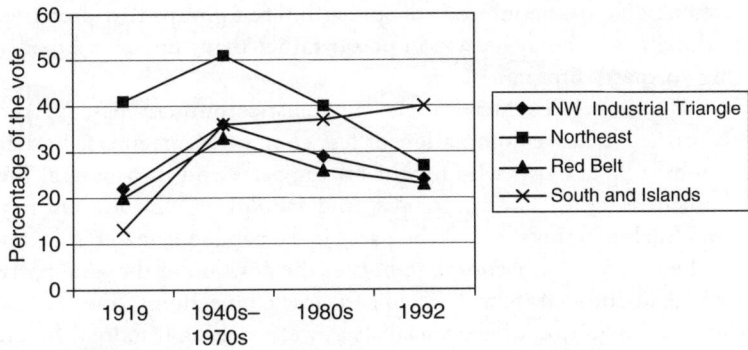

Figure 4.1 The southernization of the DC electorate

Notes: Changing share of the vote gained by the DC, in whole percentages. The 1948 vote, which was atypical for the 1940–1970s period, is omitted. Vote in 1919 for the Popular party. NW Industrial Triangle: Lombardy, Liguria, Piedmont; Northeast: Friuli-Venezia Giulia, Trentino-Alto Adige, the Veneto; Red Belt: Emilia-Romagna, the Marches, Tuscany, Umbria; South: the rest except for Valle d'Aosta, which is not included.

Source: Adapted from Mark Donovan, "A Party System in Transformation: The April 1992 Italian Election," *West European Politics* vol. 15 (1992), p. 176.

as the DC was losing support nationwide, its area of influence was becoming more restricted to the South and to the Islands, particularly Sicily, where the party's clientelism had been most effective at smoothing over any remaining secessionist sentiments left over from the early days of the postwar period.

The PSI, with whom the DC had been allied since the early 1960s, was also becoming more southern in terms of the composition of their social base. From 1983 to 1987, when Craxi was prime minister, the biggest gains for the Socialists came from southern constituencies. For example, during the provincial elections in 1990, the PSI did quite well in the three major regions of the South; it nearly doubled its seats in the provinces in Sicily and made similar gains in Campania and Puglia. However, the party declined considerably in all of the provinces in Lombardy, one of its former strongholds.[33]

The reliance of the DC and the PSI on clientelism, however, had a significantly negative effect on the organizational structures of both parties. Since the 1970s, the increasing factionalization of the DC and PSI reduced their ability to mobilize support at the grassroots level. Party discipline gave way as local and sectional pressures made their ability to aggregate interests and prioritize issues increasingly difficult. The DC's occupation of the central government had further made the party vulnerable to the interests of special interest groups that preferred to go straight to whomever was in power rather than support a broader ideology or party program.[34]

The DC and PSI's increasingly clientelistic southern base in the 1980s further led to a domination of less committed members. Rather than mobilizing activists who fought for the party and its program, the DC recruited more "family, friends, and employers who are entirely passive." Such members joined the party in exchange for material favors and in the end were only chosen to bolster the position of the local party boss who had enrolled them.[35] The PSI's close connection to the DC led to a similar corruption of the Socialists as well, making it more difficult for the party to find committed activists.

Finally, the dominance of national-level party elites reinforced a top-down dynamic within the DC and PSI, preventing the development of their regional and local levels and inhibiting the representation of subnational interests. The centralized nature of the party system was so strong that local elections were often fought on the basis of national issues, which were often obfuscated by larger ideological battles. Although both parties attempted to reform their organizations in the mid-1970s and 1980s in an effort to improve their capacity to mobilize at the grass-roots level, they were blocked by the entrenched power of the factions within the parties and their leaders.[36]

3. Clientelism and the Southern Question

The DC's clientelism and the creation of a vote bank in the South had a significant impact on Italy's political institutions. A major product of the DC's clientelism in the South was an even greater southernization of the state's bureaucratic and administrative structure, a process that had begun during the liberal and fascist periods. By the 1990s, most of the civil servants that staff the bureaucracy came from the South; out of the 100 of the highest ranking functionaries in the civil service, about 80 to 90 of them were born in the South and had studied there.[37] The same dominance of southerners exists in the lower levels of the bureaucracy—where between 60 and 70 percent are southerners—as well as in the military and the large state-holding companies.

Northerners have been less attracted to the generally low paying jobs in the public sector, which hold little prestige in comparison to the better opportunities in the private sector. In the South (excluding the capital, Rome), about 20 percent of all jobs are in the public sector, almost twice as much as those in the Center-North, and more than

15 percent of all jobs nationally.[38] As a result of this imbalance, most government field offices in the North are understaffed, while those in the South are full of extra workers.

The presence of southerners in the government is not, per se, a problem or a detriment to government services as much as how the civil servants actually received their positions. Because such jobs are handed out to secure votes for the governing party they are seen as rewards and not duties, further distorting a system that is already bogged down by numerous laws and restrictions and contributing to the problem of incompetent and unresponsive government.

Second, the DC's patronage in the *Mezzogiorno* did little to develop the region as the industrialization projects in the South did not provide the type of support the area needed. Although the *Cassa* and other initiatives facilitated an increase in the volume of industrial development in areas of the South, this did little to alleviate unemployment. Most of the state-run industries in the South "were not labor intensive and created relatively few jobs." Moreover, much of the government assistance in the South failed to "develop a long-term, coordinated investment policy or a comprehensive economic program."[39] The result has been the profusion of "cathedrals in the desert": useless or futile projects sponsored by the local ruling party to take care of short-term needs of employment, often around the time of major elections.

The more the DC used the transfer of state resources to maintain the party in power it simultaneously weakened the chances for autonomous development in the areas outside of party channels. The massive use of patronage to support the local economy encouraged a "perverse" relationship between local parties, entrepreneurs, and the state,[40] which has, among other things, created a negative business climate, driving off potential investors. Also, by forming alliances with local organized-crime groups, the DC undermined local development by encouraging a hostile and violent atmosphere in which entrepreneurs are under the stress of paying protection money.

Finally, the DC never encouraged the rise of an independent middle-class in the South, but rather created one that is dependent on the state, party, and public institutions. During the 1960s, for example, most of the state funds used to promote artisans went to those in the Center and North and not the South (more on this later),[41] further blocking the development of a class of entrepreneurs in the region. Thus, after so many years of throwing money into various development schemes and public industries in the South, there is little in the way of local entrepreneurial resources—including human capital—which might facilitate local development.

The figures alone explain the impact of the DC's action and their indifference to eradicating the Southern Question. The South continues to lag behind the Center and North, subsisting as one of the most economically underdeveloped areas of Western Europe with a per-capita GDP at around 68 percent of the national total, a figure that has not changed since the late 1960s (see table 4.2)! As of January 2002, unemployment in the North was around 4 percent, while in the South it was 18 percent, with considerably higher percentages for youth in major urban centers. While there are pockets of development in the South, the

Table 4.2   Regional per-capita GDP

Regions	GDP (in millions of lire at current prices) 1999	1970	1980	1989	1999
Piedmont	43.456	123.8	118.7	119.5	116.8
Valle d'Aosta	48.304	143.6	127.4	126.5	129.8
Lombardy	48.288	134.6	129.1	130.5	129.8
Trentino-A.A.	48.609	106.0	120.6	120.0	130.6
Veneto	43.482	106.8	109.9	115.0	116.9
Friuli-V.G.	41.757	103.3	114.6	117.4	112.2
Liguria	39.691	118.8	110.2	111.4	106.7
Emilia-Romagna	47.477	115.2	129.4	123.4	127.6
Tuscany	40.919	110.2	109.4	106.6	110.0
Umbria	35.936	90.5	98.7	92.6	96.6
The Marches	37.954	92.4	108.9	104.8	102.0
Lazio	41.188	108.5	102.0	111.4	110.7
Abruzzo	31.006	73.4	84.2	86.4	83.3
Molise	29.054	60.0	71.9	72.4	78.1
Campania	24.053	70.2	67.7	68.6	64.6
Puglia	24.626	74.0	74.0	73.1	66.2
Basilicata	26.613	63.5	67.3	59.3	71.5
Calabria	22.906	58.0	57.3	58.0	61.6
Sicily	24.543	65.8	67.7	65.2	66.0
Sardinia	28.695	79.4	73.0	72.8	77.1
South	25.117	69.0	69.3	68.7	67.5
Northwest	45.986	129.5	123.8	125.1	123.6
Northeast	45.239	109.5	118.8	118.9	121.6
Center	40.281	105.6	105.1	107.6	108.3
Italy	37.209	100.0	100.0	100.0	100.0

Indices: Italy = 100.

Sources: SVIMEZ, *I conti economici del Centro-Nord e del Mezzogiorno nel ventennio 1970–1989* (Bologna: il Mulino, 1993), p. 39; for 1999: ISTAT, *Conti economici territoriali* (October 15, 2001), www.istat.it.

region continues to depend on the largess of the state to support the local population. Although large-scale development projects like the *Cassa per il Mezzogiorno* were eventually abandoned in the 1980s after their dismal results, state transfer payments, such as false disability payments, are still a major source of income.

4. Trends in the North's Economy

In contrast to the South, the North has developed into one of the wealthiest regions in Europe. Almost 40 percent of total GDP for the country is produced in just three northern regions, Lombardy, Veneto, and Piedmont. Lombardy alone has been the most productive region, producing 20 percent of national GDP, and is currently a member of the "Four Motors of Europe," an organization that lobbies on behalf of some of the most productive and wealthy regions in Western Europe, including Baden-Württemberg (Germany), Catalonia (Spain), and Rhône-Alpes (France), in an effort to promote continued development in these regions.

Within the North, however, economic development over the past couple of decades has been concentrated in the Northeast, including the regions of the Veneto, Trentino-Alto Adige, Friuli-Venezia Giulia, and parts of Lombardy. The upturn in the economy in the Veneto, and provinces like Bergamo in Lombardy, have represented a sharp turn of events in some of these areas, which at the turn of the century were marked by economic decline and a high degree of emigration to other Italian cities or other countries abroad. It also represents a shift in industrial strength away from the northwestern Industrial Triangle of Genoa, Milan, Turin (which was responsible for economic development in Italy from the 1890s to the 1960s) to the Northeast. Moreover, while the former was built on large economies of scale, the latter is a product of more flexible small-scale enterprises (SMEs), which are more locally rooted in the territory.

The small firm emerged in the advanced industrialized world as a response to the economic crises of large firms during the 1970s when growing global competition and increasingly fragmented global markets forced companies to decentralize their operations and rely more on subcontracting.[42] Although the large firm has not disappeared from the economic map, smaller firms—which are more flexible and better able to meet changing consumer patterns and market conditions—have generally flourished.

The small firm, however, is nothing new to Italy where there has always been more small-scale industries compared to other European countries. For example, in both Germany and Italy only 1.2 and 1.7 percent of the total number of firms in each country are considered "medium and large" (employing more than 100 workers). Such firms, however, employ 58.6 percent of the German work force while it is only 30.7 percent in Italy. There are also twice as many of the even smaller artisan firms—which often comprise of only one or two workers—in Italy (1.4 million in 1991) as there are in Germany (611,000).[43]

The SMEs that have flourished in northeastern Italy have moreover benefited by being located within industrial districts: territorially delimited areas within which a number of similar firms are located. Industrial districts help small, often new enterprises by providing a forum in which entrepreneurs share important sectoral knowledge, and develop a mutually supportive network. Because industrial districts are territorially defined and often characterized by a common culture, there is a sense of community among the entrepreneurs. Therefore, it is not uncommon that the local coffee bar becomes the main locus where new product ideas are discussed and deals made. As a result of the new revitalization[44] of the industrial district over the past couple of decades, there has been a development of extremely productive areas that have been able to reverse the trend toward industrial decline in the West. In addition to Italy, other industrial districts are found in highly productive areas of Europe, like in Germany (Baden-Württemberg), Denmark (Jutland), and areas in Sweden, as well as the United States (Silicon Valley).[45]

The majority of the industrial districts in Italy can be found in the Center and Northeast (see table 4.3). With a total population of around 10 million residents, the Northeast (Friuli-Venezia Giulia, Emilia-Romagna, Veneto, and Trentino-Alto Adige) has over 65 industrial districts in a variety of industries ranging from textiles and furniture to mechanical engineering. In contrast, the Northwest (Piedmont, Liguria, Lombardy, and Valle d'Aosta), with a population of over 15 million has only 59 industrial districts, most of which are located in Lombardy, a region that sits right on the line between West and East. Within the South, there are only a total of 15 industrial districts, of which almost half are located in one region, Abruzzo, which is located near the center of the country.

The corridor of regions from the Center up through the Northeast has been dubbed the Third Italy, distinguishing it from either the large industries in the Northwest or the economically underdeveloped South. Here, the number of artisan and SMEs have and continue to be well

Table 4.3 Industrial districts by region, 1991

Piedmont	16
Lombardy	42
Trentino-Alto Adige	4
Veneto	34
Friuli-Venezia Giulia	3
Liguria	1
Emilia-Romagna	24
Tuscany	19
Umbria	5
Marche	34
Lazio	2
Abruzzo	6
Campania	4
Puglia	3
Calabria	2
Northwest	59
Northeast	65
Center	60
South	15
Italy	199

Source: Adapted from ISTAT, *Rapporto sull'Italia* (Bologna: Il Mulino, 1996), p. 76.

over the national average, accounting for the bulk of local employment and income creation. Piedmont, for example, the region most known for the growth of large industries in the late nineteenth and early twentieth centuries, has only 16 industrial districts. Similarly, Liguria—the region where the port city of Genoa is located—has only one district.

The Northeast has become a crucial area of economic growth, which has made up not only for continued losses in the South, but also in the Northwest, where the large industries of the Industrial Triangle have taken a beating in recent years as a result of industrial decline. Thus, although 4.1 percent unemployment in the Northwest is much less than in the South, it is still more than the 3.5 percent in the Northeast. The difference in youth unemployment between the Northwest and Northeast is even starker. Youth unemployment figures (people between the ages of 15 and 23) are an important indicator of the local economy as they show the degree to which local industries are able to incorporate new entrants into the workforce. The northwestern regions of Piedmont and Liguria have youth unemployment rates (1999) of 22 and 32 percent respectively. In contrast, the youth unemployment rates in the Veneto and Emilia-Romagna—together the heart of the Third Italy—are only 11.7 and 12.5 percent, respectively, about half of those in the Northwest.[46] These figures show that the SMEs of the Northeast have been much better at job creation, while the larger, less flexible industries of the Northwest continue to face challenges. Such challenges are most difficult in places like Genoa, which has been eclipsed by the processes of globalization, making the once famed port city a center of the country's rust belt.

The success of SMEs in Italy has been their capacity to dominate a high share of the export market since the 1970s, particularly during the late 1980s to the early 1990s. Part of this economic development is due to the devaluation of the Lira in the 1992, which gave the small-scale industries an edge over their more expensive competitors in Europe and the United States. In fact, during the 1992–1994 period, three regions within the Northeast (Trentino, the Veneto, and Friuli-Venezia Giulia) had the highest number of exports out of all 20 regions in Italy. Although these regions of the Triveneto area have only about 11 percent of the country's population, they accounted for 13.1 percent of total employed and 19 percent of the country's total exports in the early 1990s.[47]

The success of the Northeast has already become a national symbol of economic growth, overshadowing the old giants of the Northwest. For example, in *Schei* ("money" in Venetian dialect) a recent best selling book about the Veneto region by the Venetian journalists Gian Antonio Stella, focuses on the new wealth in the region. The book spends a great deal of time describing how the local industries have come to dominate certain world niche markets, putting a number of small towns on the map. Thus, for example, in the town of Rossano in the Veneto, only five factories produce 80 percent of all bicycle seats in the world.[48] Similar stories are also told about numerous other consumer goods produced in the Veneto and other parts of the Northeast, from ski boots to eyeglass frames. Today, some of the most well-known names of Italian industry are located in the Northeast, such as Benetton (clothing), DeLonghi (appliances), and Luxottica (eyeglasses).

5. From the Southern Question to the Northern Question

However, as Stella also makes clear in his book, while this growth has led to a new class of entrepreneurs and a new hope for Italian industry, it has also created a host of new problems that many locals feel have yet to be addressed by the country's ruling political elite. In spite of its high growth, the economy of the Northeast has faced a number of institutional barriers, which have made many local operators over the past several years concerned about future economic expansion. In particular, the local economy is confronted with the complexities of the fiscal and bureaucratic system, as well as problems associated with financing new and enlarging industry, and professional education. Although this crisis has affected all business in the North, it has taken on greater proportions in areas where the small-scale industries are most concentrated, such as the Northeast.

A 1995 report on economic development in Italy labeled this situation the "Northern Question," raising the flag that not all is well in the wealthy areas of the country.[49] The main problem that the North is facing concerns high economic growth coupled with low institutional development. The report referred to the contradiction in the regions of the Northeast that, on the one hand, are able to compete successfully on the international market and are among the "principal creators of the strong upturn of the country's economy." On the other hand, such areas are set within an old, outdated system of government institutions that are unable to meet the needs of this growing sector. The biggest issues cited by local economic operators are taxes and bureaucracy.

The concerns about taxation run from how they cut into profits, to the Byzantine nature of the system that inhibits the flow of business. Overall, Italy has experienced one of the highest increases in taxes among all OECD countries over the past 30 years. In the decade from 1980 to 1990, Italian taxes increased by 11.6 percent, just under Greece (the country with the highest increase at 13.1 percent) but well over the OECD average of 2.5 percent.[50] By the mid-1990s, total government revenue was around 44 percent of GDP compared to the EU average of 41 percent. If you break this percentage down you can further see that employers' social security payments account for 9 percent of government revenue (3 percent higher than the 6 percent average of EU countries).[51] Thus, not only have taxes in Italy risen at a rate sharper than the rest of the EU, but they have also disproportionately affected businesses and their costs.

Moreover, most of the fiscal responsibility has been borne primarily by the Center and North, where most of the small-scale industries are located (see figure 4.2). Although the South does not receive more percapita state funds than the Center-North, it contributes much less in terms of taxes. In the mid-1980s, with around 36 percent of the population, the South received about 35 percent of national funds. However, the region only generated about 18 percent of the total tax moneys used for the leading social assistance programs.

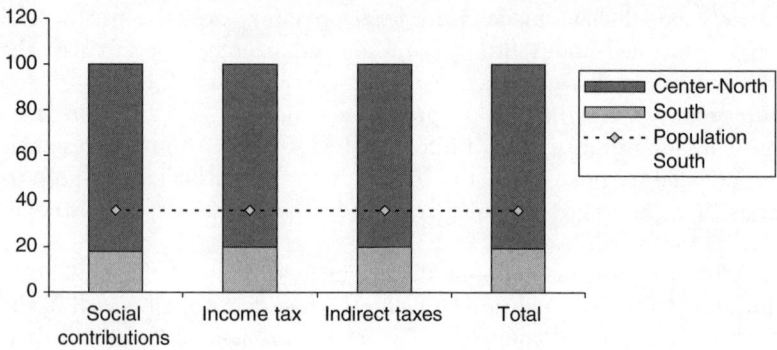

Figure 4.2 Percentage of the taxes paid to the Public Administration per geographic area (South and Center-North) in 1986
Source: Carlo Trigilia, *Sviluppo senza autonomia* (Bologna: Il Mulino, 1994), p. 61.

This unequal division of the tax burden, which is also the result of the DC's patronage to the underdeveloped South, has further consolidated the regional cleavage between the two areas of the country. In particular, it has politicized the fiscal system by making the North the country's "tax-payer" and the South, the country's "tax-receiver." The unequal contributions to the fiscal system, combined with the continuing "southernization" of the state administrative structure has further increased the perception of Rome as a predatory element that is undermining development and the future of the North.

The situation is, moreover, not helped by the inefficient and complex nature of the fiscal system itself. In general, the high number of fiscal laws—during the nine-year period from 1986 to 1993, there were over 1800 normative measures (*provvedimenti normativi*) in parliament on just fiscal matters—has created a "chronically inefficient" system.[52] Even more than the actual degree of taxation, many local economic operators in the Northeast are concerned about the way the system functions. According to Guidalberto Guidi, the president of the Federation of Industry (Federindustria) of Emilia-Romagna, "the bureaucratic-fiscal" factor is "the most fundamental thing today" that impedes industrial development in the Northeast. He further stated that the problem does not lie so much with the actual amount of taxes, as "the way one pays." "The complexity of the system," he argues, "is a dramatic problem."[53] Other leaders of local artisan associations in the North, for example, have argued that for continued economic growth, the state needs to "reduce chaotic legislation ... [and] the bureaucracy in the public administration."[54] The complexity of the Italian fiscal system is also blamed for turning away foreign investors in local industries. Innocenzo Cipolletta, director of Confindustria (Italian Confederation of Industry) argued that "foreign enterprises do not find our country appetizing in terms of investing, especially because [we have] a system which, with its uncertainty, makes planning difficult."[55]

LIFE (Liberi imprenditori federalisti europei or Free Entrepreneurs for a Federalist Europe), a radical organization that promotes small-scale and artisan industry, is most known for its anti-tax antics that have gained some publicity during the past few years.[56] Based in the Veneto, the LIFE has also called attention to the problems associated with paying a tax or filing a form, which involves going to not just one but numerous offices. Such a bureaucracy, LIFE argues, takes up precious time for small-scale entrepreneurs who have a limited number of employees and cannot afford to hire additional support staff to deal with administrative matters.

In addition to fiscal matters, the small industries in the Northeast have found the aging infrastructure an impediment to continued growth. In a recent survey of Italy by the *Economist*, the magazine noted that "there is a solid case for more public spending in the North, especially on infrastructure."[57] This same sentiment is echoed in interviews with activists working for artisans in the Veneto, who point out the need for better roadways to transport goods[58] as the volume of merchandise per kilometer has increased dramatically in the Northeast.[59] Others point out the problems related to aging train networks, and the inadequacy of local airports.[60]

A meeting of a number of politically minded entrepreneurs in the Northeast argued also that the malaise about the business climate in the Northeast was due to the "inadequacy of [government] policy" to meet the needs of local entrepreneurs and "maintain the economic system." The "manifesto" of the entrepreneurs further stated that the "flexibility of the small-scale productive system is not enough" to compete on a global level. Rather, the state still needs to address the weakness outside of the firm, that is, in the areas of infrastructure, professional formation, diffusion of research, and credit.[61] Thus, in an ironic way, the local entrepreneurs of the Northeast are asking for a combination of both less state (fewer taxes, less bureaucracy), and yet more state involvement (building of infrastructure).

Another problem is the centralized nature of the fiscal system. A research project sponsored by a regional research institute based in

Milan (IRER) compared the three regions in the Triveneto area (Trentino, the Veneto, and Friuli-Venezia Giulia) in terms of their economic productivity. The study found that, in fact, fiscal autonomy did facilitate the local economy, and that Trentino, the region with the most autonomy, had the highest level of productivity, while Friuli-Venezia Giulia was second, and the Veneto third.

The study demonstrated that, due to their fiscal autonomy, Trentino and Friuli-Venezia Giulia were able to apply more of their own resources to help the local economy. Thus, for example, in 1990 the Veneto was able to dedicate only 0.5 percent of the region's GDP to productive sectors, while Friuli-Venezia Giulia was able to dedicate 2 percent and Trentino 5 percent. Thus, although the Veneto is still a highly productive region, it faces more barriers than the regions with special statutes and more autonomy. The "quality, certainty, and programmability of the resources" available to the regions with special statutes, the study concluded, "represents a decisively important advantage."[62]

The "Northern Question" and its relationship to the growth of northern enterprises have highlighted some of the most important issues facing Italian politics today. The contradiction between high economic growth and low institutional development have shed light on the problems facing the Italian state, as well as the general gap between the North and South. The issues of taxes, bureaucracy, and the poor state of the country's infrastructure have become stark reminders of the outdated centralized administrative and fiscal system that are incapable of meeting the needs and concerns of a new class of entrepreneurs and enterprises in a changing economic and social context.

6. The Northern Question and Local Politics

As the economic changes were taking place within the North and Northeast during the 1980s, there emerged a political vacuum as no party stepped forward as the representative of the SME sector. In the early years, the DC was the strongest proponent of small-scale industries and artisans and promoted their development by establishing a number of state benefits for them. In the 1950s, the DC passed legislation that gave small firms access to low-interest loans, tax-breaks, and reductions on employer contributions. They also received "welfare benefits at reduced premiums," and "exemptions from keeping accounts and from bankruptcy proceedings."[63] On the local level, the Catholic Church was also active in financing industries in the Northeast by setting up rural *casse*—small savings and loan banks[64]—that helped industries get off the ground. As a result, 40 percent of the artisans surveyed in 1963 supported the DC, compared to their support of the PSI (19 percent) and the PCI (17 percent) that year. Similar results were also common among other sectors of the middle class, from shopkeepers, to clerical workers and executives.[65]

The promotion of the small-scale sector was central to the DC's strategy of establishing the party as the leading force for the middle class. The DC also saw a thriving class of independent entrepreneurs as a viable block to the growth of a (left-leaning) proletariat. The DC's goal in supporting entrepreneurialism was to "deproletarianize" the working class by making them all property owners, similar to the strategy by conservatives in other parts of the world that encourage, for example, home ownership. The party's saying at the time was, "*non tutti proletari, ma tutti proprietari*" (Everyone a proprietor not a proletarian), hoping that the rise in small, independent business people would reduce the number of (working class) supporters for the Left.[66]

The actions of the DC, however, did little to provide the infrastructural support or political representation that this sector needed. Rather, the party ruled in a more *ad hoc* fashion, focusing on requests by individual entrepreneurs, without any kind of long-term planning that would have taken into account the changing local economy. In most cases, the DC chose to rule by abstaining to regulate, particularly in fiscal matters as the party looked the other way when people evaded taxes and worker contributions.[67] As a result, the Northeast is not only known for its industrial success but it is also rumored to be famous for its tax cheats.

Moreover, as the DC was more interested in creating a large class of (relatively more conservative) small-scale entrepreneurs, and hence the number of firms per se, the party was less interested in the protection of existing firms and artisans. For example, eligibility for the generous government benefits that were available to artisans was based on the number of employees in a firm, rather than affiliation with a professional association or category, as it is in Germany with the *Handwerk* sector.[68] As a result of the DC's policies, the small-scale entrepreneur in Italy is less of a select "caste" of craft workers, and more a part of the semi-informal sector.

By the 1980s, the DC's focus on clientelism alienated small industries across the country as its patronage had become much more exclusive, narrowing the access to state resources. The DC's control over the credit and banking system, for example, directly favored industrial giants, like Fiat, Pirelli, Montedison, and Olivetti, who had close ties with the different factions within the party. In contrast, small- and medium-sized industries were left out of the loop and found it much harder to gain credit.[69] Big companies were also able to pay large amounts in bribes and hence guaranteed more political clout than small enterprises that could not afford this practice.

The distance between the DC and SMEs became even wider when the party adopted increasingly corporatist industrial policies in the 1970s and 1980s that favored the interests of large confederal trade unions and big business. Such arrangements, which emerged across the advanced industrialized world during the 1970s among peak organizations—ruling parties, leading trade unions, and employers associations—specifically sought to reduce conflict and arrive at agreements on wage levels and benefits.[70] The corporatist policies of the DC were part of the party's new "move to the Left" that started in the 1960s and brought the party into a coalition with the PSI.

The tripartite agreements, which occurred briefly in the early 1980s between the government and the three major confederal unions (CGIL, CSIL, and UIL), also included the Confederation of Industry (Confindustria). Although it is supposed to represent all industries in Italy, the leadership of Confindustria is dominated by the big industrial giants of the Northwest. In the end, the tripartite agreements consolidated Rome's link with the large industrial interests of the Northwest, further politicizing the growing difference between big and small industries, as well as the regional divide within the North between the Northwest and Northeast. In fact, while the DC's support in the Northeast suffered a rapid drop of 13 percent from the 1980s to the 1990s, it lost only 5 percent during this same period in the Northwest.

The corporatist positioning of the DC also moved the party further to the Left, when in 1976 the party, for the first time since 1946, brought the PCI out of the opposition and promised ruling positions in the cabinet. In exchange, the PCI promised to abstain from any votes of no confidence that would surely have brought the new government down. The DC's acceptance of the PCI in the national government was spurred by a number of factors, in particular the success of the PCI during the regional and national elections in 1975 and 1976 in which the party began to demonstrate its ability to possibly surpass the DC electorally. In addition, the DC was attempting to pass an austerity package through parliament to combat rising inflation and needed the assistance of the PCI in order to gain the acquiescence of all the major confederal trade unions for lowering wages.[71]

The move to the Left by the DC was not necessarily "anti-business" as the Communists themselves have been very supportive of small businesses (see later). Rather, such a shift went against the solidly anti-communist constituents of the party, particularly the more Catholic ones in the Northeast subculture. Moreover, the desire to cozy up with the major confederal unions put the party closer to organized dependent labor in large firms as opposed to independent workers who are by and large outside of the labor movement and linked mainly with more local small business and artisan associations.

Thus, by the late 1980s, it became clear to northern small businesses that their ties with the DC and their style of politics was less and less in their own interests. Small businesses were more outside the loop between parties and the state, and the corporatist interests of big business. By the 1990s, northern businesses had become "irritated with inefficient public services and the battery of government agencies that steered money to the South." This factor was only made worse by the fact that much of this money was making its way into the hands of organized crime groups in the South. Antonio Gava's faction in Naples, for example, grew in collusion with local crime families.[72]

The DC's incapacity to consistently represent the SME sector was not only evident in terms of its national policies, but also in terms of its incapacity to represent local interests. As the Catholic subculture began to demobilize in the 1970s, the party essentially dropped the ball by failing to replace the fall in religious-based associationalism in the Northeast with one that was more focused on the interests of the local economy and the SMEs in particular.[73] The failure of the DC to pick up on the issue of economic changes in the Northeast was the result of the party's continuing focus on building up its vote bank in the South. Moreover, the party lost touch with any of its roots in the territory as it focused on distributing national resources and less on representing local issues. Thus, just as the SMEs were growing rapidly and taking off in the 1980s, the DC was becoming more and more alienated from them, eventually contributing to the party's downfall (discussed in chapter 5).

In contrast to the DC, the party's main competitor, the PCI, emerged in the 1980s as an effective political force for small-scale industries in the central regions of the Third Italy, where the party had already gained a positive reputation for its capacity to govern local affairs. The local governments ruled by the PCI not only provided excellent services for its citizens, but also established a better business atmosphere, with better regional economic planning and more efficient local government institutions that helped smaller businesses grow and develop.[74] In addition, the PCI and its successor party, the DS, the Democratici di Sinistra (Democratic Left) continues to be effective in helping local businesses through their affiliated network of cooperatives in all sectors, particularly in local services (trash collection, energy, and the like), and providing other services for workers, like child daycare.

In the end, the DC's fear that decentralization to the regions would give more power to the locally rooted Left came true as the Communists emerged, ironically, as a real middle-class party of Italy with strong ties to the SME sector in the Center. What few resources the regions and other local authorities do have at their disposal, the PCI/DS has proven to use them in a more effective way than the DC ever did. This, however, was evident even before regional reform took hold. By the 1970s, the PCI had already begun to establish itself as the defender of this sector, "championing small business interests nationally and assisting the self-employed in areas where it controlled local government resources."[75]

As a result of the different economic strategies of the DC and PCI/DS on the local level, the development of the regional economies within the Third Italy has varied. Industries in the Veneto have emerged in a much less planned and organized atmosphere than those in Emilia-Romagna, which have been able to rely on the efforts of the PCI/DS and its allied associations to foster economic growth in the region. Thus, although both areas have been extremely productive in recent years, the growth in the Veneto and other areas that were under the DC has been more *in spite* of local politics, rather than because of it.

7. Conclusion

The divide between the North and South in Italy, which, by the 1980s had become increasingly wide, is, thus, not simply the product of a cultural gap between the two regions, but rather the concrete actions of political elites. The postwar ruling parties' use of public resources for patronage in the South led to the underdevelopment of the region, thereby hindering the development of an effective, autonomous economy. The North, however, was also adversely affected by postwar politics as it became increasingly alienated from the state, which became predatory in nature as it transferred more and more resources to the South to pay for its clientelist networks. Moreover, the institutional legacies of the DC's postwar regime, from fiscal problems and bureaucratic red tape to corporatist ties with large industry, had created a number of barriers to local, small–medium industries, particularly in the Northeast. In the end, these conditions contributed to the creation of a particular community of entrepreneurs in the North that began to shift away from the DC and more toward a new series of regionalist parties in the 1980s, an issue we confront in chapter 5.

CHAPTER 5

The Rise of the Lega in the North

1. The Liga Veneta

As the DC declined in the North during the 1970s and 1980s, the party began to be replaced by a group of new regionalist parties, the first being the Liga Veneta (Venetian League), which emerged in the northeastern region of the Veneto. The Liga (liga means league in the Venetian dialect) was started in 1979 by Franco Rocchetta, a local entrepreneur who was actively involved in promoting regional identity at the time.[1] In the beginning, the Liga was not strong enough to present candidates for elections on its own and had to briefly join forces with the French-speaking regionalists in Valle d'Aosta (the Union Valdôtaine, UV) during the elections for the European Parliament that year.

The Liga first presented its own symbol, the Lion of Venice, during local elections in 1980 in a couple of small municipalities in the Veneto region, and by the national elections of 1983 it had already gained 4 percent of the vote region-wide, an excellent showing for a new party. In particular provinces that year, such as Vicenza and Treviso, the party gained as much as 6 to 7 percent of the vote,[2] almost twice as much as its support across the whole region. In another set of local elections two years later, the Liga took a drop in support to 3.7 percent region-wide, but was still able to elect two councilors to the Veneto regional council.[3]

The rise of the Liga was in many ways consistent with the developments taking place in Europe during the late 1970s and early 1980s. At this time, regionalist movements began to emerge as both traditional political parties began to lose support and a new interest in local culture began to surge across the continent.[4] The Liga, though, was in many ways unique in Italian politics because it was the first regionalist party to gain success outside of the regions with special statutes, where parties like the UV in Valle d'Aosta, the Südtiroler Volkspartei (SVP) in Alto Adige, or the Partito Sardo di Azione (PSd'A) in Sardinia have all had a strong following.

In addition, the success of the Liga represented the first changes and mutations of the old Catholic subculture. As voters in the Northeast moved away from the increasingly southern DC, they did not necessarily shift to the traditional parties—particularly not the communist or socialist Left, which they found abhorrent to their own conservative Catholic beliefs and worldview. Rather, such an electorate was drawn to a newer and more regionally focused alternative that, possibly, provided them with another type of political subculture they could hold onto.

The Liga's political platform focused primarily on the preservation of regional culture and language. Rocchetta himself was a member of a group called the International Association for the Defense of Threatened Languages and Cultures, and had once argued that the Veneto was "like Corsica . . . one of the internal colonies in Europe that are discovering themselves."[5] Moreover, the first article in the 1983 party statute of the Liga Veneta stated that the movement seeks to defend the "ethnic and linguistic characteristics of the Venetian nation in Europe and the world."[6]

Despite the fact that the Venetians are not considered a linguistic minority in Italy, like German speakers in Alto Adige or French speakers in Valle d'Aosta, many people in the region use the distinctive regional dialect as their main language.[7] In fact, according to a recent survey, the *Veneti* communicate in dialect more than most other Italians. Around 42.6 percent of the population in the Veneto said that they speak a linguistic dialect other than Italian either exclusively or most of the time with their family. This response was just under (the northeastern province of) Trentino, where 43.6 percent said the same, and well over the 19 percent average of the whole country.[8] Overall, the Northeast and the mainland South were the areas of the country with the most dialect speakers, around 27 percent of the population, in sharp contrast with the Northwest, which had only 11 percent. In spite of the fact that the Venetian dialect is widely spoken, Rocchetta once lamented that the *Veneti* were still ignorant of their linguistic heritage.[9]

Throughout the early to mid-1980s, the Liga ran electoral campaigns on a platform that aimed to preserve the linguistic heritage of the Veneto. Thus, for example, Rocchetta had once put forward a proposal when he was a member of the Veneto regional council that the regional dialect, which is not recognized as an official foreign language in Italy, be placed on an equal footing with Italian.[10] The proposal failed, as did his request, in a 1984 letter to then socialist Prime Minister Bettino Craxi, that the Veneto be given a special statute. Rochetta argued that if other regions have been given special status on the basis of ethnicity, the Veneto—with its long history as an independent republic and distinctive local dialect—should also be granted such a distinction.[11]

On its own, the Liga never progressed beyond 3–5 percent of the Veneto regional vote-share. By 1987, the party would be undermined by its own internal dissention as a group broke off to form another regionalist party, which survived long enough to take away 2 percent of the region's vote during national elections that year and weaken Rocchetta's fledgling movement. Despite its loss, the Liga helped to spark a new drive toward regionalism that was growing more to the west in Piedmont, where the vote for similar autonomist legas had reached 4 percent of the regional vote in 1987. The most successful of the legas, however, was emerging in the region of Lombardy, the largest and wealthiest region of the country.

2. The Lega Lombarda

The Lega was formed in 1982 by Umberto Bossi, an unknown medical student from the Varese province in Lombardy. Much like the Liga Veneta, the Lega Lombarda (Lombard League) had originally emerged as a movement focusing on the preservation of local culture and language. Bossi, similar to Rocchetta, was fascinated with the local folklore of his region and had been active in a group in the late 1970s and early 1980s called *Unione Nord Occidentale dei Laghi Prealpini* or UNOLPA (Northwestern Union of the Lakes of the Alpine Foothills), a cultural organization that focused mainly on regional cooking, poetry in local dialect, and peasant festivals in the lake regions in Lombardy.[12]

Similar to the Liga, the early Lega also reflected a strong attachment to local history and folklore. In the first place, the name of the party was the same as the group of towns and villages that had banded together in the twelfth century to fight the Holy Roman emperor Federico I Barbarossa. The symbol of the party was and still is Alberto da Giussano, the sword-bearing warrior who led the original Lega Lombarda in their victory against Barbarossa's troops during the battle of the Lombard city of Legnano in 1176. Much of the party's early literature talked about the importance of preserving cultural symbols, like the regional flag of Lombardy and local dialects, which Bossi would often use in his political discourses. The Lega also began to follow a trajectory similar to the

Liga in the Veneto by seeking some form of autonomy for Lombardy. At various times the party also made noises about the secession of Lombardy from the rest of the country.

By the mid-1980s, however, it was clear that the Lega was a very different regionalist force than the Liga Veneta. In the first place, the party discussed regional identity much less in terms of local culture and folklore, and more in terms of local economic and social issues.[13] The Lega's early platform focused on autonomy not in terms of linguistic dialects, but more in terms of control over local fiscal resources ("Lombard taxes controlled by Lombards"), and also called for the reservation of jobs in the public administration for locals ("local government run by Lombards"). The Lega also called for the same kinds of reservations in terms of public assistance ("preference given to Lombards in reference to jobs, housing, and financial assistance").[14] Most interesting, Lombards were defined not in terms of ethnic or blood ties, but rather anyone who resided in the region for at least five years.[15]

Moreover, Lombard, and later northern identity, is conceived by the Lega in more generic cultural terms, such as the supposedly widespread Protestant-like work ethic that exists among the population, to their strong sense of entrepreneurialism and disdain for the bureaucratic sluggishness of Rome. The North's status as a "producer" region is further contrasted with the status of the South as a "dependent" region. For example, one of the more colorful propaganda posters of the party depicts Lombardy as a hen, with the caption that the "Lombard hen lays a golden egg for Rome and below."

The Lega also emerged with an economic program that expressed a number of neoliberal themes, from the privatization of state industries to policies in favor of the self-employed, like easier access to credit, a reduction of taxes, and an end to bureaucratic red tape. The neoliberal position of the Lega distinguished the party on the right side of the political spectrum, which was still dominated at the time by the more statist DC. At the same time, the Lega expressed a more protectionist view toward small-scale industry and small business in general, championing this sector as the "backbone" of the local economy. The party even created ALIA or *Associazione Liberi Imprenditori Autonomisti* (Association of Free Entrepreneurs for Autonomy) that claimed to represent artisans, retail merchants, small-scale industrialists, independent professionals, and managers of private and public firms. In a 1993 pamphlet, ALIA presented itself as "an association of autonomous workers" that wants to defend the "traditional values of our population: work–honesty–professionalism." ALIA's propaganda focused on the concerns of small-scale entrepreneurs and the issues they confront, from high taxes and state inefficiency to the corporatist tendencies between big business and the state.

The party's focus on neoliberal economics also went hand in hand with its emphasis on devolution and federalism. "With centralism," Bossi argued, lies "a large part of the public employees, big capital, finance and industry, which, in a unitary state, can better control and corrupt the political class." "Meanwhile," Bossi continued, "small-scale entrepreneurs, autonomous workers, employees in private firms, students, and the elderly," are united in their interest in federalism, an institution "closer to the dimensions and interests of small business and the citizen."[16] Bossi summed up the debate stating that the battle is between the "parasitic and clientelistic capital of Rome" and the "capital of the economy" in Milan.[17]

3. The Regional Nativism of the Lega

From the beginning, the Lega's regionalism has been expressed not only in positive terms, but also, equally, in a strongly negative view toward the South and southern Italians. Playing on latent anti-southern sentiments across the North, Bossi and other Lega leaders have used crude and racist speech, such as persistently referring to southerners as "*terrone*" or "dirty peasants"—a widely used pejorative for people from the South. Moreover, the party has depicted southerners as being everything from lazy to corrupt and backward.

Taking a page from movements like MARP in the 1950s, the Lega also expressed a strong antipathy toward the thousands of southerners that have migrated to the North over the past several generations. The Lega's early campaigns against southern "immigrants," for example, petitioned against everything from southern-born schoolteachers in public schools in the North to the presence of Mafia turncoats who have been relocated to the North under assumed names. The Lega, however, made a crucial shift in the late 1980s when it extended its discourse of intolerance to not just immigrants from the southern regions of the country, but also to non-European immigrants. This was a crucial move by the Lega in part because they risked alienating potential support from southerners residing in the North (for at least five years, thereby passing the party's own test for regional "citizenship").

Moreover, by this time, increasing numbers of migrant laborers began to arrive in the country, particularly from North Africa and Albania. This was a considerable change in a country that for generations was strictly a country of emigration. Slowly, the growing number of nonwhite foreigners in the peninsula, such as Senegalese street vendors selling trinkets on beaches and in piazzas, started to become a social issue with, among other things, incidences of racist violence toward immigrants. Around this time, the national media also began to focus on issues such as the incorporation of undocumented workers, racism, and multiculturalism in Italy. Despite the public concern over the issue—in both Italy and the rest of Europe—the traditional political parties expressed little desire to exploit it.

The Lega was really the first party in Italy to take an explicitly anti-immigrant position, a move that not only politicized the issue considerably, but also put the party squarely in the camp of other new populist Right parties, which were emerging across the continent at the time. Interestingly, the neo-fascist MSI party had failed to pick up on the immigration issue at this early stage despite the fact that the party's support base was strongly anti-immigrant.[18] Immigration did not fit visibly within the MSI's platform, which at this time was still strongly focused on nostalgia for the country's fascist past.

In early 1990, the Lega started a campaign against a newly passed immigration law, the *legge Martelli* (Martelli Law) named after the socialist parliamentarian who introduced it. The focus of the law, which was the first attempt by the state to effectively deal with the issue since the rise in immigration during the 1980s, was to both limit the number of immigrants and also improve the condition of those who are already residing in the country. The Lega argued that although the law was strict in some respects,[19] it was soft on immigrants because it recognized undocumented workers and granted them access to some social and welfare rights (housing and health care).

Much like other populist Right parties in Europe, the Lega's anti-immigrant tactics exploited latent feelings of intolerance and attempted to raise the specter of a "black invasion" overrunning social order. In his first of several books, *Vento dal Nord*, Bossi harangued against multiracial, multiethnic, and multireligious societies. He argued that increasing immigration into Italy would lead to what he called the "American system" or a general decline of society into drug abuse, suicides, teenage delinquency, and an overall increase in social hostilities and tensions.[20] Similarly, in an interview in 1990, Bossi made the assertion that "excessive social differences are fatal to social peace," especially when there are differences of color. "If your streets and plazas are full of people of color," Bossi says, "citizens feel that this is no longer their own world."[21]

The Lega's anti-immigrant position has not been limited to just official discourse, but also considerable action on the local level, where the party has attempted to hinder the growth of immigrant communities. In 1990, for example, a group of Lega members in the town council of Seveso, a small village just north of Milan, tried to block plans to renovate an existing center to house new immigrants. The councilors were eventually able to limit the size of the center and, according to them, "save" the town from an "invasion" of about 1,500 new immigrants. The Lega further argued in their party newspaper that their actions were necessary to stop the development of a "multiracial Seveso." Similarly, the Lega ranted against the high number of immigrants in Bovezzo, another small town in Lombardy where, according to the story in the party's newspaper, "for every ninth Bovezzo resident, there is an immigrant."[22]

In 1995, Erminio Boso, a Lega member of parliament advocated the use of excessive force against immigrants. He said that he "looks to defend white people from blacks," because, "today, everyone is against the whites. The white race has to defend itself, because white faces are becoming extinct."[23]

Finally, the xenophobic position of the Lega goes hand in hand with its regionalist position as the party presents immigrants as simply another threat to northern interests, using them as scapegoats for other problems, such as unemployment, rising crime, and drug abuse. Like much of the populist Right in Europe, the Lega raises the specter of immigrants bringing numerous social problems into Europe, without addressing the role of Europeans themselves. For example, the Lega organizes vigilante groups (*ronde*) to chase away African and Albanian prostitutes from the highways in the North, yet does little to condemn the (Italian) men who frequent them. The Lega, further, blames immigrants for the growing problem of drug addiction in the North, without criticizing the more "pure" Italians for being clients of Moroccan drug dealers. The party uses xenophobia to drum up support, without really addressing the pressing social issues that face the North and the rest of Italy.

4. The Lega Nord

In the early 1980s, the Lega was still far from being a challenging political force and up to 1987 did not even run as an independent party. Rather, during these initial years, the Lega ran its own candidates under the Liga Veneta's symbol or as part of a coalition with other regionalist movements in the North.[24] When the Lega finally did enter electoral races on its own during the national elections in 1987, it gained only 3 percent of the regional vote share, a little less than what the Liga had gained at its peak. Despite this small percentage, the Lega was able to elect two representatives, one in the Chamber of Deputies and Bossi in the Senate.

Despite a slow start, the Lega would eventually experience considerably more support than the Liga Veneta had. Only two years after its first solo elections in 1987, the Lega's support almost tripled to 8.1 percent of the vote in Lombardy, making it the fourth largest party out of the 13 that had presented candidates in the region during the 1989 elections for the European Parliament. Support for the Lega would continue to grow and by the regional elections in 1990, the party's regional vote share shot up to almost 19 percent, making the Lega the second largest party in Lombardy after the Christian Democrats. Early support for the Lega was strongest in ex–Christian Democrat strongholds in Lombardy, such as the provinces of Varese, Como, and Bergamo.[25]

As the Lega's electoral support began to rise, the party also began to expand outside of its own base in Lombardy to the rest of the northern and central-northern regions. In 1989, Bossi formed *Alleanza Nord* (Northern Alliance), an electoral alliance with the Liga Veneta and other regionalist forces in the areas of the Center and North, some of which were new and had emerged in response to the success of the Lega. By this time, the Lega had pretty much dropped the focus on just Lombardy and began calling for unity among all the northern regions to form a "*Repubblica del Nord*" (Northern Republic).

In 1991 Bossi created the Lega Nord that effectively took over the control of the much smaller and weaker legas of the Alleanza Nord, including the Liga Veneta, the Piemont Autonomista (Piedmont League), the Union Ligure (Ligurian Union), the Lega Emiliano-Romagnola (Emilia-Romagna League), and the Alleanza Toscana (Tuscan Alliance). By the end of the Lega Nord's first congress in 1991, the statute of the party superseded those of the existing regionalist forces that were then transformed into "national sections" of the Lega.

Despite the fact that the new party represented an aggregation of all the new regionalist leagues in the North, the Lega Lombarda remained the dominant force in the Lega Nord. In the first place, the symbol of Alberto da Giusano was retained by the party and the leaders of the Lega Lombarda gained leading positions within the Lega Nord. The new party also had an impact on the local organizations of the other smaller leagues. As one observer describes in the province of Belluno, Veneto, the Lega Nord "brought on the marginalization of the original party leaders [of the Liga]" with a change of guard that "favored the emergence of a new group of leaders who began to penetrate the valleys of the province and introduce the embryonic organization of the Lega Nord."²⁶

The shift in power to the leaders of the Lega Lombarda particularly increased the stature and power of Umberto Bossi. To this day Bossi remains the Federal Secretary of the Lega Nord, the highest-ranking officer in the party. He represents the "movement politically in its entirety" and is also the "only one [in the party] who can speak for the movement as a whole."²⁷ Bossi has, moreover, used his power to maintain a relatively high degree of party discipline, constraining the different legas to adhere to centralized directions, "silencing and even firing dissenters."²⁸ In short, the Lega Nord is Bossi.

Bossi also emerged as a strongly charismatic leader who eschewed the traditional political speak—which in Italy has often been expressed in a highly formal and technocratic language—in favor of a more populist style of rhetoric that brings politics down to the lowest common denominator. Bossi captivated audiences and attracted the national media by using everyday language in his speeches, peppered with occasional lapses into local dialects, obscenities, and sexually laden innuendoes.²⁹ Bossi would also make frequent threats of secession from the rest of the country. Although the threats of the Lega were never backed up by force and, at least in the early 1990s, were not seen as an immediate danger to national unity, they were still able to generate a considerable degree of discussion and concern about regional divisions within the country. Many of these threats were based on simple symbolic acts by the party, like creating their own northern "identity cards" that mimicked the national ones the Italian state issues to all citizens.

The Lega also portrayed itself as the antiparty party, being adamant about keeping a "clean" image of the organization and separating it from other political forces. As other observers have noted, the populism of the new Right in Europe has appealed to voters who have become increasingly disenchanted with the traditional political actors.³⁰ The Lega's antipartyism, however, has appealed to more than just a disgruntled electorate faced with few interesting choices. Rather, the party has mobilized on a specific antiparty cleavage directed toward the traditional political parties, a cleavage that had been growing since the mid-1970s. Overall anti-institutional sentiment is evident from the responses that Italians give to the yearly Eurobarometer polls, registering one of the lowest regards for the functioning of their democratic system compared to other European countries.³¹ Before the Lega, other parties like the libertarian Radical party had similarly capitalized on the antiparty cleavage in the 1970s and early 1980s by running porn stars and convicted terrorists as candidates.[32] The Lega turned the issue into a regional dimension, identifying the traditional political forces with the South and Rome, and the North with change.

The antiparty position of the Lega also put the party in the same camp as others seeking to reform the political system. In 1991, there was a referendum to limit the number of preference votes to only one per party as a way to reduce the "corrupt market in vote trading," which had developed between the main factions in parties and local representatives, particularly in the DC and PSI.[33] Led, ironically, by an ex-Christian Democrat, Mario Segni, whose name became synonymous with electoral reform, the referendum was an overwhelming success with 95 percent of the electorate voting in favor of abolishing multiple preference votes. Although the referendum—which intended to rid the system of one of the most important tools that local party bosses used to keep power— was supported by other reformist Catholics and most of the Left, the DC actually abstained from support or condemnation of the referendum, hoping in private that it would fail.[34] Bettino Craxi, the leader of the PSI, was also against the referendum and was more vocal, encouraging the electorate to abandon the polls and "go to the beach" instead of voting.[35]

Finally, the Lega began to create links with the local population through membership drives, registering about 18,000 members in 1989. A little over a year later, membership more than doubled to 40,000[36] and by 1992 the Lega commanded about 140,000[37] members—comparable to the rolls of the other Italian political parties of similar size.[38] The Lega was also effective in the late 1980s at mobilizing militants and facilitating active participation at a time when the traditional political parties had lost a lot of their original appeal and were finding it hard to maintain such enthusiasm within their own ranks.[39] Although Italian parties are much more mass-based and active compared to American political parties (which essentially lack any consistent system of membership), they have become considerably more bureaucratic in their organization since the combative days of the early postwar period.

The early militants of the Lega were mostly young people who had previously played only a minor or no role in politics and found little in common with the traditional political parties and ideologies.[40] The young militants, many of whom came from the smaller villages in the North rather than the big urban centers like Milan, were attracted to the Lega because it gave them a sense of "group identity" and a chance to get involved in politics.[41] The early activism of the Lega, particularly during the late 1980s and early 1990s, is reminiscent of the earlier years of European socialist and communist parties with young militants participating in political campaigns, putting up posters, organizing protests, and attending periodic meetings.

The Lega also added more collateral organizations to the party, including an artists' association, sports clubs, and a trade union, which by 1990 had gained over 1,000 members working in major industries, from the ATM (the transport company of buses, trams, and subways that services Milan) to ILVA, a major industrial firm in the Lombard province of Bergamo. The union's delegates were also elected in "factory councils" (*consigli di fabbrica*) in firms across Lombardy, a practice started originally by the CGIL, the large confedal trade union, in the early part of the century.

5. *Mani Pulite* and the Demise of the Postwar Party System

The big break for the Lega came in the early 1990s when the clientelism and corruption of the DC and its partners in government was brought to light during the *Mani Pulite* (Clean Hands) trials. The first of their kind in postwar Italian history, *Mani Pulite* led to the implication of literally thousands of politicians and business people in the illicit financing of political parties. The trials started in Milan when a journalist published a story about complaints by business people who had to pay *tangenti* (kickbacks) to politicians. In February, 1992, the socialist politician Mario Chiesa, director of a public nursing home in Milan, was the first to be accused when he extracted a relatively small bribe of 7 million lire (about $3,500.00) from a local businessman who was seeking to acquire a cleaning contract at the home.[42] Soon, the seemingly minor and isolated event blew up into a national crisis as the growing number of cases of corruption implicated almost all of the political parties, most of the *enti* or state agencies, and major private companies. By 1994, thousands of politicians and business people had been arrested and numerous others had been given the *avviso di garanzia*, the official notification of criminal investigation that allows authorities the right to briefly detain suspects for a period of time.

The trials were a watershed in Italy for a number of reasons. The extraordinary activism of judges like Antonio Di Pietro put to shame the major political leaders of the postwar period, such as Giulio Andreotti, the seven-time prime minister and longtime DC chief, and Bettino Craxi of the PSI. Andreotti went on trial for illicit party financing and collusion with the Mafia, while Craxi was tried and proven guilty of corruption in absentia while in hiding in Tunisia, where he eventually died in 2000. The trials not only destroyed the power of the traditional ruling party formations of the postwar period, but also the longtime complacency Italians felt toward endemic corruption in their political system.

The public response to the trials was one of euphoria. Di Pietro was made a national hero as people scrawled "Grazie Di Pietro" on walls across Milan where the trials took place. In 1992, the writer and historian Alexander Stille described the atmosphere in Italy as being similar to the Velvet Revolutions in Eastern Europe in 1989: "Suddenly Italians are rebelling against a system they had regarded as eternal and inevitable." Across Italy, he continued, people are "eager to report cases of bribery and extortion."[43]

The Lega was an instrumental player in the general public furor against politicians and the deeply embedded system of corruption. One of the confessed bribe-takers at the time said that "[t]he investigation became unstoppable because of the great ability of the judges . . . but also because of the rise of the Lega and the general distrust towards people in the parties."[44] The Lega turned the focus of its campaign on the ideological bankruptcy of the ruling parties and the corrupt basis of the party system. The Lega, moreover, played up *Mani Pulite* as a battle between a clean North and a corrupt Rome that favors the South.

The *Mani Pulite* trials, however, demonstrated that corruption was in no way limited to the South. In addition to Chiesa, Craxi, whose antics made him the poster boy of the greed and corruption that escalated in the 1980s, represented the Milan district in parliament. Moreover, an ex-mayor of Milan, Carlo Tognoli, had received an *avviso di garanzia* to appear before the magistrates and testify, as did the then Mayor Paolo Pillitteri, Craxi's brother-in-law, who was accused of "personally accepting suitcases full of cash."[45] Other prominent business people who were either *Milanese* or resided in the city, such as Raul Gardini, were brought up on charges of making bribes to politicians in return for political favors. Gardini, at one time the second wealthiest man in Italy and head of the Montedison Group, which was a major client of the DC, paid a bribe that amounted to 140 million dollars.[46] Gardini, however, eventually committed suicide before his court appearance, as did several others accused during this period.

The North did, though, become a bastion of antiparty sentiment as evidenced by the results of a referendum a year into the trials to end public funding for political parties. Since 1974, political parties have had access to public funds, based on a flat rate with an additional amount calculated according to the number of seats they occupy in the

Table 5.1 Abrogative* referendum on public financing of parties, 1993

	National	North	Center	South	Islands
Yes	90.3	92.9	90.2	85.9	85.5
No	9.7	7.1	9.8	14.1	14.5
Total	100	100	100	100	100

* No vote represents support for party financing.
Source: Ministry of the Interior.

Chamber of Deputies (the lower house). Although public funding of political parties is intended to reduce such things as kickbacks, which actually led to the *Mani Pulite* trials in the first place, the initiative was seen at the time as a referendum of the parties per se. As a result, when 90 percent of the voters favored "abrogating" the law on public funding of parties, it was seen at the time as a widespread rejection of the traditional parties and revulsion toward the *partitocrazia*, the domination of the country's democracy by hegemonic parties (see table 5.1).

In the North, almost 93 percent favored abrogating public support of parties, while the South was lower than the national average with "only" around 86 percent supportive. The most "pro-party" region was Sicily, where only 83 percent agreed with abrogating public support and 17 percent wanted to keep it. Overall, the referendum showed a sharp change in the attitudes toward the country's parties when a similar referendum was held in 1978 and a majority of the voters (56 percent) nationwide supported keeping public funding of parties.

Only a few months into the trials, the DC took a beating during the April 1992 elections, getting only 29 percent of the vote, the first time in 40 years that the party had slipped below 30 percent. Much of the party's support was drained by the Lega, which was able to mobilize considerable support during the 1992 elections on a wave of antiparty sentiment, gaining almost 9 percent of the vote nationwide and 55 seats in the national parliament. During these elections, the Lega had officially moved from its former marginalized status of a small, obscure folkloristic movement, to a party with a regional base but a national presence.

It was also in 1992 that the Lega demonstrated its capacity to mobilize support within the industrial districts of the North. The results of the election show that the Lega was the first party in 13 out of 28 industrial districts in Lombardy and the second party in the other 14 districts, just under the DC. The only district where the Lega was the third party in Lombardy was in Suzzara, which happens to be a stronghold of the DS.[47] The Lega appeared at this time to offer the entrepreneurs and workers in the SMEs and industrial districts a new, alternative voice to replace the increasingly illegitimate DC.

By 1993 many of the postwar political parties that were tarnished from the *Mani Pulite* trials started to fall apart or break up into different formations. By 1994, the DC had divided into three much smaller parties, the Popular party (PPI), the Christian Democratic Union (CDU) and the Christian Democratic Center (CCD). The PSI dissolved, with its members finding their way into other parties or forming other small socialist factions. All of the "lay" parties that had faithfully joined the DC in numerous coalition governments over the years (the PRI, PLI, and PSDI) had disappeared. The DS (which until recently was called the PDS) and the more radical communist splinter, Rifondazione Communista (RC), were relatively unscathed by the trials. Having been out of national government, the Left was relatively clean. The fall of the ruling parties officially marked the end of the First Italian Republic and the start of the Second Republic with the rise of new parties like the Lega.

6. The Shift to the Practical Politics of Federalism

As the early 1990s brought the Lega Nord greater electoral success, the party also began to position itself as a more serious force for federalist reform. During the first congress of the Lega Nord in February 1991, Bossi had presented a project for the division of Italy into three "macro regions" named the Republic of the North, Center, and South, respectively. A few months later, during another meeting, Bossi spoke on a much larger scale than in the past, discussing the issue of federalism within the context of national institutional reform and not just the interests of the North. While the Lega Lombarda and then the Lega Nord had always talked of the need to devolve power to the regional level, it was only at this point that the party actually made some initiatives in this direction. Bossi did not, however, completely toss out the baby with the bath water but rather kept its threat of secession on the backburner. "Rome be forewarned," Bossi stated, "the North will have federalism or it will leave."[48]

The propaganda of the Lega during this period demonstrated an attempt by the party to move away from its primarily protest appeal, presenting itself as a serious contender for power with a clearer program for reform. At the time, the party published a pamphlet series entitled

"Ideas and Syntheses that Support Federalism." The pamphlets confronted, in a professional way, a number of institutional issues, from the organization of local authorities, to fiscal and electoral reform, and European integration.

The Lega also made tentative alliances with other political forces[49] and began to ally with people and groups outside of its immediate orbit of regionalist parties. In 1992, Gianfranco Miglio, an established scholar of constitutional law as well as a professor of political science at the Catholic University in Italy and a longtime proponent of federalist reform, joined the Lega and was elected a senator under the party's banner. Miglio's experience with federalist ideas also went back to the Resistance when he was active in the many groups advocating the creation of a federalist republic during postwar reconstruction of the country. Miglio supplied the Lega with a number of ideas for federalist reform, such as the notion of a federal Italy divided into three macro regions.

In their congress at the end of 1993, Bossi reaffirmed the federalist trajectory of the party and announced the willingness of the Lega to form additional coalitions with other political leaders. Earlier that year the Lega attempted to break out of the North to mobilize support in other areas of the country, including the South! At a press conference, Bossi argued that the Lega is

> already able to present a political program for the whole Peninsula. In the Mezzogiorno our battle against the party-state (*partitocrazia*) is understood as well as our total war against the culture of dependency (*assistenzialismo*).[50]

Later that year, the Lega opened offices across the South without the "Nord" in the title of the party, presenting itself as the Italian Federal League during local elections across the country. Bossi even visited Sicily on a campaign tour in March, where he praised the region's own traditions of autonomy and argued that their own special statute provided a good model for the rest of the country.[51] The Lega also softened its anti-southern message in favor of one that presented the South as a victim of the system of dependency rather than the perpetrator of it. The party even talked about the additional problems of southern businesses that have to pay "unofficial taxes" to the Mafia as well as official ones to the state,[52] an issue that northern businesses are less likely to face.

During this period, the Lega was also able to mobilize support against a new Minimum Tax. A major populist strategy of the Lega has been its occasional calls for a tax revolt in the North. Similar to its sporadic threats of secession, the Lega's tax revolts are intended to spotlight the divide between the North and South and the anger among northerners that their tax resources are going primarily to support a dependent South. They are also very symbolic, with, apparently, few people participating and posing little threat to the country's accounting.[53]

The new Minimum Tax, however, had a particular impact on the economic base of entrepreneurs in the North as it was directed at independent artisans and other small businesses, the groups most known to evade taxes. The tax was intended to make up lost revenue from tax evaders by setting "'assumed' minimum income levels for the various categories of self-employed business people." If the assumed amount happened to be higher than what the taxpayer actually had to pay, he/she would have to prove it in order to get a refund.[54] Because the burden of proof was on the taxpayer, the new law was perceived as a form of discrimination against the self-employed,[55] and appeared to favor the interests of large industry over small. The CGIA, a leading association for artisans in the North, further argued that the government's assumption that artisans and other types of smaller industries and businesses are the worst tax evaders was not accurate. Their reports demonstrated that evasion was greatest among large industries, 60 percent of which frequently declare either a loss or no profit every year.[56]

The Minimum Tax was a perfect issue for the Lega to exploit as it impacted disproportionately on small-scale entrepreneurs, a group the party had been trying to win over. The Lega's propaganda argued that the new law was only a method to "extort taxes from the productive world, in particular those who are most at risk: merchants and small businesses who, more than others, are exposed to the fluctuations of the market."[57] The Lega sponsored a signature campaign to abolish the new law and, once again, threatened a tax strike. The Lega argued for the tax revolt in order to "restore dignity to the productive world and to beat that unproductive and parasitic economy, which is favored by this system and lives on the backs of those who work, produce and take risks."[58]

On March 26, 1993, the Lega's employers' association ALIA sponsored a major protest in Milan. The rally took the form of a mock "funeral" that marked the "death" of small enterprise. There were banners at the protest that compared the new tax to a form of protection money for the state ("*Il pizzo dello Stato*"). ALIA further presented to the Prefecture of Milan a program on behalf of the commercial sector of the city. The program's "national objectives" included, among other things, the abolition of the Minimum Tax, a cut in fiscal pressures, and a simplification of the tax system.[59]

The fiscal revolt gained such momentum that by October of 1993 protests were coming from groups who were affected, including merchants, artisans, and several professional groups—such as journalists and medical doctors. On October 18, around 100,000 people, primarily artisans, came from all over Italy to march in Milan and call for the government's repeal of the Minimum Tax. The protestors also called for lower fiscal pressures in general and for government incentives to turn the economy out of the recession the country was in at the time.

The protests put such pressure on the state that the Minimum Tax was eventually abolished. The protest against the Minimum Tax also helped to galvanize support for the Lega. Although in previous years the Lega's calls to avoid paying particular taxes have generally passed without great enthusiasm, the Minimum Tax provoked resentment across the country, particularly in the business oriented city of Milan where the Lega's support was growing at the time.

7. Victory in Milan

The next big victory for the Lega came in the summer of 1993 when it won the mayoral seat in Milan, the second largest city in the country after Rome. The fall of the postwar parties provided the Lega with a unique space in the early 1990s to mobilize support in Milan, where the party had became the leading center-right force in the city. Moreover, the victory demonstrated that the Lega was capable of attracting a more educated, urban electorate. This was a significant shift for the party, which, up to this point, had found its strongest supporters in smaller communes where the voting population is much less diversified.

Many of the issues that the Lega brought to the campaign were also new to the political agenda, previously untouched by other political parties, such as the growing immigrant population in the city, which was second to that of Rome. During the campaign, the Lega framed the issue not only in terms of race but also in terms of public order, associating a perceived rise in crime with the increasing presence of immigrants in the city. For example, the party called for the establishment of the beat-cop system (*vigili di quartiere*) to confront issues like "clandestine immigrants, micro-criminality, drug abuse, and prostitution."[60] The Lega had, thus, become one of the first xenophobic parties in Europe to run a major urban center.

The party also focused on the question of European integration, a leading issue in the country at the time. Italy was one of the founding members of the European Community and has always been an enthusiastic supporter of European integration and unification. Italians, for example, have expressed considerable support of European institutions in Eurobarometer polls since they have been taking them in the early 1970s. The image of Italy as a leading member of the EU, however, took a blow in 1992 when it had to withdraw from the Exchange Rate Mechanism—the forerunner to the European Monetary Union and the Euro—when it reduced the price of the Lira in order to encourage much needed investment. Although this move had a positive impact on the country's economy by increasing the number of exports, it hurt the country politically, confirming the image of Italy as an underdog of the EU countries. In the end, Italy would eventually adopt the Euro along with most of the other EU members, however, skepticism about the country's commitment to maintaining the necessary austerity measures remained well into the late 1990s.

The Lega also benefited from the regionalist tensions between the North and South that were exacerbated by closer European integration. First, the Center and North in Italy have consistently been more enthusiastic toward European integration, actively utilizing EU regional development funds (particularly to support the SME sector) and generally seeking a stronger role in the Community's decision-making process. Although the southern regions have also shown support for European integration, they have generally been more skeptical of the potential side effects that integration, and the necessary austerity measures that go along with it, would have on relatively poorer regions.[61]

The Lega exploited the fact that the country's difficulty in maintaining the convergence criteria set up in the Maastricht Treaty stems largely from southern dependency on the state. During the campaign for Milan, the Lega toyed with the idea of the North entering into monetary unification, while the South waited until it was ready.[62] The slogan of the campaign was in fact, "*Portiamo Milano in Europa*" or "Let's bring Milan into Europe." The Lega also presented a candidate who had considerable experience with the EU, Marco Formentini, an independent businessman, who, according to the electoral propaganda, had previously worked for the European Economic Community and had even participated in the drafting of the norms for the European Common Market.[63]

Finally, the Lega was able to ride on a new wave of regionalism that was initiated by the Maastricht Treaty, which set up the Committee of the Regions, a consultative body made up of regional and local authorities and deliberates on local and regional issues. Although the Committee does not have decision-making powers like the European Parliament or Commission, its formation has been a major step for regionalists who seek greater autonomy from their national capitals. Since the beginning of the European integration process, there has been a conflict between those who see a Europe of the regions versus a Europe of nation states. The treaty was the first to recognize this conflict and gave the subnational level greater legitimacy in making their claims for greater autonomy. The treaty also gave hope to regionalists all over Europe who see unification as a positive step toward reducing the power of national governments and giving more opportunities for the subnational level to make claims and gain power.

Finally, the Lega emerged not only as a regionalist force but also a more clearly defined right-wing party. Although the Lega continued to declare its ideology as "centrist," the party's issues—which included such things as greater privatization of state industries, budget cuts, closer European integration, and limits on immigration—appealed to the center-right tendencies of Milan's middle-class electorate. The Lega offered this electorate a decidedly new option after the clientelist and statist politics of the Christian Democrats and the Socialists.

8. Conclusion

During the late 1980s and early 1990s, the Lega started to peak when the party was able to expand and grow on the issues of regional identity and interests, as well as antiparty sentiment. The crucial moment occurred when the party shifted from regional Lombard identity to a more broad-based northern identity in the late 1980s. This shift, moreover, involved a move away from identity as a manifestation of local language and culture, to one of a "community of interests,"[64] which took the region's economy and political institutions more into account. The Lega had effectively intertwined the issues of the Northern Question, particularly taxation and the inefficient bureaucracy, within the context of the conflict between the North and Rome and the divide between the North and South.[65]

The Lega was also capable of mobilizing support among the sector of the population that worked in the industrial districts. In these areas the Lega appealed both to their interests as a group as well as their increasing alienation from the political center. Moreover, the party's focus on taxes struck a chord in a population that has seen its livelihood threatened by a system of redistribution that appears to favor the interests of the South. What is most interesting, however, is that the Lega had found support almost solely in areas of the Third Italy that were governed by the DC, as opposed to those governed by the PCI/DS, where voters remained faithful to the Left. The varying appeal of the Lega in the Third Italy demonstrated that the party's populist message of regional autonomy had much less of an impact on the areas governed by the Left, which were already experiencing a relatively good local/regional government. The Lega was most successful at mobilizing support in ex-DC areas where the increasingly southern DC alienated the local level and where its policies at the center went counter to the interests of northern small industries.

The real key to the Lega's sharp rise in success at this time, however, was most likely its capacity to capitalize on the general distrust with the traditional political parties and state institutions. Although the Lega had effectively brought the issue of federalism to the political agenda, its bread and butter was its antiparty rhetoric. The antiparty status of the Lega gave them a degree of legitimacy during the turbulent years of 1992 and 1993, when it was discovered that almost all of the traditional parties were involved in the illicit financing of party organizations.

CHAPTER 6

The Lega and Federalist Reform in the Late 1990s

1. The Lega as a Party of Government

By the mid-1990s, the Lega faced a number of considerable challenges that threatened its continuing success. The first challenge came from the emergence of a new political party on the Right, Forza Italia (FI), that had formed in early 1994, only a few months before another series of national elections that were held after the fall of the last DC-led government. Led by Silvio Berlusconi, the Milanese media magnate and one of the wealthiest men in the country, FI emerged as a conservative force with a strongly neoliberal platform that focuses on issues one would find dear to American republicans, such as reform of the bureaucracy, privatization, and lower taxes. Berlusconi also took a page from the old Cold War DC, emerging as a strong critic of the Left and even calling the now thoroughly democratized DS a communist threat, a weak issue so long after the fall of the Berlin Wall.

FI, however, did emerge in a clear vacuum on the center-right as the DC splinter groups have only been able to mobilize a small following. Moreover, the Lega was too small and regionally confined to take the place of the DC. The only other potential contender for the DC's old support base was the neo-fascist MSI, which went through a transformation in 1993 when the party's leadership, headed by Gianfranco Fini, officially denounced their fascist past. During the conference the party changed its name to Alleanza Nazionale (AN, National Alliance) and declared a new, democratic trajectory for the party. Although the AN is not a specifically regionalist party, it mobilizes the bulk of its support in the South, where the MSI was also strong.

From the start, FI threatened the Lega's dominance in the North. Berlusconi's party appealed to the same constituency of the Lega, but offered a more "stable" political option,[1] without the radical views of the Lega. Berlusconi spoke to those Lega supporters who aspired for a truly conservative party that represented a "return to the old certainties—to traditionalist values that had long been suppressed, to confidence in the future, and to a desire for security and social cohesion."[2] More specifically, the FI was able to take away potential Lega supporters by focusing on issues like taxes and law and order, issues that had allowed the Lega to captivate the Milanese in 1993. Moreover, Berlusconi was able to mobilize this middle-class electorate in both the North and South because it lacked the regional limitations of the Lega.[3] Finally, although FI is not a specifically federalist party, it also began to address the issue of decentralization by putting forth a plan for devolution in its party platform.

Although during the election the Lega gained about the same as it had in 1992, most of this support came from its existing strongholds in the North, particularly in the smaller towns in the former regions of the Catholic subculture. The greatest gains for the Lega were in the Northeast, particularly in the Veneto region. The party, however, had lost its support in areas outside of its core where it had previously been able to attract supporters, such as major urban centers. Most disturbing for the Lega were its losses in Milan, which became a stronghold of FI over night.

The elections also presented all parties with the challenge of a new electoral system. During the postwar period, the Italian party system suffered from a plethora of political parties that emerged as a result of a liberal system of proportional representation (PR). Because PR provides seats to parties based on the proportion of the votes they receive, such a system has a tendency to create multiparty systems.[4] The reintroduction of PR (Mussolini had previously abolished it) was seen as the best way to prevent the rise of another hegemonic force in government. In the end, however, such a system led to the problems of revolving door governments that changed on average every nine months. Moreover, although PR did prevent the rise of any absolute majority party in the Chamber of Deputies, it still allowed the DC to dominate the system; in fact it facilitated it. The numerous parties in the system gave the DC endless partners with which it was able to form governing coalitions, preventing any alternation of power to the more "natural" competitor on the Left, the Communist party. A more restrictive plurality (first-past-the-post) system—such as the current systems in the United States and the United Kingdom—generally leads to a more bipolar (2-party) system, forcing smaller parties to merge into two large forces on the Left and Right.[5]

After overwhelming support in a referendum in 1993 to introduce more "plurality" into the system, a new law went into effect on the national level in 1994. As a result, 75 percent of the deputies in parliament are now selected on a first-past-the-post (plurality) system, while the remaining 25 percent are selected on a PR basis. In order to prevent smaller parties from proliferating, the new law also institutes a 4 percent threshold that parties have to cross in order to win seats on a PR basis.

The reform has led to a more bipolar system because it forces parties to form cartels, or large coalitions on the Left and Right (see table A.5).[6] On the Left, the DS formed the "Progressive" coalition (the name would be changed in later years to the Ulivo or Olive Tree), which includes numerous Left parties, such as RC (in 1994 only) and different Green formations. Berlusconi took the upper hand on the Right and formed the Polo coalition along with the AN and some of the smaller right-wing splinters of the DC. Facing potential losses in the elections as a result of the new, more restrictive, electoral law, the Lega reluctantly joined the Polo coalition, which eventually won the election after beating a weaker Left.

Once in government, the coalition was under the strains of having two territorially based parties, the Lega in the North and the AN in the South. In addition, both the Lega and the AN came from two distinctly different positions in terms of their views on the state and the economy. The Lega was more neoliberal and pro–free market, while the AN— a party that emerged from the neo-fascist Italian Social Movement—was more statist, favoring a strong welfare state and continued support to the South. In order to make the unwieldy coalition work, Berlusconi had to agree to a territorially based pact with his two partners. As a result, the Lega and FI ended up presenting candidates together in the North under a list called the Pole for Liberty (*Polo delle Libertà*). The AN and FI presented candidates in the South under a list called the Pole for Good Government (*Polo del Buon Governo*).

Berlusconi also gave the Lega considerable power within the coalition. Although the Lega only received 8.3 percent of the vote nationwide (compared to FI's 20 percent and the AN's 12 percent), the party commanded a leading role in the coalition. The pact with Berlusconi gave the Lega 117 seats in the Chamber of Deputies and 60 seats in the senate, much more than what it would have gained on its own. This was not only more than the share of FI (99/32) and the AN,(109/47), it was the largest number of seats of any single party in the parliament![7] Moreover, the Lega was also given five ministries, three with portfolio (Interior, Industry, and Budget), and two without (European Union Affairs, Institutional Reform).

In the end, the Lega conflicted more with FI than the AN in the coalition. The first and last major upset in the new government came when a bill was presented by the (FI) Minister for Justice that limited the use of preventive detention for only suspects of terrorism and Mafia crimes. The bill was widely seen as a way for Berlusconi, himself a target of the *Mani Pulite* investigations, to weaken the power of the anticorruption judges, who had frequently used preventive detention during the trials as a way to force suspects into plea bargaining. The Lega and the AN distanced themselves from the bill in order to preserve their status as "clean" parties. Roberto Maroni, the Lega Minister of the Interior, threatened to quit his post unless corruption was also added as a crime for which investigating judges could use preventive detention.

Although the bill was eventually modified along the lines of the Lega's requests, the conflict highlighted the tenuous relationship between Bossi and Berlusconi. The government eventually fell in December 1994, only nine months after it was formed, after a series of inconclusive meetings that were held to patch up the alliance between the two parties. Finally, after a secret meeting between Bossi and opposition leaders, the Lega decided to leave the coalition and return to its more familiar adversarial position. This move brought down the forty-ninth postwar government in Italy and put into question the future of a united Right in Italy.[8]

Overall, the Lega's status as a party of government was not sustained by the party's electorate. The party's support fell nearly 2 percent nationwide during the elections for the European parliament in June 1994, just three months after the national elections. The position of responsibility had shifted the party away from its original role as a noncooperative protest force, whose enemy was Rome and the traditional political parties. Political compromising while in government had put the party in an awkward position, reneging on many of its promises of federalism and local autonomy. In spite of the fact that the Lega held the Ministry of Institutional Reform—the department in charge of things like devolution—it did nothing to implement federalist reform, even though Bossi had promised this as the first order of business. Even the Lega's Irene Pivetti, a member of parliament who was voted in as Speaker of the Chamber of Deputies, admitted at the time of the coalition's failure that the party in power had not given any concrete proposals for federalism.[9]

In fact, the "Revision of the Constitution in a Federal Sense," written by the senators of the Lega, was presented to parliament only in January 1995, after the government had fallen. Similarly, although it held the Ministry of Industry, no unique legislation appeared to emerge in favor of small-scale enterprises.

Moreover, accusations of corruption against the party and Bossi also added to the Lega's image problems. Bossi too was accused, in 1993, of taking kickbacks in 1992 from Raul Gardini, the Milanese industrialist who later killed himself, to finance the Lega's electoral campaigns. The treasurer of the party, Alessandro Patelli, admitted to taking 200 million Lire, but later said that the money was eventually stolen when the party offices in Milan were ransacked. The case weakened the image of the Lega as a "clean" political force and instead made it look more like the other traditional parties it had so desperately tried to distance itself from.

2. Padania and the Return of Ethno-Regionalism

Shortly after the disastrous coalition with Berlusconi, the Lega began to move toward a more extremist position that advocated the secession of the North from the rest of the country. During the Lega's annual meeting in the spring of 1996—which was held, as usual, out in the open in the Lombard village of Pontida—Bossi announced that the party was shifting its focus to a more radical call for the independence of the North from the rest of the country. The Lega backed up its calls for secession by drawing up a "Constitution of the North" that led to a split within the party's leadership between Bossi and the more moderate, pro-federalist wing of the party that was led by Pivetti. One of the founding members of the Lega Lombarda, Pivetti, would eventually leave the Lega in the late 1990s and form her own federalist movement.

The party also began to emphasize more "ethnic" issues in its propaganda, a major turn for the Lega that up to this point had shied away from ethno-regionalism, preferring instead to define the region primarily in terms of the social and economic interests of the North. The party began to refer to the North as "Padania," a little used historical denomination of the area north of the Po River Valley, the *Valle Padana*, which runs through the central-northern regions of the country. Along with the name change came a renewed focus on the cultural origins of Padania, such as its ties to Celtic culture, and the adoption of green as the party's color.[10]

The Lega compared the party's new focus with those of other regionalist minorities in Europe, like the Catalans and Basques in Spain and the Corsicans in France, or as simply part of the "re-awakening" of the people of Europe and the rise of "ethno-federalism." The leaders of the Lega put their struggle alongside the unification of Germany, the rise of the ex-Soviet successor states, the divisions of Yugoslavia and Czechoslovakia, as well as the referendum for autonomy in Quebec in the earlier part of the decade.[11]

The more radical position of the Lega appeared to work well during the 1996 national elections, a year and a half after the fall of the short-lived Berlusconi government. The Lega gave its best performance ever, winning a little over 10 percent of the national vote, with around 20 percent in the North, where it surpassed FI and restored its position as the leading party in the region. During the elections, Bossi took a calculated risk and decided not to enter into a coalition with Berlusconi again, but, instead, go it alone as a third force.

During the election, the Lega was able to capitalize on the growing disenchantment about the country's business climate, an issue that was further politicized by a nationwide "Tax Day" organized by Berlusconi's Polo coalition along with Confcommercio, the national association which represents, among other things, retail merchants. The daylong event, which was publicized in English as a "Tax Day," took place a month before the election in early March and was intended to focus the campaign on taxes and other problems associated with local businesses. The day also included a general protest during which all businesses, including grocery stores, coffee bars, and restaurants, were asked to close their doors for two hours to protest high taxes. Confcommercio also held a videoconference in its offices in 40 cities across the country. In addition, the two main candidates for prime minister, Romano Prodi for the Ulivo and Berlusconi for the Polo, were brought together for a debate on the issue of taxes.

Although not all stores adhered to the protest, the Tax Day event raised a number of issues that surround the concerns of businesses and business people in Italy, such as the divisions between small and large industry as well as the divide between family-run stores and the increasing number of large supermarkets. Although the Tax Day was an attempt by the conservative Polo coalition to co-opt the issue of taxes, the Lega was in fact the political force that was best able to capitalize on the sense of malaise with its radical talk of secession.

Business issues were, in fact, most politicized in the Northeast, where the Lega had made its most significant gains. Leading up to the elections, *La Repubblica*, the leading national newspaper, described the atmosphere in the northeastern regions as a "rebellion of the rich," where voters in the Veneto and Friuli-Venezia Giulia felt "unsatisfied," "abandoned," and "betrayed" by the state.[12] The Lega's radical secessionist message had a strong appeal in an area that had not only a widespread middle class with a high standard of living, but also one that depends on small, private enterprise for its livelihood. In the Veneto, the Lega was able to gain almost 30 percent, better than its support in Lombardy, which was around 25 percent. In these areas, the Lega consolidated its support in the provincial towns where the party had developed a base and had skillfully articulated the local sense of alienation from the central state, which was widely regarded as "blocking local development."[13]

The success of the Lega created a considerable buzz about the political climate in the Northeast, an issue that would remain strong for the next couple of years. After the increased electoral support for the Lega in 1996, Massimo Cacciari, the then leftist mayor of Venice, began to sound the alarm of secession and discontent in the region. In reference to the Lega, Cacciari argued that the party had "interpreted the intolerance toward" the deficiencies in the state, such as over bureaucratization, and that such sentiments are only growing and leading to "unforeseen consequences."[14]

In fact, a survey in early 1996, just a few months before the national elections, showed an alarmingly high number of supporters for secession in the North (see table 6.1). Asked what they felt about the "independence of the North," around 23 percent of the respondents in the North saw such a move as "favorable and desirable," while another 30 percent saw such a move as "favorable" but not possible ("unacceptable"). Overall, more than half of the respondents were open to the idea of secession of the North, a striking turn of events for an area (the whole

Table 6.1 Survey question: "What does independence of the North represent for you?" (1996) (percent)

An unacceptable hypothesis	34.7
A path that would lead to disaster	8.1
A favorable prospect, but on the whole unacceptable	29.2
A favorable and desirable prospect	23.2
No response, no opinion	4.8
Total	100.0
Number	904

Source: Limes vol. 1 (1996), p. 17.

Table 6.2 Survey question: "What does independence of the North represent for you?" (1996) (percent)

	Northwest	Lombardy	Northeast
An unacceptable hypothesis	40.5	33.7	31.0
A path that would lead to disaster	10.5	8.6	5.1
A favorable prospect, but on the whole unacceptable	24.9	29.1	33.6
A favorable and desirable prospect	21.0	23.5	25.2
No response, no opinion	3.1	5.1	5.1
Total	100.0	100.0	100.0

Source: Limes vol. 1 (1996), p. 18.

North) that had up to then never expressed such views. Secession had been an issue in places like Sicily in the 1940s and later in Alto-Adige, but never the whole North. Even more surprising was the fact that only 8 percent saw an extremist solution like secession as something highly negative, that is, something that would "lead to disaster."

While support for secession was evident across the whole North, the degree to which people agreed varied from the West to East. Within the Northeast, almost 59 percent of the respondents viewed secession as being favorable in some way or form (possible or otherwise), while only 5 percent saw it as something disastrous (table 6.2). On the other hand, in the Northwest, twice as many people (10 percent) saw secession as something disastrous, while about 46 percent saw such a move as something favorable. The region of Lombardy was somewhere in the middle of the range of responses.

3. Marches and a Referendum for Secession

After the election, the Lega went full gear in its drive for secession, organizing a series of events that were intended to evoke a serious effort toward northern independence, starting with a "March to the Sea" on September 13, 1996. During this event, the party organized a flotilla down the Po River and set up a series of gatherings and rallies that celebrated local culture culminating two days later during a "March on the Po," where Bossi declared an "independent and sovereign Padania." It is also interesting to note that this declaration took place in Venice, the capital of the Veneto, and not in Milan, demonstrating the party's increasing shift toward the Northeast.

This was one of the most publicized events of the party and received a great deal of media attention, covered heavily by all the mainstream newspapers and television stations during that summer, including international press organizations. In some cases, the press simply ridiculed the Lega saying that the party lacked a great deal of originality in their approach to secession, pointing out the fact that they had borrowed numerous phrases from the American Declaration of Independence and other independence movements, including the one in Quebec.[15] *The New York Times* (September 16, 1996) reported that the "long-awaited independence day rally by the [Lega Nord] fell far short of expectations, as an estimated 10,000 supporters gathered on the banks of the Grand Canal." *The Times* further mentioned that the event was like many other Lega-sponsored gatherings in its festive and relaxed atmosphere: "As the crowd milled below a sea of colorful flags, shopping for Padania memorabilia, the mood was more of a small town party than the beginnings of a separatist rebellion."

Many other people and groups, though, took the March seriously. The Lega's actions sparked a number of articles in newspapers and discussions in television programs about the state of the country's union. It was also met by numerous counterdemonstrations of all political stripes, from the far Left to the far Right. The largest counterdemonstration, in fact, was organized by the rightist and considerably nationalist AN, in which around 200,000 people showed up in Milan to protest the Lega's call for secession. The event gave the AN a perfect chance to present itself as a more moderate Right party and to appeal to potential voters in the North, where the party's support had been relatively weak compared to its base in the South.

The March was followed by another flamboyant Lega event: a "referendum" for the independence of Padania. On May 25, 1997, the Lega set up voting booths under portable gazebos in cities across the North that were open to all citizens that could prove residency in one of the northern regions by showing, ironically, their *national* identity card (and not the phony "Republic of Padania" cards that the party sells at its events). The ballot asked participants to vote either "yes" or "no" to the question: "do you want Padania to become an independent and sovereign federal republic?" to which over 90 percent of the participants answered "yes." The Lega claimed that over a million voters came to their gazebos, with the largest turnout in Lombardy, which has a population of about nine million people.

Similar to the March on the Po, the referendum for Padania was met with a mixture of fear, scorn, and veiled support. One of the most vocal criticisms came from the Vatican, which has been a frequent target of the Lega since the 1980s for the Church's emphasis on national solidarity. The *Osservatore Romano*, the official organ of the Vatican, called the homemade referendum "absurd" and "alarming." However, the Vatican also conceded that the party and its success were not simply a reflection of an extremist electorate but a product of the centralized nature of the state and the need to decentralize power. Thus, the Vatican, like many other critics of the Lega, saw a semi-legitimate side to the Lega's protest against the centralized state.

The leftist Ulivo government also began to take a more aggressive position toward the Lega. While in the past, the ruling parties frequently ignored the exhortations of the Lega as the rantings of a fringe movement, during the March on the Po the Minister of the Interior warned in an interview that Umberto Bossi was going in a "dangerous" and possibly "unconstitutional" direction. This kind of attention, however, only gave further encouragement to Bossi, a populist leader who has always valued the ability to shock and mobilize media attention to himself and his party.

4. A More Extremist Party

The radicalization of the Lega was, moreover, manifested in the formation of a series of controversial new organizations within the party, including a northern "shadow government," called the *Governo Provvisorio per L'Indipendenza della Padania* (Provisional Government for the Independence of Padania). The party also started its own Parliament of the North or *Parlamento del Nord* that was originally located in the Lombard city of Mantova, allegedly chosen for its location as the most central point in the North. In addition, the Lega also created a voluntary organization called the *Camicie Verdi* (Green Shirts), a name that evokes the *Camicie Neri* or Black Shirts, the violent organization that formed the core of Mussolini's Fascist movement. The Green Shirts, which is the unofficial name for the *Guardia Nazionale Padana* (Padania National Guard), usually operate as security guards for Lega-sponsored events and have aroused much criticism and concern about a potentially violent turn for the party. In an interview after their formation, the then head of the Green Shirts described the all-volunteer organization as a nonviolent "army with a smile." He then responded, ironically, in the same interview that if "someone asks me one more time about violence in the Green Shirts, I'll kick them in the ass."[16]

During this period, the party also unveiled a new symbol for the Lega, which it calls the "Sun of the Alps" and looks like a green cartoon daisy. Although the Lega does not have any roots in neo-Nazi ideology, their own propaganda describe the new symbol as originating in part from the swastika, the Nazi symbol.[17] Thus, in an ironic twist, the new images of the Lega evoke more and more the authoritarianism of fascism—not something you would expect from a party whose battle is against Rome and the centralized state! Although the Lega continues to argue that it is a nonviolent organization, its new strategy has only led to increasing skepticism about the party's democratic credentials.

Since the mid-1990s, the actions of Bossi and other Lega leaders have been under the continual scrutiny of the Italian judicial system for possible crimes against the constitution—declaring secession and other offenses, like insulting the country's flag. In 1997, magistrates requested that Bossi be brought on trial for telling a woman during a rally that she could clean her toilet with the Italian flag she was hanging from her balcony. In early 2002, Bossi was let off when a special house panel in the Chamber of Deputies voted to not put him on trial.[18] In another case of irony, members from the AN, which traces its lineage to its neo-fascist predecessor, the MSI, denounced Bossi for violating a 1952 law that prohibits the reformation of the Fascist party. According to the exponents of the AN, Bossi had broken the law in August 1995 when he "publicly invited the participants at a party rally" to find "the names of all those who had voted for the AN so the Lega could go 'house by house to round them up.'"[19]

The flag incident and Bossi's "fascistic" remarks were not the first time the Lega had to face the courts over constitutional issues. Bossi had also been under investigation for exhortations made at other rallies, like when he had claimed in 1995 that he had known about an aborted coup attempt to "liberate" the North in 1993. Further, Bossi has paid fines related to things he said during the 1993 mayoral campaign, in which he insinuated that the Left's candidate, Nando dalla Chiesa, was a member of the Mafia.[20] Most recently, Bossi and a number of other Lega leaders were given suspended sentences of four months each for resisting an investigation by the Italian police into the activities of the Green Shirts, which ended in a scuffle at the party's headquarters in Milan in 1996.

The apparent "fascistfication" of Bossi and the Lega demonstrate a number of nuances about the Lega and the changes it was going through at this time. In particular, the party was not necessarily the "liberal" force for freedom and liberty that it had always claimed to be. The party also has a clearly visible authoritarian side. In this way, the party seems to be appealing less to the "liberal" sensibilities of a business-oriented middle class, than a more working-class electorate that desires a "strong man" to take care of problems like immigration, crime, and unemployment.

In fact, the Lega's support base began to shift during the mid-1990s, losing some of its appeal among certain sectors of the middle class (see table 6.3). Of the entrepreneurs, professionals, and managers interviewed in 1991, only 14 percent responded that they intended to vote for the Lega, a figure that would drop to around 12 percent in 1996. In contrast, the number of working-class people who stated that they intended to vote for the Lega grew during this period from 16 to 31.2 percent, the largest of any group interviewed. The next largest group comprised the retail merchants, artisans, and farmers, of whom around 24 percent intended to vote for the Lega in both 1991 and 1996.

These figures demonstrate that although the Lega's support has emerged from within some of the wealthiest regions of the country, the

Table 6.3 Those who intended to vote for the Lega from 1991 to 1996; by profession and education (percent)

	1991		1994		1996	
	Votes Lega	Number	Votes Lega	Number	Votes Lega	Number
Profession						
Entrepreneurs, professionals, managers	14.0	50	15.8	202	12.4	88
Teachers, white collar employees	13.3	249	16	675	18.8	609
Retail merchants, artisans, farmers	24	96	26.5	260	23.9	94
Workers (manual laborers)	16.6	157	21.4	393	31.2	290
Housewives	10.7	168	14.2	592	21.6	370
Retirees	10.7	234	15.1	764	13.8	429
Students	14.6	158	16	224	18.2	132
Unemployed	21.4	28	17	83	21	52
Education						
None-elementary	9.4	276	14.7	735	20.5	275
Middle school	19.3	373	19.4	1057	23.9	700
High school	15.1	317	17.6	1157	18.9	957
Some university-university graduates	8.6	174	9.8	284	6.6	166
Total for Northern Italy	14.1	1140	16.9	3233	19.8	2099

Source: Roberto Biorcio, *La Padania promessa* (Milan: Il Saggiatore, 1997), p. 252.

people supporting the party are not necessarily "rich." The party appeals to those sectors of the northern middle and working class (artisans, small farmers, and laborers), who are most susceptible to the changes in the global economy. The latter group of workers are finding globalization a threat as, for example, they compete with immigrants, legal and otherwise, who are being hired by local entrepreneurs for their skills as well as their greater flexibility and willingness to work for less pay.

It is also interesting to notice how this change in the Lega's class base has affected the actual institutions of the party. In the early 1990s, the party's leading association was ALIA, the collateral organization for entrepreneurs that headed the protests against the Minimum Tax in 1993 in Milan. ALIA, which was later changed to PIU (*Padani Imprenditori Uniti*) during the organizational changes in 1996, appears to have disappeared entirely from the party's organization sometime in the late 1990s.[21] In contrast, the party's trade union, *Sindacato Padano*, which is more associated with the party's working-class base, remains an integral part of the party. By the mid-1990s, the Lega began to show that it was less a revolt of the rich than a revolt of the middle to lower middle classes within the rich areas.

Overall, the social base of the Lega is similar to that of the rest of the parties in the North, with slightly more working-class voters than other parties. Almost 26 percent of the Lega's total electorate can be described as working class, compared to 21.5 percent of all other parties in the North (see table 6.4). Further, in terms of education, the percentage of university graduates among the Lega's supporters (2.4 percent) is about half that of all other parties (4.1 percent) in the North. However, the number of party supporters without any schooling or just elementary schooling is lower than the average for the North and the electorate of other parties in the region. The Lega's electorate is, thus, moderately educated and more likely to attend a technical college to learn a specific trade rather than the university, a not too uncommon path for someone who wants to become an artisan in a small enterprise.

What distinguishes the Lega from other parties in northern Italy is the fact that it has considerably more support from men (66.6 percent) than from women (33.8 percent), which contrasts drastically with the more or less even distribution of male and female voters for all other parties. Moreover, the party is also slightly overrepresented by youthful voters (18–29 years of age), and underrepresented by the elderly, 60 years and older. In this way, the Lega's support base is similar to that of other populist Right parties that have found their greatest audiences among younger men in smaller towns with a little to average education.

Table 6.4 Electorate of the Lega Nord in comparison to the electorate of other parties and the northern electorate in general (excluding Emilia-Romagna); percent distribution according to gender, age, education, and profession

	Lega Nord	Other parties in the North	The North
Gender			
Male	66.2	49.9	51.8
Female	33.8	50.1	48.2
Total	100	100	100
Number	209	1593	1802
Age			
18–29	27.9	21.2	21.9
30–39	22.1	21.7	21.8
40–49	20.3	17.7	18.0
50–59	19.7	16.8	17.2
60–above	10.1	22.6	21.1
Total	100	100	100
Number	209	1593	1802
Education			
None-elementary	30.5	40.7	39.6
Middle school	48.1	36.1	37.5
Diploma	19.0	19.0	19.0
University degree	2.4	4.1	3.9
Total	100	100	100
Number	209	1593	1802
Profession			
Employee	19.5	16.8	17.1
Worker	25.7	21.5	22.0
Self-employed	16.3	14.8	15.0
Housewife	5.9	14.6	13.6
Student	5.7	5.5	5.6
Retired	22.3	23.7	23.6
Unemployed	4.6	2.9	3.1
Total	100	100	100
Number	209	1593	1802

Source: Ilvo Diamanti, *Il male del Nord. Lega, localismo, secessione* (Rome: Donzelli, 1996), p. 118.

5. Growing Restlessness in the Northeast

Just as the Lega was becoming increasingly more extremist in its position, the party also started to face competition from other pro-federalist movements in the Northeast. One of the most noted movements during this period was a coalition of activist mayors called simply the

Movement of the Mayors (*Movimento dei Sindaci*). At the time, the new electoral law on the national level was complemented by one on the local level, which came into effect in 1993 and provided for the direct election of mayors through a two-turn system. Prior to this period, the ruling party or coalition had selected mayors after the election. The new law, which was instituted in order to facilitate more stable ruling coalitions on the local level, also guaranteed the winning party or coalition 60 percent of the council seats, regardless of their actual vote share. The mayors who came in under this new procedure were given a new mandate to govern, being more autonomous from the local party apparatus. A similar law would go into effect for the direct election of regional presidents in 2000.

Bolstered by this change, a group of these officials took on a new role in setting the national political agenda, particularly in the Northeast where the movement was strongest. One of the most visible and outspoken members of the movement, which was nonpartisan in nature, was Massimo Cacciari, who was voted in as mayor of Venice in 1993 and who was a member of the DS. In an interview in late 1995, Cacciari argued that the main goals of the mayors were essentially "more authority, more responsibility, and thus, more power" for the local level.[22] In a later interview, he stated that, in contrast to the Lega, "the mayors are not asking for the Republic of the North, nor the state of Padania. They are simply asking to liberate local administrations which not only lack autonomy but exist in a state without liberty."[23]

Cacciari and other mayors in the Northeast also directly addressed the concerns related to the Northern Question that had been brewing for years in the region. For Cacciari and others, there is a "lack of a true political reference point of the entrepreneurial world" in the Northeast. "It is a society which," after the fall of the DC and the failure of the Lega to initiate reforms, "has lost trust in politics."[24] Cacciari has focused on the need for greater fiscal federalism and the development of local infrastructure. He has, for example, stressed the need to reorganize local taxes to clearly define the "source for financing municipalities" and the "sovereignty" of communal authorities.[25] He, furthermore, argued that in the Veneto there is a need for a better relationship between the central state and the local authorities, particularly on the level of planning and infrastructure, "which is essential for the economic life of the region."[26] By late 1997 and early 1998, Cacciari and other mayors in the Northeast had formed another coalition, this time not with politicians but with leading industrialists and entrepreneurs in the region, which they dubbed the "Party of the Northeast" (*Partito del Nord-Est*).

Although the Party of the Northeast would end up being a short-lived experiment, suffering from divisions and eventually fading, it made an impact on national politics. In particular, the movement put a more "moderate" face (Cacciari and others) on the desire for economic and institutional reform in the North, and the Northeast in particular, and how this was seen primarily in some form of devolution. The movement also removed the spotlight from Bossi and the Lega, and in fact demonstrated another threat to the party, which up to this point had done little in concrete terms toward federalism.

Moderates voices, however, were not the only ones in the Northeast, particularly during the spring of 1997 when the 8 Venetian youths invaded the bell tower in Venice's San Marco Square. The separatists caught the top leadership of the Lega by surprise. At first, the Lega condemned the actions of the eight youths, calling it a "provocative act" "orchestrated" by the Italian secret services in order to delegitimize and discredit the party. However, after realizing the public outpouring of support for the youths in the Veneto, the Lega quickly reversed its position and came around to backing them. In fact, it was later discovered that a few members of the Lega and the party's Green Shirts paramilitary organization were tied to the Veneto Serenissima group. As a result, during a special meeting of the Venetian municipal council, the Lega councilors opted to abstain from a vote that was called to condemn the act of the youths.

Finally, the events in Venice became a pivot around which other pro-federalists and regional autonomists rallied in the region, including LIFE (The Free Entrepreneurs for a Federalist Europe), which emerged as one of the most outspoken groups in favor of the actions of the youths. Calling the 8 of Venice "patriots," LIFE's president, Fabio Padovan, an ex-member of the Lega, raised substantial funds for their legal fees and became a permanent fixture in the constant crowds in front of the courthouse where the youths were being tried and eventually convicted to six years in prison.[27] Also protesting in front of the courthouse were members of extreme Left groups who surprised the press by arguing that they too were "*federalisti.*" Citing the example of sub-commander Marcos in Chiapas and his support for self-government, the leftist groups called themselves the "radical wing of federalism" in Italy.[28]

6. The Bicameral Committee for Reform

At this time, the pressures from the surge in support for the Lega, along with the rise of other pro-federalist/secessionist movements in the

Northeast, were creating a crisis for the Ulivo government, which had been in power since winning the 1996 elections. By 1997, the government began an extensive process toward reform of the state in a federalist direction, starting with a nonpartisan bicameral committee, which was instituted in early 1997. The purpose of the committee was to rewrite the second, more substantial part of the constitution, making a number of reforms in the areas of electoral laws, the judicial system, the parliamentary and presidential system, and, in an effort toward federalist reform, the state structure. The committee was entrusted with a number of ambitious reforms that had been bounced around for years, from a directly elected president (rather than an appointed one) to the reduction of the number of parliamentarians. The hope was that the committee would be able to discard outdated aspects of the 50-year-old constitution that had contributed to such problems as a politicized judiciary and a legislative process that is frequently stalled by weak coalition governments. Moreover, there was hope that the reforms would eventually decentralize more power to the regions and to the other subnational levels of government.[29]

The bicameral committee was one of the most ambitious attempts at devolution in Italy since the regional reforms of the 1970s. The committee was also another serious challenge to the Lega, which had monopolized the debate on federalism since the mid-1980s. Although the Lega had members in the bicameral committee, they had refused to play a consistent role in the debates of the Form of the State subcommittee that was assigned to work on this area. The committee threatened to take the issue of federalism out of the Lega's hands, and as a result, it came as no surprise that Bossi's response to the initiatives of the committee was cold at best.

The document that was eventually presented to parliament by the Form of the State subcommittee called for considerable decentralization with the formation of twenty "small Italies," with "very strong powers," held together by a pact of national unity. From the beginning, however, the committee's recommendation came under heavy criticism, particularly from the different lobby groups that represent the various subnational levels of government. The Conference of Regional Presidents presented a number of objections to the bicameral committee, including the lack of a "regional senate" to "permit true territorial representation," a common criticism of the committee's findings. The conference also objected to the fact that certain functions that were reserved to the central state already fell within the remit of the regions.

The committee further sparked a familiar debate on the question of which level of government should benefit the most from federalist reform. On its own, the committee's proposals more or less favored the regional level, giving it more default powers. However, Enzo Bianco, the president of the National Association of Italian Communes (ANCI), a well-established lobby for the municipal level, criticized the committee's view of federalism, arguing that they discriminated against the communes. Bianco too called for the institution of a representative house like a regional senate, but argued that it should have seats for delegates from the communes and other local authorities, not just the regions. A wider, more representative "house of autonomous units" (*Camera delle autonomie*), Bianco argued, would fix this imbalance in power. The ANCI echoed in many ways the views of the Action party during the Constituent Assembly in 1946–1947 by calling for a presidential system in order to strengthen the executive office: "a strong federalism assumes a strong parliament and a strong executive." Antonio Bassolino, mayor of Naples and member of the Movement of the Mayors, echoed the opinion of many of his municipal colleagues, when he argued for a federalism that "recognizes the indispensable role of the city as the hinge to democracy" in Italy.[30]

In addition to the conflicting voices from the representatives of the regions and other local authorities, there were also some outright opponents to decentralization. The rightist AN emerged as one of the most visible critics of the process of decentralization, voicing words of caution about how such a reform will affect the poorer South, the party's base. According to the AN, federalism risks penalizing "small regions and those less developed in the Mezzogiorno" putting them into a "permanent" state of marginalization. However, unlike the Lega, the AN went along with the bicameral committee in the hopes of gaining its own goal of a stronger and directly elected president.[31]

7. Devolutionary Reforms of the Late 1990s

Despite the failure of the bicameral committee, the Ulivo government continued to press for federalist reforms as part of its own legislative agenda. The leftist government was also under considerable pressure from the EU to introduce a number of institutional reforms. Italy had been under the gun since the Maastricht Treaty, to meet the convergence criteria for monetary union. A general reform of the administrative structure and fiscal system was needed to reduce the country's mounting deficit, which was still high in 1997. Decentralization of powers emerged not only as a response to secessionist pressures from the Northeast, but also as part of a general plan to introduce greater efficiency and accountability into the system of governance.

The reforms the Ulivo government initiated both simplified the administrative system and strengthened the subnational level. First, the so-called *Bassanini I* law of 1997 essentially transferred a number of administrative responsibilities to regional and local levels, which up to this point had been carried out by the central state, including the provision of health care and education, industrial incentives, urban planning, public works, and environmental protection. Overall, the regions and other local authorities were given extensive control over the administration of government functions,[32] except for those with explicit national interests, such as foreign affairs and trade, defense, public order and safety, justice, university and scientific research, and large infrastructural projects. The government was given discretionary powers to gradually devolve responsibilities, keeping within certain guidelines that respect the need for both local autonomy and overall efficiency and national unity. The reform also enhanced the role of the Conference on State and Regions, the main liaison organization between the state and the regions, giving the group a greater say in legislative initiatives that deal with regional issues. In addition, two new organizations were created to enhance the relationship between the center and periphery, the Conference on State and Communes and the United Conference on State–Regions–Communes.

In the language of the OECD, the reforms are based on the principle of "subsidiary," and are "closely linked to the process of decentralization."[33] It was not outright devolution because it did not, at this point, give the regions the capacity to pass their own legislation over these issues, but simply gave them the power to administer programs. The reforms did, however, require a considerable shake up of the *status quo*, as thousands of civil servants who used to work for the central government came under the control of regional and local governments.

The reforms also addressed specifically the concerns of local industry and the needs of SMEs in the Northeast, as the regions were specifically given powers over local economic development, particularly over industrial incentives, while the central state retained its control over general industrial policy.[34] In addition to decentralization of functions, the reforms of 1997–1999 also intended to simplify the problematic administrative system that has been the source of great angst for Italian entrepreneurs. This process involved a reduction of the number of government ministries from twenty-two in 1995 to only twelve in 2001, as well as a number of reforms that were intended to reduce the red tape that frequently bogged down businesses. For example, a series of new laws simplified the procedures for filing documents and certifications with the government and created a "one-stop-shop" for businesses seeking administrative approvals. This last reform will help new, start up companies by instituting a single authorization procedure that replaces the previous forty-three needed in the past.[35]

Another major cause of inefficiency in Italy arises from the numerous administrative laws that govern the bureaucracy. As a result, many regulations have been streamlined through numerous "delegislation" decrees that simplify administrative procedures.[36] Moreover, the *Bassanini I* law calls for more stringent requirements for civil servants in the public administration, making them more accountable and giving citizens greater recourse for legal action when they are given inefficient service. Finally, government agencies have been reorganized to encourage a more "consumer-friendly" approach by defining greater standards of quality in service.

However, the most celebrated reform during this period for pro-federalists was an extensive reorganization of the tax system, which included a considerable decentralization of fiscal powers to regional and local authorities. First, the government introduced a new, regional tax call IRAP or *Imposta regionale sulle attività produttive* (regional tax on productive activities), which went into effect in 1998, replacing a number of smaller central and local government taxes. IRAP, which taxes business profits, is intended to increase regional fiscal autonomy as the revenue earned will go directly to the regions (not via Rome like in the past), and cover around 40 percent of the regional budget. Regions will, moreover, be allowed to vary the rate of the tax (within limits) according to their own economic situation.

This reform also directly addresses the needs of entrepreneurs in the Northeast, in part because IRAP further simplifies the fiscal system by replacing a number of smaller taxes on independent professionals and small-scale businesses. The new tax further claims to reduce the cost of labor for employers by abolishing some employer contributions and thereby giving incentives for increasing employment.

In addition to IRAP, the reform further decentralized fiscal powers by replacing state transfers with regional and local surcharges on existing national taxes, giving local authorities additional autonomy over their own resources. The imbalances between the different regions and their capacity to collect revenue are evened out in part through a National Equalization Fund, which, however, does not come from the central purse but is financed by the regions themselves.

Overall, fiscal autonomy has increased considerably during the past five years since the reforms were first implemented. In 2002, it is

Table 6.5 Tax receipts and contributions in Italy (in billions of Italian Lire)

	1996	1999	2002*
Supranational level	9,739	7,190	8,450
Central administration	446,653	530,913	545,726
Local administrations	64,960	112,159	206,232
Of which:			
Regions	39,665	83,787	165,025
Provinces and communes	25,295	28,372	41,207
Contributions	286,166	270,819	301,775
Total	807,518	921,081	1,062,183
As a percentage			
Supranational level	1.2	0.8	0.8
Central administration	55.3	57.6	51.4
Local administrations	8.0	12.2	19.4
Of which:			
Regions	4.9	9.1	15.5
Provinces and communes	3.1	3.1	3.9
Contributions	35.4	29.4	28.4
Total	100.0	100.0	100.0

* projections.
Source: OECD, *Territorial Reviews, Italy* (Paris: OECD, 2001), p. 154.

projected that tax receipts from local administrations combined (regions, provinces, and communes) will be a little more than 19 percent of the total, a considerable jump from 1996, when it was only 8 percent (see table 6.5). Italy has moved from being one of the most centralized nations in fiscal terms to one of the most decentralized in the OECD, where, on average, local tax receipts make up only 13 percent of the total. Today, the OECD puts Italy somewhere between the United States (where states have extensive fiscal autonomy) and Germany (where shared national tax revenues allow for little local autonomy).[37]

Although it is too early to judge the impact of these new initiatives, they represent a considerable shift in the dynamics of the Italian state. First, they represent a move in a federalist direction in terms of the administration and fiscal system. New initiatives like the *Bassanini I* law and IRAP regional tax demonstrate the increasing awareness that the Italian state needs to further decentralize in order to meet the needs of its changing society and economy. In addition, the new initiatives demonstrate that decentralization is not enough. Rather, there needs to be a greater degree of simplification in the administrative system that had become bloated and inefficient due, especially, to the clientelist practices of the ruling parties in the past.

Second, the increase in fiscal autonomy will make the regions a more independent and eventually a more relevant arena of government in Italy. As the regions have more control over local resources, they will have to become more accountable and responsible. Increased regional autonomy should also have a major impact on the party system, encouraging the parties to take the regional level more seriously as an arena for political initiatives and policy-making.

8. Constitutional Changes

Most recently, the Italian parliament passed a bill just before the Ulivo was voted out of office in the spring of 2001, which made another major jump in a federalist direction. The new law specifically calls for changes in the articles of the second part of the constitution that deal with the powers of the regions and other subnational levels of government. In the original constitution, there is a "residual clause" that guarantees that any power not specifically attributed to the realm of the regions, or other subnational units of government, automatically falls under the jurisdiction of the central state. The new law reverses this, giving all legislative powers to the regional level, unless they are "expressly reserved to the legislative remit of the state."[38] In essence, this change would be similar to the spirit of the tenth amendment of the United States Constitution that reserves all powers to the states, except the "expressed" powers of Congress. While the constitutional changes do not allow for Italian regions to have nearly as much power as an American state (as much is still reserved to the central level), it gives the regions, provinces, and communes a constitutional guarantee of their own autonomy, something that was lacking in the old constitution.

In October of 2001, the bill was put to test in a national, constitutional referendum, which was the first since the formation of the republic in 1946. The referendum, which is needed for any effort to change the constitution, was passed by a wide margin with over 60 percent of the voters agreeing with the changes. The turnout for the referendum, however, was quite low, around 34 percent, primarily due to the terrorist attacks of September 11th in New York, which consumed the world, particularly NATO countries like Italy. Despite the low turnout, a quorum was not necessary and so the results have the force of law. The changes to the constitution are a major step for Italy, giving the regions greater legislative powers to complement the new administrative functions that were passed down with the *Bassanini I* initiative.

Like the bicameral commission, the Ulivo's constitutional bill threatened to take the federalist issue out of the Lega's hands. During the weeks leading up to the referendum, the Lega ran a "no" campaign, putting it in the same camp as the AN and the far Left RC. However, while the latter two parties argued that the reform went too far, the Lega argued that it did not go far enough in the way of decentralization. Although the referendum was passed in all regions of the country, except Valle d'Aosta,[39] its weakest supporters could be found in Lega strongholds, like the Lombard provinces of Como and Bergamo, and the Veneto provinces of Verona, Vicenza, and Treviso. The strongest support came from the central regions that are ruled by the DS, the party that originally sponsored the bill. The southern regions widely supported the bill despite fears from the AN that such a move would threaten the region by cutting it off from the central government. The South's support, however, was most likely based on the fact that the bill included a provision that guaranteed weaker regions support.

CHAPTER 7

Conclusions

1. The State and Regionalist Politics in the North

This book has focused on the political and economic factors that have contributed to the rise of the Lega Nord, and the regionalist tensions that have propelled it over the past decade and a half. A crucial factor has been the nature of the Italian state, which reached a crisis point in the late twentieth century, when its bureaucratized and inefficient administrative system became a barrier to the country's new economic "engine," the Northeast. The centralized state structure also failed to provide the local economy with a much-needed institutional basis for continued economic growth. As a result, a reform of the state in Italy has meant not only a better administration, but also a more decentralized one that can more effectively manage the changing needs of industrial districts in the North and the rest of the country.

This book has also shown that the enduring divide between the North and South in Italy is not simply a product of differences in culture, but the specific actions of political elites. Specifically, the regional gap between these regions has been perpetuated by the clientelist politics of the DC, a policy the party inherited from its liberal and fascist predecessors and involved the trading of state resources for votes. The DC's strategy had resulted in a dependent South that lacks many of the necessary resources to help autonomous growth and development, causing it to lag behind the rest of the country. Moreover, the DC's strategy had the effect of increasingly "southernizing" the state structure as it filled the administrative system with patronage appointments from the South, thereby adding to its inefficiency.

The cracks in the DC's clientelist system began to appear in the 1980s as the party's foundation crumbled. In particular, the DC began to lose its support in the once solid "White" regions of the Catholic subculture of the Northeast, the network of Catholic institutions that had in the past supported the party and were now either declining themselves or simply becoming more independent of the DC. The DC had also lost favor within its base among small-scale entrepreneurs in the Northeast, a sector that was experiencing considerable transformations in the 1980s. Although the DC had supported this sector in the 1950s and 1960s, its increasing focus on clientelism in the South had alienated them from the party. In addition, the DC's center-left strategies in the 1970s and 1980s shifted the party further away from this sector as it attempted to consolidate corporatist links with big business.

The final blow for the DC came in the early 1990s, when a combination of corruption scandals and an expanding public sector debt both disillusioned Italian voters and threatened to keep the country behind the rest of their European partners. By 1993, the DC, its partner the PSI, and a series of other smaller forces that had made up the *partitocrazia* (party-state) had all fallen apart, opening the way for the Lega. The decline and eventual exit of the DC from the party system provided a perfect "political opportunity" for the Lega to emerge and succeed as a new regional force.

Since its emergence, the Lega has capitalized on two salient cleavages in Italian politics, which have grown as a result of the legacies of the DC. First, the Lega has focused on the regional cleavage between the North and South and the burden that this divide has placed on the North. A crucial factor behind the Lega's success has been its capacity to depict the North as a victim of a predatory central state that favors the South and treats the North as a political periphery. Second, the Lega has been able to mobilize support as a "new" party in opposition to the political *status quo* by campaigning against decades of *partitocrazia* and the domination of the DC and its partners like the PSI.

The Lega has, moreover, had a significant impact on the Italian political system, forcing the issue of federalist reform of the state onto the political agenda, an issue that had been floating around since the Risorgimento in the mid-nineteenth century. The reforms of the past few years offer a significant move in a federalist direction for the country and a break from the centralized state and the Napoleonic legacies of the past. However, as the reforms are still new, their ability to truly improve Italy's institutional structure—and solve problems like the Northern Question—needs to be measured at a later date.

2. The Recent Decline of the Lega

In spite of its spectacular rise during the mid-1990s, the Lega has declined in recent years, even in its strongholds in the Northeast. During the elections to the European Parliament of June 1999 the Lega was able to gain only 4.5 percent of the national vote share, less than half of its support in 1996. Since then, the Lega has gained only about 4 percent of the national vote, a decline that is due in part to the ongoing federalist reforms that have undermined the central issue of the party. In addition, the impracticality of the party's secessionist plans may have put off many voters in the North, who eventually found a home in the less radical FI. Moreover, the antiparty sentiment that propelled the Lega in the late 1980s and early 1990s has begun to wane, particularly after the last of the *Mani Pulite* trials.[1] Despite these losses at the polls, however, the party remains a contending force in the North, though with most of its support in the Veneto, Lombardy, and Friuli-Venezia Giulia.

The Lega, however, has moderated its position on the issue of northern independence, moving back in a pro-federalist direction and officially dropping the issue of secession during a special party convention in late 1998. The moderation was met with some objection within the party, particularly in the more secessionist Veneto, where Fabrizio Commencini, the popular leader of the Liga Veneta, split from Bossi shortly after the convention to form his own movement, *Liga Fronte Veneto* (Venetian Front League). In spite of this split, however, the Veneto continues to be a stronghold for the Lega as Comencini's new party has only gained marginal results.

In 2000, the Lega decided to rejoin its former foes on the Right in an electoral alliance for the regional elections that year. Together with FI, the AN, and a number of other, small right-wing parties, the coalition was able to dominate the elections across the North, winning the regional councils in all areas of Padania, except Emilia-Romagna in the center-north that remains a stronghold of the Left. The Lega remains in an alliance with FI and the AN today, in a coalition that is now called the *Casa delle Libertà* (House of Liberties), which most recently entered national elections in 2001 and won by a wide margin against the leftist Ulivo coalition.

The victory of the Right was reminiscent of the elections in Austria only a year earlier, when the populist Right Freedom Party of Jörge Haider entered the ruling coalition, bringing on seven months of diplomatic sanctions from the rest of the EU. Although Italy did not have to endure a similar ordeal, there was a considerable degree of concern from other EU members about the inclusion of the Lega and the rambunctious Bossi in a governing position. The EU decided not to punish Italy as the boycott against Austria was considered a disaster that had only brought on widespread anti-EU feelings.

There were a number of incentives for Bossi to keep his party in the coalition, including the fact that it was able to gain seats in parliament only as a coalition member, demonstrating the considerable strain that the new electoral law is having on the party. On its own, the Lega had only received about 3.9 percent of the national vote during the elections, just under the 4 percent threshold needed to attain seats on a proportional level. But as a member of the broader coalition, Bossi was able to receive 30 seats for his party as part of the agreement with Berlusconi. In addition, the Lega received three ministerial positions, including two with portfolio, Social Services and the Judiciary, and a noncabinet ministry without portfolio, the ministry for Institutional Reform and Devolution, which is aptly filled by Bossi himself. As Minister of Institutional Reform and Devolution, Bossi has presented another constitutional bill that will go to the floor of both houses of parliament for a vote in the near future. If it passes, it will devolve more exclusive powers to the regions.

The Lega's move to drop secession, however, was met with an increased focus on its anti-immigrant position, expressing many of the same themes as other populist Right parties in Europe today. Much of this xenophobia was evident during the 1997 mayoral elections, which happened to coincide with a second exodus of Albanian refugees who landed on the Adriatic coast and caused a major political crisis in the country. During the election, the party's slogan was "one more vote [for the Lega], one less Albanian" ("*un voto in più, un Albanese in meno*"). At the local level, the Lega's many mayors also continue to make life difficult for immigrants living in the North, such as Giancarlo Gentilini, the mayor of Treviso (the Veneto), who has stated that the country should ship illegal immigrants out of the country in "lead wagons." Gentilini, who is a close friend of Jörge Haider, was also accused by an Italian court of inciting racial hatred when he made public statements that hypothesized the use of immigrants as targets for gun practice. Although the charges against him were eventually dropped, the actions of the "sheriff of Treviso" and other Lega representatives continue to put into question the democratic character of the party.

The Lega was also able to get a highly restrictive immigration bill passed in both houses of parliament, which calls for, among other things, the finger printing of all non-EU permanent residents in Italy and harsh penalties for people who hire illegal immigrants. The bill was a clear victory for the Lega, which, despite its diminished status, has had a considerable influence on the ruling coalition. The bill's passage was also an important demonstration of the capacity of far Right parties like the Lega and the AN, which co-sponsored the legislation, to influence the national agenda on the issue of immigration.

At the same time, the anti-immigrant position of the Lega runs counter to the interests of entrepreneurs in the North, who may or may not be as intolerant of immigrants as the rest of the country but whose livelihood depends on them more. Many of the SMEs in the North depend on cheaper foreign labor for factory jobs that younger Italians do not want. In fact, the organization of young industrialists recently criticized the Lega's new immigration bill for, among other things, not giving amnesty to illegal immigrants working in factories as it does for domestic workers.[2] In many ways, the immigration bill shows how the Lega has become out of touch with the entrepreneurial base of the North. Although the Lega still supports the SME sector and champions it as the backbone of the North's economy, they have failed to align themselves effectively with this class of voters.

3. The Lega as a Party against Globalization

In recent years, the Lega has adopted a number of new themes in its campaign, the latest being the defense of Western, Christian values, expressing a strongly anti-Muslim position by protesting such things as the construction of mosques in the country. Like other far Right parties, the Lega's fears regarding an "islamicization" of the country are highly exaggerated, given the fact that only about a third of the immigrants in the country today are actually Muslim, while half are Christian.[3] Despite this fact, the party appears to have capitalized on this issue in all of its campaigns, outpacing, at times, its focus on regional autonomy. The Lega has also become strongly antigay, against civil unions between same-sex couples and the adoption of children by gay couples, as well as a virulent opponent of controversial fertility advances. In one of his rallies, Bossi called for the "natural against the artificial," praising "natural things," like "natural families, natural children, and natural Padania."[4] Despite this position, the party still maintains a relatively ambiguous view toward the Vatican, siding with the Church on a number of conservative issues but criticizing them for their universalist position, which emphasizes national and global unity, as well as a generally pro-immigration stance. The Vatican is also an easy target for the Lega because of its former ties to the DC and, hence, the old politics of the First Republic.

The Lega has also become increasingly opposed to globalization, saving its biggest criticism for the EU, which Bossi has called the "Soviet Union of Europe," or simply a "fascist" conspiracy that is run by big businesses and Free Masons.[5] This is a considerable shift for a party that, in the early 1990s, had presented itself as a pro-EU force that wanted to bring the North, alone, into the union among the leading members. The Lega has also moved significantly from its former support of freer markets, expressing considerably more skepticism about the increasing integration of the European market. For example, in his 1998 book, *Processo alla Lega*, Bossi complains that the

> supermarkets and hypermarkets arrive from the center of Europe, with their competitive prices and their global commercial networks, and they bring to our country the honey from Paris, the *prosciutto* from Hamburg, Bavarian and French cheese, Belgian and Dutch milk. Goodbye commerce, goodbye Padanian agriculture; the stores close and the commercial networks pass under the control of the large foreign groups.[6]

The Lega's anti-EU views have also moved the center–right *Casa* coalition into a more anti-Europe position. Although Italy is still one of the most supportive nations of the EU, the current government is much more skeptical of increasing integration, and has been protesting a number of new European initiatives, the latest being a post-September 11th EU-wide arrest warrant intended to catch terrorists.[7] In general, members of the coalition that were once solidly pro-EU, particularly those in the more neoliberal FI, have begun to follow Bossi's lead.

At first glance, the Lega's increasingly xenophobic and inward looking views are simply a desperate attempt to find new "enemies" after the disappearance of old ones, like the postwar ruling parties. However, the party also appears to have tapped into a growing sense of unease in the North about current changes in the economy that have led to things like immigration and multiculturalism and the breakdown of the traditional family and lifestyles. In many ways, the Lega's new issues are indicative of tensions in regions like the Veneto that, on the one hand, are highly integrated into the global economy, yet, on the other hand, are still strongly rooted in local and regional traditions, like pride in speaking the Venetian dialect. The feeling that national institutions are not effectively protecting the region from global economic and cultural changes has simply exacerbated the fear of these changes.

Overall, the Lega's shifting positions on free trade and globalization over the years reflect the contradicting tendencies in places like northern Italy. On the one hand, northerners benefit from access to liberal markets that boost the local economy and help local entrepreneurs become world leaders in certain niche markets. The entrepreneurs of the North, moreover, express their own desire to operate with fewer barriers to trade, like bureaucratic red tape and high and complex taxes. On the other hand, the people in the North want to protect themselves from the destructive side of global competition that makes the economy more unstable—especially for the working class—and has the potential to undermine local culture.

4. Globalization and the Populist Right in Europe

The regionalist tensions in northern Italy demonstrate that globalization has politicized territorial issues today more than ever.[8] An increasingly competitive global economy continues to exacerbate the divide between dynamic, vibrant regions and the less productive, dependent ones. This divide will only become worse as states are forced to follow more neoliberal policies that limit their capacity to support lagging regions, and international agreements like the WTO prevent states from instituting tariffs that might help nascent industries in regional economies. In addition, the increasing trend toward regional economies, like the one in the Italian Northeast, have forced states to take a different, more decentralized approach to deal with economic and industrial growth. While such devolutionary trends do not pose a direct threat to the sovereignty of nation-states, it presents policy makers with a considerable challenge and the need to breakdown the centralized institutions of the postwar period.

Increasing globalization and the territorial fissures it causes will also provide further fuel for inward looking, xenophobic parties like the Lega Nord. Ironically, just as the national borders of the world appear to be falling, new walls have emerged from populists seeking to block the influence of global economic and cultural trends. As it is, territory and the preservation of boundaries have become the hallmarks of other populist Right parties, whether they are expressly regionalist, like the Lega or even the Vlaams Bloc in Flanders (Belgium), or simply nationalists like the French National Front. These parties have mobilized a great deal of support by arguing that the current rise in free trade, immigration, and multiculturalism is a threat to borders, whether national or regional. Further, as more parties like the Lega emerge out of the margins and into positions of national prominence—as have the populist Right in Austria and Denmark—they will continue to have considerable influence on national agendas and public policy, making Europe a more inward looking place.

Appendices

Table A.1 Electoral results of Italian parties, Chamber of Deputies (lower house) First Republic: 1948–1992

Parties	1948 %	1948 Seats	1953 %	1953 Seats	1958 %	1958 Seats	1963 %	1963 Seats	1968 %	1968 Seats	1972 %	1972 Seats	1976 %	1976 Seats	1979 %	1979 Seats	1983 %	1983 Seats	1987 %	1987 Seats	1992 %	1992 Seats
DC	48.5	305	40.1	263	42.3	273	38.3	260	39.1	266	38.7	266	38.7	263	38.3	262	32.9	225	34.3	234	29.7	206
PCI/PDS	31.0	183	22.6	143	22.7	140	25.3	166	26.9	177	27.1	179	34.4	227	30.4	201	29.9	198	26.6	177	16.1	107
PSI	*	—	12.7	75	14.2	84	13.8	87	14.5	91	9.6	61	9.6	57	9.8	62	11.4	73	14.3	94	13.6	92
PSDI	7.1	33	4.5	19	4.6	22	6.1	33	#	—	5.1	29	3.4	15	3.8	20	4.1	23	2.9	17	2.7	16
MSI	2.0	6	5.8	29	4.8	24	5.1	27	4.5	24	8.7	56	6.1	35	5.3	30	6.8	42	5.9	35	5.4	34
PNM/PMP	2.8	14	6.9	40	4.8	25	1.7	8	1.3	6	—	—	—	—	—	—	—	—	—	—	—	—
PRI	2.5	9	1.6	5	1.4	6	1.4	6	2.0	9	2.9	15	3.1	14	3.0	16	5.1	29	3.7	21	4.4	27
PLI	3.8	19	3.0	13	3.5	17	7.0	39	5.8	31	3.9	20	1.3	5	1.9	9	2.9	16	2.1	11	2.8	17
SVP	0.5	3	0.5	3	0.5	3	0.4	3	0.5	3	0.5	3	0.5	3	0.5	4	0.5	3	0.5	3	0.5	3
Valle d'Aosta lists	—	—	—	—	0.1	1	0.1	1	—	—	—	—	0.1	1	0.1	1	0.1	1	0.1	1	0.1	1
Radicals/Pannella	—	—	—	—	—	—	—	—	—	—	—	—	1.1	4	3.5	18	2.2	11	2.6	13	1.2	7
Liga Veneta	—	—	—	—	—	—	—	—	—	—	—	—	—	—	—	—	0.3	1	—	—	—	—
Lega Lombarda	—	—	—	—	—	—	—	—	—	—	—	—	—	—	—	—	—	—	0.5	1	8.7	55
Green lists	—	—	—	—	—	—	—	—	—	—	—	—	—	—	—	—	—	—	2.5	13	3	16
RC	—	—	—	—	—	—	—	—	—	—	—	—	—	—	—	—	—	—	—	—	5.6	35
Other legas	—	—	—	—	—	—	—	—	—	—	—	—	—	—	—	—	—	—	—	—	1.2	1
Others	0.5	2	—	—	0.6	1	—	—	4.4	23	0.1	1	1.5	6	1.6	7	1.8	8	2.1	10	2.3	13
Parties without seats	1.3	0	2.3	0	0.5	0	0.8	0	1.0	0	3.4	0	0.2	0	1.8	0	2.0	0	1.9	0	2.7	0
Total	100.0	574	100.0	590	100.0	596	100.0	630	100.0	630	100.0	630	100.0	630	100.0	630	100.0	630	100.0	630	100.0	630

* PCI and PSI ran together in a Popular Front coalition.
# PSI and PSDI ran together in a United Socialists coalition.

DC, Christian Democratic party; PCI/PDS, Communist party/Democratic Party of the Left; PSI, Socialist party; PSDI, Social Democratic party; PNM/PMP, Monarchist parties; MSI, Italian Social Movement; PRI, Republican party; PLI, Liberal party; SVP, South Tyrol People's party; RC, Refounded Communists.

Source: Adapted from David Hine, *Governing Italy* (Oxford: Clarendon, 1994), pp. 71–76.

Table A.2 Electoral results of Italian parties, Chamber of Deputies, Second Republic: 1994–2001

Parties/electoral lists	1994 %	1994 Seats	1996 %	1996 Seats	2001 %	2001 Seats
PDS/DS	20.4	109	21.1	156	16.6	138
RC	6.0	39	8.6	32	5.0	11
PPI	11.1	33	6.8	67	—	—
PSI	2.2	14	—	—	—	—
Greens	2.7	11	2.5	21	2.2	18
Patto Segni	4.7	13	—	—	—	—
La Rete	1.9	6	—	—	—	—
Alleanza Democratica	1.2	18	—	—	—	—
Lista Dini	—	—	4.3	24	—	—
La Margherita	—	—	—	—	14.5	76
Communisti Italiani	—	—	—	—	1.7	9
FI	21.0	99	20.6	123	29.4	189
AN	13.5	109	15.7	93	12	96
Lega Nord	8.4	117	10.1	59	3.9	30
CCD/CCD-CDU	*	29	5.8	30	3.2	40
Nuovo PSI	—	—	—	—	0.9	2
Parties not winning seats #	6.9	0	4.5	0	10.6	0
Other parties winning seats	—	33	—	25	—	21
Total	100.0	630	100.0	630	100.0	630

PPI, Popular party (P-S-P-U-P in 1996); PDS/DS, Democratic Party of the Left (since 2001, DS or Democrats of the Left); PSI, Socialist party; Nuovo PSI, New Socialists; FI, Forza Italia; AN, Alleanza Nazionale; RC, Refounded Communists; CCD, Christian Democratic Center (CCD-CDU since 1996).
Since 1994, 75% of the seats are allocated on a majoritarian basis, in single-member districts.
The rest of the seats are allocated on a PR (Proportional representation) basis.
Numbers in italics: Seats allocated on a single-member district basis to smaller parties and lists that failed to gain seats on a PR basis, but gained seats as part of their alliance with larger party "cartels."
See appendix A. 3 for cartels since 1994.
* CCD ran as part of the FI list in 1994.
# Smaller parties and lists that failed to win seats allocated on a PR basis.

Sources: Stefano Bartolini and Roberto D'Alimonte, "La competizione maggioritaria: le origini elettorali del parlamento diviso," in *Maggioritario ma non troppo* (Bologna: Il Mulino, 1995), p. 320 (for 1994); www.parlamento.it (for 1996); *La Repubblica*, May 16, 2001 (for 2001).

Table A.3 Party cartels

	1994		1996		2001	
Progressisti (Progressives)	PDS		Ulivo (Olive Tree)	PDS	Ulivo	DS
	RC			PPI (P-S-P-U-P)		La Margherita
	PSI			Greens		Greens
	Greens			Lista Dini		Communisti Italiani
	La Rete			Sardinian Action party		Other parties/lists
	Alleanza Democratica					
	Cristiano-Sociali					
	Rinascita Socialista					
	Indipendenti di Sinistra					
Polo per il Buon Governo/ Polo per le Libertà (Pole for Good Government/ Pole for Liberty)	FI		Polo per le Libertà (Pole for Liberty)	FI	Casa delle Libertà (House of Liberties)	FI
	AN			AN		AN
	Lega Nord			CCD-CDU		Lega Nord
	CCD					CCD-CDU
	Unione di Centro					Nuovo PSI
	Polo Liberal-Democratico					
	Riformatori					
	Lista Pannella					
Patto per l'Italia (Pact for Italy)	Patto Segni					
	PPI					

Table A.4 Electoral results of the Lega parties in central and northern Italy, 1983–2001

Region	1983 Nat	1985 Reg	1987 Nat	1989 Eur	1990 Reg	1992 Nat	1994 Nat	1994 Eur	1995 Reg	1996 Nat	1999 Eur	2000 Reg	2001 Nat
Valle d'Aosta	—	1.1	—	—	—	—	—	5.7	7.6	8.1	1.9	3.4	—
Piedmont	—	—	2.9	2.1	5.1	16.3	16.2	11.5	9.9	18.4	7.8	7.6	6.0
Liguria	—	0.9	1.3	1.4	6.1	14.3	11.4	8.1	6.5	10.2	3.7	4.3	3.9
Lombardy	—	0.5	4.1	8.1	18.9	23.0	22.6	17.7	17.7	24.8	13.1	15.4	11.3
Trentino-A.A.	—	—	—	0.7	—	8.9	7.5	4.5	9.6	13.2	2.4	4.7	3.6
Veneto	4.2	3.7	3.1	1.7	5.9	17.8	21.6	15.6	16.7	29.8	10.7	12.0	10.5
Friuli-V.G.	—	—	0.8	0.5	—	15.3	16.9	11.2	26.7	23.2	10.1	17.3	8.2
Emilia-Romagna	—	0.4	0.5	0.5	2.9	9.6	6.4	4.4	3.4	7.2	3.0	3.3	2.6
Tuscany	—	0.5	0.3	0.2	0.8	3.1	2.2	1.6	0.7	1.8	0.6	0.6	0.6
Marche	—	0.5	0.5	0.1	0.2	1.3	—	0.8	0.5	1.5	0.4	0.3	—
Umbria	—	0.4	0.4	0.1	0.2	1.1	—	0.6	—	1.0	0.3	0.3	—

Nat, national elections; Eur, elections to European Parliament; Reg, regional elections.
The regional elections in Valle d'Aosta, Trentino-Alto Adige and Friuli-Venezia Giulia were held in 1993 and 1998, not 1995 and 2000.
1983: Liga Veneta; 1985: Liga Veneta; for Lombardy: Liga Veneta-Lega Lombarda; 1987: Liga Veneta-Pensioners' Union; for Piedmont: Liga Veneta-Pensioners' Union and Piedmont List; for Lombardy: Lega Lombarda and Liga Veneta-Pentioners' Union (which ran as a separate list); from 1989: Alleanza Nord and then Lega Nord.

Sources: Table adapted from Marco Tarchi, "The Lega Nord," in *Regionalist Parties in Western Europe*, edited by Lieven de Winter and Hüri Tursan (London: Routledge, 1998), p. 153. For 1995, 1999 and 2000: *La Repubblica* www.repubblica.it/elezioni2000/regionali. For 1999 (Valle d'Aosta, Trentino and Friuli), 1996 (Valle d'Aosta) and 2001 (all regions): Ministry of the Interior, www.interno.it. For 1995 (Valle d'Aosta): www.cattaneo.it/archivi.

Notes

Chapter 1 Overview

1. *La Repubblica*, May 10, 1997, derisively referred to them as "Hezbollah alla polenta," making references to both the Lebanese group and the local northern Italian dish.
2. See, for example, the classic works by Giovanni Sartori, *Parties and Party System* (Cambridge: Cambridge University Press, 1976); Paolo Farnetti, *The Italian Party System, 1945–1980* (New York: St. Martin's Press, 1985); and Joseph LaPalombara, *Democracy Italian Style* (New Haven: Yale University Press, 1987).
3. For more on these debates, see Enrico Ruisconi, *Ce cessiamo di essere una nazione: Tra etnodemocrazie regionali e cittadinanza europea* (Bologna: Il Mulino, 1993). See also Roberto Cartocci, *Fra Lega e Chiesa: l'Italia in cerca di integrazione* (Bologna: Il Mulino, 1994).
4. See in particular, Hans-Georg Betz, *The Populist Right in Western Europe* (New York: St. Martin's Press, 1994); Hans-Georg Betz and Stefan Immerfall, ed., *New Politics of the Right: Neo-Populist Parties and Movements in Established Democracies* (New York: Palgrave, 1998); Martin Schain, Aristide Zolberg, and Patrick Hossay, ed., *Shadows Over Europe: The Development and Impact of the Extreme Right in Western Europe* (New York: Palgrave, 2002); Herbert Kitschelt, *The Radical-Right in Western Europe* (Ann Arbor: University of Michigan Press, 1996); Paul Hainsworth, ed., *The Extreme Right in Europe and the USA* (New York: St. Martin's Press, 1992); and Luciano Chiles, Ronnie Ferguson, and Michalina Vaughan, eds., *The Far Right in Western & Eastern Europe*, 2nd ed. (London: Longman, 1995).
5. André Taguieff, "From Race to Culture: The New Right's View of European Identity," *Telos* (Winter/Fall 1993/94), pp. 99–125.
6. Umberto Bossi, *Processo alla Lega* (Milan: Sperling & Kupfer, 1998), p. 14.
7. For more on the Committee of the Regions, see Bruce Millan, "The Committee of the Regions: In at the Birth," *Regional & Federal Studies* vol. 7, no. 1 (Spring 1997), pp. 5–10. For more on the general process of regional

mobilization in Europe, see Liesbet Hooghe and Gary Marks, "'Europe with the Regions': Channels of Regional Representation in the European Union," *Publius* (Winter 1996), pp. 73–91; Martin Rhodes, ed., *The Regions and the New Europe* (Manchester: Manchester University Press, 1995).
8. Daniel J. Elazar, "From Statism to Federalism: A Paradigm Shift," *Publius* vol. 25, no. 2 (Winter 1995), pp. 5–18.
9. See, for example, Kenichi Ohmae, *The End of the Nation-State: The Rise of Regional Economies* (New York: The Free Press, 1995). Ohmae argues that globalization has essentially made the nation-state an obsolete unit for organizing the economy. Global economic trends, he argues, have created what he calls "regional states," areas where economic and social developments have formed natural economic zones that are similar in their economic and social/cultural make up. Such zones do not necessarily coincide with national borders but often across them, such as between northern Italy and its neighbors across the Alps. Ironically, the future of economic development for Ohmae is for states to take a hands-off approach, allowing such regions to grow with as little interference as possible and allow them to form closer relationships with their nonnational neighboring regions.
10. See John Loughlin, "'Europe of the Regions' and the Federalization of Europe," *Publius* vol. 26, no. 4 (Fall 1996), pp. 141–162.
11. Michael Keating, *The New Regionalism in Western Europe: Territorial Restructuring and Political Change* (Cheltenham, U.K.: E. Elgar, 1998).
12. See "Italia bocciata in libertà economica," in *Il sole 24 ore*, July 15, 1997.
13. For more on regionalization and devolution across Europe, see L.J. Sharpe, *The Rise of Meso Government in Europe* (London: Sage Publications, 1993). For the Italian situation, see Robert Putnam, Robert Leonardi, and Rafaella Nanetti, *La pianta e le radici: il radicamento dell'istituto regionale nel sistema politico italiano* (Bologna: Il Mulino, 1985).
14. See Carlo Trigilia, "Italy: The Political Economy of a Regionalized Capitalism," *South European Society and Politics* vol. 2, no. 3 (1997).
15. For more on regional divisions and the role of national institutions in Italy, see Cartocci, *Fra Lega e Chiesa*.
16. For more on the concept of a "community of interests" in northern Italy, see Ilvo Diamanti, *La Lega* (Rome: Donizelli, 1993).
17. Michael Keating, "Regional Autonomy in the Changing State Order: A Framework of Analysis," *Regional Politics and Policy* vol. 2, no. 3 (Autumn 1992), pp. 45–61.
18. Robert Putnam, *Making Democracy Work: Civic Traditions in Modern Italy* (Princeton: Princeton University Press, 1993).
19. See also Filippo Sabetti, *The Search for Good Government: Understanding the Paradox of Italian Democracy* (Montreal: McGill-Queens University Press, 2000).

Chapter 2 The Origins of the Centralized State in Italy

1. At the time, the region was part of the Kingdom of Sardinia, which included Piedmont and Sardinia.
2. For more on the history of Italian unification see Denis Mack Smith, *Modern Italy: A Political History* (Ann Arbor: The University of Michigan Press, 1997); Denis Mack Smith, *The Making of Italy 1796–1870* (New York: Harper & Row, 1968); Raymond Grew, *A Sterner Plan for Italian Unity: The Italian National Society in the Risorgimento* (Princeton: Princeton University Press, 1963); Clara Lovett, *The Democratic Movement in Italy 1830–1876* (Cambridge: Harvard University Press, 1982); and Antonio Gramsci, *Prison Notebooks* (New York: International Publishers, 1971), pp. 44–120.
3. Mack Smith, *Modern Italy*, p. 5.
4. See Sidney Tarrow, *Between Center and Periphery* (New Haven: Yale University Press, 1977).
5. Ibid., p. 61.
6. P.A. Allum, *Italy—Republic without Government?* (New York: W.W. Norton & Company, 1973), p. 48.
7. Raphael Zarisky, *Italy: The Politics of Uneven Development* (Hinsdale, Ill.: The Dryden Press, 1972), p. 19.
8. Mack Smith, *Modern Italy*, pp. 59–65.
9. Allum, *Italy—Republic without Government?* pp. 7–8.
10. P.A. Allum and G. Amyot, "Regionalism in Italy: Old Wine in New Bottles?" *Parliamentary Affairs* vol. 24, no. 1 (Winter 1970/71), p. 54.
11. Zarisky, *Italy: The Politics of Uneven Development*, p. 27.
12. Ibid., pp. 18–19.
13. Cavour, for example, identified more with the English tradition of local rule, as opposed to the French emphasis on centralization.
14. R. Romanelli, *L'Italia liberale* (Bologna: Il Mulino, 1979), p. 40, cited in Lucy Riall, *Sicily and the Unification of Italy: Liberal Policy and Local Power, 1859–1866* (Oxford: Clarendon Press, 1998), p. 122.
15. Tarrow, *Between Center and Periphery*, pp. 58–59.
16. James Fesler and Donald Khel, *The Politics of the Administrative Process* (Chatham, N.J.: Chatham House, 1991), p. 70.
17. B.C. Smith, *Decentralization. The Territorial Dimension of the State* (London: George Allen & Unwin, 1985), p. 9.
18. Ibid.
19. See, for example, Margaret Levi, *Of Rule and Revenue* (Berkeley: University of California Press, 1988).
20. Cited in Howard Machin, *The Prefect in French Administration* (New York: St. Martin's Press, 1977), p. 19.
21. Royal Decree no. 3702, October 23, 1859.
22. Robert C. Fried, *The Italian Prefects: A Study in Administrative Politics* (New Haven: Yale University Press, 1963), p. 65.

23. Adrian Lyttleton, "Shifting Identities: Nation, Region and City," in *Italian Regionalism*, ed. Carl Levy (Oxford: Berg, 1996), p. 40.
24. For a brief period Tuscany was able to retain a separate local government act.
25. Ibid., p. 39.
26. The position was first termed governor and then prefect.
27. Fried, *The Italian Prefects*, p. 67.
28. For more on the difference between French and Italian prefects, see Tarrow, *Between Center and Periphery*, pp. 47–75. See also Smith, *Decentralization. The Territorial Dimension of the State*.
29. Fried, *The Italian Prefects*, p. 134.
30. Ibid., p. 149.
31. Tarrow, *Between Center and Periphery*, p. 59.
32. Fried, *The Italian Prefects*, p. 90.
33. Lyttleton, "Shifting Identities: Nation, Region and City," p. 40.
34. Givoanni Sabbatacci and Vittorio Vidotto, eds., *Storia d'Italia*, vol. 2 (Rome: Laterza, 1994), p. 267. Sabbatacci and Vidotto's figures are drawn from the estimates of P. Ercolani, "Documentazione statistica di base," in *Lo sviluppo economico in Italia*, vol. 3, ed. G. Fuà (Milan: Angeli, 1975).
35. Ibid.
36. Ibid., p. 261.
37. Gianni Marongiu, *Storia del fisco in Italia*, vol. I (Turin: Einaudi, 1995), p. 65.
38. Ibid., p. 254.
39. Ibid., p. 329.
40. Ibid.
41. Ibid., p. 338.
42. Ibid., p. 339.
43. See Riall, *Sicily and the Unification of Italy*, p. 122. See also R. Romanelli, "Il comando impossibile: la natura del progetto liberale del governo," *Il comando impossible: stato e soceitá nell'Italia liberale* (Bologna: Il Mulino, 1988), p. 7.
44. Fried, *The Italian Prefects*, pp. 92–93.
45. Allum and Amoyt, "Regionalism in Italy," pp. 54–55.
46. Mack Smith, *Modern Italy*, p. 47.
47. For more on this, see R. Romeo, *Il Risorgimento in Sicilia* (Bari: Laterza, 1950).
48. According to Gramsci, in the South the gentry easily withdrew their support of their former Bourbon rulers in order to save their property, and quickly formed an alliance with northern industrialists. This alliance, referred to by Gramsci as the *blocco storico* (historic bloc), prevented social change by making potential social reformers in the South instruments of northern interests. See Gramsci, *Prison Notebooks*, p. 94.
49. Sabino Cassese, *Questione amministrativa e questione meridionale* (Milan: Giuffrè, 1977), p. 71.
50. Ibid., p. 73.

51. See Luigi Graziano, "Center–Periphery Relations and the Italian Crisis: The Problem of Clientelism," in *Territorial Politics in Industrial Nations*, ed. Sidney Tarrow et al. (New York: Praeger Publishers, 1978), p. 303.
52. Sabbatacci and Vidotto, *Storia d' Italia*, p. 265. See also Gianni Toniolo, *Storia economica dell'Italia liberale* (Bologna: Il Mulino, 1988), pp. 104–105.
53. Bruno Brunello, *Il pensiero di Carlo Cattaneo* (Turin: P. Gobetti, 1925), p. 168.
54. Gianfranco Morra, *Breve storia del pensiero federalista* (Turin: Oscar Mondadori, 1993), pp. 72–82.
55. Lovett, *The Democratic Movement in Italy, 1830–1876*, p. 44.
56. Fried, *The Italian Prefects*, p. 84.
57. Lyttleton, "Shifting Identities: Nation, Region and City," p. 43.
58. David Hine, "Federalism, Regionalism and the Unitary State: Contemporary Regional Pressures in Historical Perspective," in *Italian Regionalism*, ed. Carl Levy (Washington-Oxford: Berg, 1996).
59. Lyttleton, "Shifting Identities: Nation, Region and City," p. 36.
60. Ibid.
61. Fried, *The Italian Prefects*, p. 91.
62. L. Franchetti and S. Sonnino discuss the various abuses of the fiscal system in the South during this period in their work, *Inchiesta in Sicilia*, vol. 1 (Florence: Vallechi, 1974), p. 194, which was cited in Marongiu, *Storia del fisco in Italia*, p. 339.
63. Moreover, the communes were incapable of establishing an effective and profitable system of taxation, as they only had numerous small local tributes, which the autonomous political *Consorzi* were able to institute. Ibid., p. 331.
64. Lyttleton, "Shifting Identities: Nation, Region and City," p. 44.
65. These are the same brigands described by E.J. Hobsbawm in his classic work, *Primitive Rebels* (New York: W.W. Norton, 1959). See, for example, "A Bourbon Brigand Examined," p. 180, in the appendix.
66. Mack Smith, *Modern Italy*, p. 66.
67. Ibid., p. 68.
68. Ibid., p. 4.
69. Ibid., p. 77.
70. Fried, *The Italian Prefects*, p. 128.
71. Ibid., pp. 131–132.
72. Ibid., p. 133.
73. Gramsci, *Prison Notebooks*, p. 94. For a more recent discussion of this issue, see John A. Davis, "Changing Perspectives on Italy's 'Southern Problem,'" in *Italian Regionalism*, ed. Carl Levy (Washington-Oxford: Berg, 1996).
74. For more on the corporatist state of the fascist period, see Sabino Cassese, *La formazione dello stato amministrativo* (Milan, 1974); L. Franck, *Il corporativismo e l'economia dell'Italia fascista* (Turin: Einaudi, 1990).

75. Fried, *The Italian Prefects*, p. 208.
76. Ibid., p. 204.
77. Paul Ginsborg, *A History of Contemporary Italy* (London: Penguin Books, 1990), p. 147.
78. Ibid., p. 146.
79. Sabino Cassese, "Hypotheses on the Italian Administrative System," *West European Politics* vol. 16, no. 3 (1993), p. 318.
80. Ibid.
81. Sabino Cassese, *Il sistema amministrativo italiano* (Bologna: Il Mulino, 1983), p. 116.
82. Ibid.
83. A. De Stefani, *Una riforma al rogo* (Rome: Giovanni Volpe, 1966), cited in Paul Ginsborg, *A History of Contemporary Italy*, p. 147.
84. Riall, *Sicily and the Unification of Italy*, p. 122.

Chapter 3   Centralization in the Postwar Period

1. Luigi Einaudi, "Via il prefetto!" originally printed in *La gazzetta ticinese*, July 17, 1944. Reprinted in *Federalismo & Società* vol. 2, no. 1 (1995), pp. 228–232.
2. Allesandro Vitale, "Il federalismo di 'Giustizia e Libertà,'" *Federalismo & Società* vol. 2, no. 1 (1995), p. 91.
3. Ibid., p. 90.
4. *La Carta di Chivasso*, December 19, 1943. Reprinted in *Federalismo & Società* vol. 2, no. 1 (1995), pp. 233–235.
5. Roberto Gremmo, *Contro roma: storie, idee e programmi delle leghe autonomiste del Nord* (Aosta: Il Gral, 1992). See also the interview with Leo Valiani by Paolo Bertaccini in *Federalismo & Società* vol. 2, no. 1 (1995), who was a member of the Action party at the time of the Resistance and discusses the role of the CLN as models for a federalist system in Italy.
6. "Le tesi politiche della fondazione del movimento federalista europeo," *Federalismo & Societa* vol. 2, no. 1 (1995), pp. 236–239.
7. "I progetti federalisti degli Alleati," *Federalismo & Societa* vol. 2, no. 1 (1995), p. 219; see also Harley A. Notter, *Postwar Foreign Policy Preparations* (Washington, 1949); David W. Ellwood, "L'occupazione e la restaurazione istituzionale: il problema delle regioni," *Italia contemporanea* vol. 1, no. 3 (1974), pp. 23–41; and N. Gallerano, "L'influenza dell'amministrazione italiana sulla riorganizzazione dello stato italiano, 1943–1945," *Italia contemporanea* vol. 1, no. 3 (1974), pp. 4–22.
8. Adrian Lyttleton, "Shifting Identities: Nation, Region and City," in *Italian Regionalism: History, Identity, Politics*, ed. Carl Levy (Washington: Oxford-Berg, 1996), p. 47. The original document is the "Memorandum dei socialisti di Palermo al commissario civile per la Sicilia" (1896).
9. Mussolini, for example, banned the use of foreign languages and even prevented parents from giving their children non-Italian names.

10. Cited in Paul Ginsborg, *A History of Contemporary Italy* (London: Penguin, 1990), p. 103.
11. For more on the origins of the conflict, see Dennison I. Rusinow, *Italy's Austrian Heritage 1919–1946* (Oxford: Clarendon Press, 1969).
12. See P.A. Allum, *Italy—Republic without Government?* (New York: W.W. Norton & Company, 1973), p. 25.
13. Denis Mack Smith, *Modern Italy: A Political History* (Ann Arbor: The University of Michigan Press, 1997).
14. Allum, *Italy—Republic without Government?* p. 29.
15. Ibid., p. 35.
16. The origins of southern support for neo-fascism is discussed in Piero Ignazi, *Il polo escluso* (Bologna: Il Mulino, 1989).
17. At the time of the Constituent Assembly, the Liberals ran a list called National Democratic Union (UDN). They would later run in Italian elections as the Partito Liberale Italiano (PLI).
18. For recent works on the DC, see Giorgio Galli, *Mezzo secolo di DC* (Milano: Rizzoli, 1993); Agostino Giovagnoli, *Il partito italiano. La Democrazia Cristiana dal 1942 al 1994* (Bari: Laterza, 1996).
19. Robert Leonardi et al., "Devolution as a Political Process: The Case of Italy," *Publius* (Winter 1981), p. 99.
20. See Robert Fried, *The Italian Prefects* (New Haven: Yale University Press, 1963), p. 228; Robert Leonardi and Douglas Wertman, *Italian Christian Democracy: The Politics of Dominance* (New York: St. Martin's Press, 1989).
21. See Pasquale Hamel, ed., *La regione nella nazione* (Palermo: La Zisa, 1992); and his *Le autonomie regionali e il mezzogiorno* (Rome: Edizioni "Il commento", 1944).
22. Luigi Sturzo, "Relazione dell 23 ottobre, 1921 al congresso di Venezia," cited in P.A. Allum and G. Amyot. "Regionalism in Italy," *Parliamentary Affairs* vol. 24, no. 1 (Winter 1970/71), p. 55.
23. Gianfranco Morra, *Breve storia del pensiero federalista* (Turin: Oscar Mondadori, 1993), p. 109.
24. Ginsborg, *A History of Contemporary Italy*, p. 15.
25. Leo Valiani. Interview by Paolo Bertaccini, *Federalismo & Società* vol. 2, no. 1, p. 84.
26. See the statement by Leo Valiani, in Assemblea Costituente vol. 1, p. 467, cited in *Il parlamento italiano, 1861–1988*, vol. 14 (Nuova CEI), pp. 12–13.
27. *Atti dell' Assemblea Costituente*, July 27, 1946, p. 830, cited in Antonio Iannello, *L'inganno federalista e l'opposizione all'ordinamento regionale nel dibattito all'Assemblea Costituente* (Naples: Vivarium, 1998), p. 26.
28. Antonio Iannello, *L'inganno federalista e l'opposizione all'ordinamento regionale nel dibattito all'Assemblea Costituente*, p. 25.
29. *Atti dell' Assemblea Costituente*, March 11, 1947, p. 333, cited in ibid., pp. 28–29.
30. There were also those who argued that decentralization did not pose a threat to the poorer South, but rather a solution to its problems. For Sturzo,

a Sicilian, some type of federalist reform was necessary to cure the economic and social ills that plagued the South. According to Sturzo, the solution to the underdevelopment of the Mezzogiorno rested in a "sober decentralization of administrative and financial power to the regional level and a federation of the regions." Along with Sturzo, there were others who saw decentralization as the answer to poverty in the South, such as the socialist historian Gaetano Salvemini who argued that it was better to "leave it to the municipalities and a federation of regions and municipalities" to take care of issues surrounding local governance, from the judicial system to schooling, public order, and local finances. See Morra, *Breve storia del pensiero federalista*, p. 109.

31. Martin Clark, *Modern Italy 1871–1982* (London: Longman, 1984), pp. 322–323.
32. Ginsborg, *A Contemporary History of Italy*, p. 117.
33. For example, a poster in 1956 depicted tanks in the streets of Hungary, threatening that this is the true "socialist road." See European People's Party picture archive at www.eppe.org/archive/posters_ital.asp.
34. In all of Western Europe, Italy was possibly the country that received the bulk of the attention from U.S. foreign policy makers in their efforts to prevent what they saw as the spread of communism from the East.
35. Ginsborg, *A Contemporary History of Italy*, p. 115.
36. Fried, *The Italian Prefect*, pp. 247–248.
37. For more on how the powers of the prefect were reduced with the regions, see Enzo Sanantonio "Italy," in *Central and Local Government Relations*, ed. Edward Page and Michael Goldsmith (London: Sage, 1987), p. 108.
38. Leonardi et al., "Devolution as a Political Process: The Case of Italy," p. 100.
39. Allum, *Italy—Republic without Government?* p. 237.
40. Fried, *The Italian Prefects*, pp. 239–240.
41. Allum and Amyot, "Regionalism in Italy," p. 68.
42. See, for example, the analysis of Emilia-Romagna in Robert Putnam's *Making Democracy Work* (Princeton: Princeton University Press, 1993), p. 84. Putnam ranks Emilia-Romagna, along with Umbria—another leftist region—as the best region in institutional performance from the 1970s to the 1980s out of all of the 20 regions in Italy.
43. The special statute for Friuli-Venezia Giulia does not give specific linguistic rights to Slovenian speakers as do the statutes in Valle d'Aosta and Trentino-Alto Adige for the French and German speakers, respectively. Rather, it simply establishes the equality of all citizens within the region of Friuli-Venezia Giulia, regardless of their language.
44. *Diritto regionale* 7th ed. (Naples: Esselibri-Simone, 1995), p. 16.
45. Putnam, *Making Democracy Work*, p. 15.
46. Sidney Tarrow, "Local Constraints on Regional Reform: A Comparison of Italy and France," *Comparative Politics* vol. 7 (October, 1974), p. 36.
47. Allum, *Italy—Republic without Government?* p. 213.

48. Ibid., p. 229.
49. OECD, *OECD Economic Surveys, Italy 1995–1996* (1997), p. 93.
50. Ibid., p. 96.
51. See Enzo Sanantonio, "Italy," p. 121; and *OECD Economic Surveys, Italy 1995–1996*, p. 89. See also Alan Norton, *International Handbook of Local and Regional Government: Comparative Analysis of Advanced Democracies* (Aldershot: Edward Elgar Limited, 1994), p. 220.
52. David Hine, *Governing Italy* (Oxford: Clarendon Press, 1993), p. 261.
53. The regions with special statutes in the North receive a proportion of the taxes collected within the region. Sicily has the most fiscal autonomy of any region as it collects all of its own taxes, except tobacco and production taxes and lotteries. Norton, *International Handbook of Local and Regional Government*, p. 222.
54. See Massimo Ilardi, "Analisi dei dibattiti degli organi dirigenti dei partiti, 1970–1985, sulla regionalizzazione del partito come organizzazione," *Autonomia politica regionale e sistema dei partiti* (Milan: Dott. A. Giuffre Editore), 1988, p. 69.
55. Ibid.
56. Sanantonio, "Italy," p. 111.
57. Ibid.

Chapter 4   The Christian Democrats and the North–South Divide

1. For more on Catholic Action see Gianfranco Poggi, *Catholic Action in Italy: The Sociology of a Sponsored Organization* (Stanford: Stanford University Press, 1967).
2. Patrick McCarthy, *The Crisis of the Italian State* (New York: St. Martin's Press, 1995), p. 26.
3. Ginsborg, *A Contemporary History of Italy*, p. 169.
4. By religious we mean that the majority of the DC electorate was attending Church regularly. In 1972, 64 percent of all DC voters attended Church weekly. See Robert Leonardi and Douglass Wertman, *Italian Christian Democracy: The Politics of Dominance* (New York: St. Martin's Press, 1989), p. 176.
5. Allum, *Italy—Republic without Government?* (New York: W.W. Norton, 1973), p. 54.
6. Ibid., p. 98.
7. In Trentino, the DC was the dominant party while in Alto Adige it was and still is the SVP, or South Tyrol People's Party.
8. Vittorio Capecchi et al., *Il comportamento elettorale in Italia* (Bologna: Il Mulino, 1968), cited in Renato Mannheimer and Giacamo Sani, "Electoral Trends and Political Subcultures," in *Italian Politics: A Review* vol. I, ed. Raffaella Nanetti and Roberto Leonardi (London: Pinter, 1986), p. 164.

9. Paul Ginsborg, *A Contemporary History of Italy: Society and Politics 1943–1988* (London: Penguin, 1990), p. 156.
10. Judith Chubb, *Patronage, Power and Poverty in Southern Italy* (Cambridge: Cambridge University Press, 1982), p. 70.
11. Ginsborg, *A Contemporary History of Italy*, p. 139.
12. Ibid., p. 162.
13. Joseph LaPalombara, *Interest Groups in Italian Politics* (Princeton: Princeton University Press, 1963), p. 344.
14. Frederic Spotts and Theodor Wiser, *Italy, a Difficult Democracy: A Survey of Italian Politics* (Cambridge: Cambridge University Press, 1986), p. 235.
15. Carlo Trigilia, "Italy: The Political Economy of a Regionalized Capitalism," *South European Society & Politics* vol. 2, no. 3 (Winter 1997), p. 73.
16. Patrick McCarthy, *The Crisis of the Italian State* (New York: St. Martin's Press, 1995), p. 70.
17. Ginsborg, *A Contemporary History of Italy*, p. 290.
18. Ibid., p. 288.
19. The lower membership numbers in the Northeast can also be attributed to the fact that membership had fewer benefits there than in the South where it was more instrumental. For this reason, the ideologically committed voter had little reason to actually join the party and, as a result, the number of DC members in the Northeast had remained relatively constant (around 10 members out of 100 voters) from the 1940s to the 1980s. In return, because the DC could rely on the "transmission belt" effect in which Catholic associations automatically provided the party with supporters, there was little incentive for the DC to actively seek members.
20. McCarthy, *Crisis of the Italian State*, p. 70.
21. Mario Caciagli, "The Movimento Sociale Italiano-Destra Nazionale and Neo-Fascism in Italy," *West European Politics* (1988), p. 22.
22. Roberto Chiarini, "The Italian Far Right: The Search for Legitimacy," in *The Far Right in Western and Eastern Europe*, ed., Luciano Cheles et al. (London: Longman, 1995), p. 25.
23. Piero Ignazi, *Il polo escluso* (Bologna: Il Mulino, 1989), pp. 146–147.
24. Riots erupted in Reggio di Calabria in 1970 when the regional capital was moved to Catanzaro and, along with it, the many government jobs in the regional government.
25. Mannheimer and Sani "Electoral Trends and Political Subcultures," p. 172.
26. Ibid.
27. Leonardi and Wertman, *Italian Christian Democracy: The Politics of Dominance*, p. 212.
28. Also, after Vatican II, Catholic associations were encouraged to become more independent of both the Church and Christian Democratic parties.
29. Two new Catholic groups that emerged in the 1980s were *Comune e Liberazione* and *Movimento Popolari*. For more on these, see ibid., p. 218.
30. Mario Caciagli, "Il resistibile declino della Democrazia Cristiana," in *Il sistema politico italiano*, ed. Gianfranco Pasquino (Bologna: Il Mulino,

1984) cited in Leonardo Morlino, "The Changing Relationship between Parties and Society in Italy," *West European Politics* vol. 7, no. 4 (1984), p. 61.
31. Leonardi and Wertman, *Italian Christian Democracy: The Politics of Dominance*, p. 171.
32. Ibid.
33. For more on the PSI's local support, see Giorgio Galli and Daniele Comero, *Partiti storici e nuove formazioni* (Milan: Franco Angeli, 1992).
34. David Hine, *Governing Italy* (Oxford: Clarendon Press, 1993), p. 118.
35. Ibid.
36. See ibid., pp. 117–121; Gianfranco Baldini, "The Failed Renewal: The DC from 1982–1994," in *The Organization of Political Parties in Southern Europe*, ed. Piero Ignazi and Colette Ysmal (Westport: Praeger, 1998).
37. Sabino Cassese, "Hypotheses on the Italian Administrative System," *West European Politics* vol. 16, no. 3 (July 1993), p. 319.
38. OECD, *OECD Economic Surveys: Italy* (1999), p. 157.
39. Spotts and Wiser, *Italy, a Difficult Democracy: A Survey of Italian Politics*, p. 235.
40. Carlo Trigilia, *Sviluppo senza autonomia* (Bologna: Il Mulino, 1994), pp. 37–70.
41. Linda Weiss, *Creating Capitalism: The State and Small Business Since 1945* (London: Basil Blackwell, 1988), p. 63.
42. Charles Sabel, "Flexible Specialization and the Re-emergence of Regional Economies," in *Reversing Industrial Decline?*, ed. Paul Hirst and Jonathan Zeitlin (Oxford: Berg, 1989), p. 18; see also Michael Piore and Charles Sabel, *The Second Industrial Divide* (New York: Basic Books, 1984).
43. Jürgen R Grote, "Small Firms in the European Community: Modes of Production, Governance and Territorial Interest Representation in Italy and Germany," in *Organized Interests and the European Community*, ed., Justin Greenwood (London: Sage Publications, 1992), p. 137.
44. Such trends represent a "revitalization" because they share many of the same characteristics of the nineteenth-century industrial districts described by Alfred Marshall in his *Industry and Trade* (London: 1919).
45. Sabel, "Flexible Specialization and the Re-emergence of Regional Economies," p. 22. For more on the Italian case, see Charles Sabel, *Work and Politics* (New York: Cambridge University Press, 1982).
46. ISTAT, 1999.
47. See *La Repubblica*, March 8, 1996, p. 4.
48. This figure includes global production, excluding China. See Gian Antonio Stella, *Schei* (Milan: Baldini & Castoldi, 1996), p. 57.
49. CENSIS, *Rapporto sulla situazione sociale del paese* (Milan: Franco Angeli, 1995).
50. *Corriere della sera*, July 8, 1997.
51. OECD, *Economic Surveys, Italy 1995–1996* (1997), p. 91.
52. Silvia Cippolina, "Una nuova fiscalità per la piccola e media impresa: ipotesi di breve periodo," *La società della piccola impresa. Sfide e opportunità per la piccola e media industria* (Treviso: Unindustria, 1996), p. 228.

53. CNEL, *Laboratori territoriali: competizione e leadership nella questione settentrionale* (Rome, 1996), p. 80.
54. *Il sole 24 ore*, July 8, 1997, p. 6.
55. *Il sole 24 ore*, July 16, 1997.
56. For example, in July 1996, LIFE staged a tax revolt against a special transport tax (*Bolle di accompagnamento*), which was eventually reduced. In addition to the issue of taxes, LIFE has taken on the problems of inefficiency in the state and other problems for the small-scale entrepreneur. For more on the LIFE, see their website at www.life.it.
57. *The Economist*, November 8, 1997, p. 14.
58. Interview with Giuseppe Bortolussi, President of the Confederation of Artisans, Mestre, April 19, 1997.
59. See CENSIS, *Rapporto sulla situazione sociale del paese*, p. 411.
60. CNEL, *Laboratori territoriali*, p. 78.
61. *Manifesto delle libere regioni del Nordest in un'Italia federale.* Flyer handed out at a press conference, Mestre (Veneto) Town Hall (February 15, 1997).
62. *Il sole 24 ore*, July 16, 1997, p. 8.
63. Weiss, *Creating Capitalism*, p. 57.
64. Carlo Trigilia, *Grandi partiti e piccole imprese* (Bologna: Il Mulino, 1986), p. 118.
65. Weiss, *Creating Captialism*, p. 46.
66. Grote, "Small Firms in the European Community," p. 126.
67. Trigilia, *Grandi partiti e piccole imprese*, p. 179.
68. Grote, "Small Firms in the European Community."
69. Waters, "'Tangentopoli' and the Emergence of a New Political Order in Italy," *West European Politics* vol. 17 (January 1994), p. 176.
70. See Philippe Schmitter, "Still the Century of Corporatism?" in *Trends Towards Corporatist Intermediation*, ed. Philippe Schmitter and Gerhard Lehmbruch (Beverly Hills: Sage, 1979).
71. For more on labor politics during this period, see Miriam Golden, *Labor Divided: Austerity and Working Class Politics in Contemporary Italy* (Ithaca: Cornell University Press, 1988).
72. McCarthy, *Crisis of the Italian State*, p. 75.
73. Trigilia, *Grandi partiti e piccole imprese*, pp. 178–179.
74. See for example, Daniele Mazzonis, "The Changing Role of ERVET in Emilia-Romagna," in *Local and Regional Responses to Global Pressure: The Case of Italy and Its Industrial Districts*, ed. Francesco Cossentino (Geneva: ILO, 1996), pp. 131–142.
75. Weiss, *Creating Capitalism*, p. 49.

Chapter 5   The Rise of the Lega in the North

1. Agostino Amantia, "Note sulla penetrazaione della Liga Veneta in provincia di Belluno, distretto dell'alta piave, 1979–1993," in *Lega e localismi in*

montagna. Il caso Belluno, ed. Agostino Amantia and Ferruccio Vendramini (Belluno: Tipografia Piave, 1994), p. 27.
2. Ilvo Diamanti, "La mia patria e il Veneto. I valori e la proposta politica delle leghe," *Polis* (August 1992).
3. During these elections the party was in a coalition with the nationally based Pensioner's party.
4. See Thomas O. Hueglin, "Regionalism in Western Europe: Conceptual Problems of a New Political Perspective," *Comparative Politics* vol. 18, no. 4 (July 1986), pp. 439–458.
5. Amantia, "Note sulla penetrazaione della Liga Veneta," p. 15.
6. Statute of the Liga Veneta (1983), printed in Amantia and Vendramini, *Lega e localismi in montagna*, p. 66.
7. Although postwar developments have made Italy a highly literate country with a common national language, people continue to use dialects among friends, family, and coworkers.
8. ISTAT, "Lingua italiana e dialetti in Italia" (March 12, 2002), www.istat.it/anotizie/aaltrein/statinbrev/menu.html.
9. Amantia, "Note sulla penetrazaione della Liga Veneta," p. 15.
10. P.A. Allum and Ilvo Diamanti, "The Autonomous Leagues in the Veneto," in *Italian Regionalism: History, Identity, and Politics* (Washington: Oxford-Berg, 1996), p. 160.
11. Liga Veneta, "Promemoria per l'onorevole Bettino Craxi," in Amantia and Vendramini, *Lega e localismi in montagna*, p. 70.
12. For more on this, see the firsthand account by Roberto Gremmo, *Contro roma: storie, idee e programmi delle leghe autonomiste del Nord* (Aosta: Il Gral, 1992).
13. Referring to this shift in the mid-1980s, Bossi said that his decision to change the strategy of the Lega away from "ethno-nationalism" was because the issue had little impact on the region itself. See Daniele Vimercati, *I lombardi alla nuova crociata* (Milan: Mursia, 1990), p. 19.
14. Ilvo Diamanti, *La Lega* (Rome: Donzelli, 1993). Diamanti's book still provides one of the best accounts of the Lega's shifts and turns in strategy. See also his *Il male del Nord* (Rome: Donzelli, 1996).
15. Vimercati, *I lombardi alla nuova crociata*, p. 21.
16. Umberto Bossi, V*ento dal Nord* (Milan: Sperling & Kupfer Edizioni, 1992), pp. 168–169.
17. Ibid., p. 170.
18. A survey conducted in 1989 showed that the strongest anti-immigrant sentiments in the country existed among the electorate of the MSI. The Lega's electorate was second. See Roberto Biorcio, "La Lega come attore politico: dal federalismo al populismo regionalista," in *La Lega Lombarda*, ed. Renato Manheimmer (Milan: Feltrinelli, 1991), p. 63.
19. The *legge Martelli*, among other things, limited tourist visas for visitors from select countries. Misuse of tourist visas has been one of the most

common ways "illegal" immigrants enter Italy. For more on this, see Maria Macioti, *Gli immigrati in Italia* (Rome: Laterza, 1991), p. 39.
20. Bossi, V*ento dal Nord*, p. 148.
21. *Epoca*, May 30, 1990.
22. *Lombardia Autonomista*, October 1990.
23. Gian Antonio Stella, *Dio Po* (Milan: Baldini & Castoldi, 1996), p. 49.
24. In 1984, the Lega Lombarda ran along with the Liga Veneta and the Moviment Arnassita Piemonteisa, a regional list in Piedmont, for the European Parliament in a coalition called the "*Unione per L'Europa Federalista*" (Union for a Federalist Europe).
25. For more on the electoral shifts from the Christian Democrats and other parties to the Lega, see the following studies sponsored by the region of Lombardy: Paolo Natale, "Le elezioni europee del 1989 in Lombardia. Un'analisi dei flussi elettorali," *Notiziario statistico regionale* supplement to no. 59 (March 1990); and Paolo Natale, "Le elezioni regionali del 1990 in Lombardia. Un' analisi dei flussi elettorali," *Notiziario statistico regionale* supplement to no. 60 (April 1990).
26. Amantia, "Note sulla penetrazione della Liga Veneta," p. 31.
27. Lega Nord, *Struttura federale* (Milan, 1993), photocopy.
28. Ruzza and Schmidtke, "Roots of Success of the Lega Lombarda: Mobilization Dynamics and the Media," *West European Politics* vol. 16, no. 2 (1993), p. 23.
29. One of the most colorful expressions of Bossi is a comparison of the power of the Lega Nord to an erection ("*La Lega ce l'ha duro!*").
30. Roberto Biorcio, "La Lega come autore politico," pp. 44–45.
31. See, for example, Roberto Biorcio, "The Rebirth of Populism in Italy and France," *Telos* no. 90 (Winter 1991–1992), p. 43. Despite the low regard that Italians feel toward the functioning of their democratic system, the electoral turnout in Italy continues to be one of the highest in the world. Thus, unlike in the United States, antiparty sentiment in Italy is not expressed in apathy toward elections.
32. The Radical party presented the porn star Iona Staller ("Cicciolini") in the 1980s as a candidate. Before her, the party was able to elect Toni Negri, a university professor who was convicted of conspiring with the Red Brigades terrorist group in the 1970s. As a parliamentarian, Negri was given immunity and was able to escape, for a period of time, a prison sentence.
33. Simon Parker, "Electoral Reform and Political Change in Italy, 1991–1994," in *The New Italian Republic*, ed. Steven Grundle and Simon Parker (London: Routledge, 1995), p. 41.
34. Ibid., p. 42.
35. Ibid.
36. Vittorio Moioli, *Il tarlo delle leghe* (Milan: Comedit2000, 1991), p. 58.
37. Leonardo Morlino, "Crisis of Parties and Change of Party System in Italy," *Party Politics* vol. 2, no. 1 (January 1996), p. 15.

38. Rifondazione Communista (RC) with a similar vote share of the Lega at the time had about 120,000 members. For party member rolls, see also the Cattaneo Institute's website, www.cattaneo.it.
39. This refers mainly to the PCI/DS that started to lose members even before the party changed its name in 1991 and suffered the separation with RC. The membership rolls for the DC and PSI, however, which were instrumental in terms of their relationship to the parties' patronage structures, actually rose during the 1980s.
40. See article by Roberto Biorcio in the communist daily *Il manifesto*, June 16, 1993.
41. Carlo Ruzza and Oliver Schmidke, "The Making of the Lombard League," *Telos* (Winter 1991).
42. Sarah Waters, "'Tangentopoli' and the Emergence of a New Political Order in Italy," *West European Politics* vol. 17, no. 1 (January 1994), p. 170.
43. Alexander Stille, "Italy's Bribery Scandals," *Italian Journal* vol. 6, no. 4 (1992), p. 19.
44. Ibid., p. 19.
45. Ibid., p. 20.
46. Jan Kramer, *The New Yorker* (March 28, 1994), pp. 70–81.
47. Anna Cento Bull, "The Politics of Industrial Districts in Lombardy: Replacing Christian Democracy with the Northern League," in *The Italianist* vol. 13 (1993), p. 214.
48. Bossi, *Vento dal Nord*, p. 160.
49. In December 1992, the DS in Monza and Varese, two medium-sized communes in Lombardy, agreed to support the Lega "externally" in the communal councils, without actually playing any role in the governing coalition led by the Lega. See Stella, *Dio Po*, p. 123.
50. Ibid.
51. Bossi stated that Sicily's statute "is the one closest to the classic federalist system, the kind that stands at the base of federalist states like the US, Brazil and Argentina," *Il giornale di Sicilia* (March 11, 1993). Quoted in *Lombardia autonomista* (March 24, 1993). Bossi's comments about Sicily were an exaggeration (the island does not have nearly as much autonomy as an American state does). However, his statement was indicative of an effort by the party to win over other areas of the country on a general federalist platform, as opposed to just focusing on the North.
52. *Lega Nord*, May 9, 1993.
53. Although some people do avoid paying taxes in the North, this is done primarily out of selfish/monetary reasons as opposed to political/ideological ones.
54. Umberto Venturini, "Political and Economic Turmoil," *Italian Journal* vol. 6, no. 5 (1992), p. 8.
55. *Il giornale di Vicenza*, September 23, 1993. In order to avoid the Minimum Tax artisans would have had to change the status of their businesses, and

subsequently lose any of the other benefits they have access to, like state subsidies.
56. *Il giorno*, January 9, 1993, p. 13.
57. *Lega Nord*, March 24, 1993, p. 2.
58. Ibid.
59. ALIA's official organ, *L'imprenditore*, April 1993, p. 2.
60. *Lega Nord*, May 9, 1993.
61. Robert Leonardi, "The Regional Reform in Italy: From Centralized to Regionalized State," in *The Regions and the European Community*, ed. Robert Leonardi (London: Frank Cass, 1992), pp. 237–239.
62. At the time, Bossi even made a formal request to the European Commission for the North to reenter the EMU without the rest of the country. The request was eventually denied.
63. Lega Nord, "Portiamo Milano in Europa," electoral campaign pamphlet (1993).
64. This term is taken from Diamanti's analysis in his book, *La Lega*.
65. For more on the Lega and the Northern Question, see Anna Cento Bull and Mark Gilbert, *The Lega Nord and the Northern Question in Italian Politics* (New York: Palgrave, 2001).

Chapter 6   The Lega and Federalist Reform in the Late 1990s

1. Ilvo Diamanti, "The Northern League: From Regional Party to Party of Government," in *The New Italian Republic*, ed. Steven Grundle and Simon Parker (London: Routledge, 1996), p. 123.
2. Ibid., p. 122.
3. Ibid., p. 123.
4. See William Riker, "Two Party Systems and Duverger's Law," *American Political Science Review* vol. 76 (December 1982), pp. 753–766.
5. This assumption rests on the theory of Duverger's Law. See ibid.
6. Ironically, there are more parties today, after the reform, than before. This is due to a number of reasons, in part because the few seats that are allocated on a PR basis give smaller parties a fighting chance. Also, smaller parties have been able to win seats in plurality districts by running as part of the larger party cartels.
7. For a good analysis of the 1994 electoral results, see Stefano Bartolini and Roberto D'Alimonte, "La competizione maggioritaria: le origini elettorali del parlamento diviso," in *Maggioritario ma non troppo*, ed. Stefano Bartolini and Roberto D'Alimonte (Bologna: Il Mulino, 1993).
8. For more on the desire for a more "normal" right in Italy, see Furio Colombo and Vittorio Foa, *Il sogno di una destra normale* (Rome: Donzelli, 1995).
9. Gian Antonio Stella, *Dio Po* (Milan: Baldini & Castoldi, 1996), p. 135.
10. Gilberto Oneto, *L'invenzione della Padania* (Bergamo: Foedus Editore, 1997), p. 75.

11. Lega Nord party document, *Filodiretto* (1997), p. 20.
12. *La Repubblica*, March 8, 1996, p. 4.
13. Interview with Ilvo Diamanti in *La Repubblica*, April 30, 1997, p. 7.
14. *La Repubblica*, April 24, 1996.
15. See *La Repubblica*, September 20, 1996, p. 9.
16. *La Repubblica*, August 18, 1996, p. 4.
17. Lega Nord party document, *Quaderni padani* (1995), pp. 1–6
18. Speaking for himself on the floor of the Chamber of Deputies during the special session, a contrite Bossi stated that his remarks were "unfortunate" and made during "the heat of a rally during a particularly tense moment in the struggle for federalism." He continued, "I no longer recognize myself in those words" (BBC Monitoring International Reports, January 23, 2002).
19. *La Repubblica*, August 21, 1996, p. 3.
20. Bossi called him "Nando *dalla Cosa Nostra*," replacing his last name (dalla Chiesa) with the name of the famous Mafia organization, the *Cosa Nostra*.
21. P.I.U. is no longer listed on the Lega's website, which is updated regularly.
22. *Il gazzettino*, October 13, 1995.
23. *La Repubblica*, April 24, 1996.
24. CNEL, *Laboratori territoriali: competizione e leadership nella questione settentrionale* (Rome: CNEL, 1996), p. 239.
25. *Il gazzettino*, May 15, 1996.
26. *La nuova Venezia*, July 10, 1996.
27. Fabio Padovan's brother was also under investigation for his ties to the Veneto Serenissima group. See *La Repubblica*, June 23, 1997, p. 16.
28. *La Repubblica*, June 5, 1997, p. 15.
29. For more on the bicameral committee, see Gianfranco Pasquino, "No Longer a Party State? Institutions, Power, and Problems of Italian Reform," *West European Politics* vol. 20 (1997), pp. 34–53; and Mark Gilbert, "Transforming Italy's Institutions? The Bicameral Committee on Institutional Reform," *Modern Italy* vol. 3, no. 1 (1998), pp. 49–66.
30. *Il sole 24 ore*, June 5, 1997, p. 12.
31. See, for example, interview with Maurizio Gasparri, second in command of the AN in *Il mattino* May 24, 1997, p. 3.
32. The subnational level was given "all administrative functions and tasks relating to the interests and promotion of development of their respective communities, and all the administrative functions and tasks located in their territories." OECD, *Territorial Reviews, Italy* (Paris: OECD, 2001), p. 145.
33. OECD, *Economic Surveys, Italy* (Paris: OECD, 1999), p. 65.
34. OECD, *Territorial Reviews, Italy*, p. 146.
35. Ibid.
36. The new law also targets the language of administration in its attempts to simplify the bureaucracy and make the public sector more consumer friendly. In the summer of 1997, the state printed a "Manual of Style" for public offices across the country. The manual changes the numerous and

complicated terms in "bureaucratese" that have permeated the public administration for generations, to a simpler, more everyday language. The changes focus mainly on reversing the traditional habit of making the public administration inaccessible with long, complicated phrases, often with archaic terms and Latinisms. For example, the manual changes "executive order of release" (provvedimento esecutivo di rilascio) to the more direct, "eviction" (sfratto). *La Repubblica*, July 9, 1997, p. 18.
37. OECD, *Territorial Reviews, Italy*, p. 152.
38. Legge costituzionale (Constitutional Law) no. 3, October 18, 2001.
39. The initiative most likely did not pass in Valle d'Aosta as the region already enjoys considerable autonomy.

Chapter 7   Conclusions

1. By the mid-1990s, the *Mani Pulite* trials would eventually lose steam as many of the accused went free. At the peak of the trials in 1993–1994, when over 5,000 people were under suspicion, the magistrates handed out 1,200 indictments. However, in the end only about 600 of those accused received convictions and around ten people were sent to prison, of which only a handful are still serving sentences today, ten years after the first trials. Moreover, pressure by Berlusconi, who was prime minister in 1994 and himself under suspicion, eventually forced the judges to abandon their efforts by 1995. Antonio Di Pietro, the crusading judge during the trials, would eventually resign in protest and make a brief but failed attempt to enter politics.
2. *La Repubblica*, June 8, 2002.
3. *The Economist*, January 11, 2001.
4. *La Repubblica*, September 18, 2000.
5. In addition, the Lega's new fight against globalization targets the United States and the growing influence of American culture on northern Italy. Bossi argues in *Processo alla Lega* that the "capitalist system" has essentially created a "great consumer," which is "fattened by hamburger and drowned in a sea of Coca Cola" (p. 13). Such views, however, are not unusual as they are consistent with other parties and movements of the New Right and much of the mainstream in Europe today.
6. Umberto Bossi. *Processo alla Lega* (Milan: Sperling & Kupfer, 1998), p. 144.
7. According to Bossi, the extension of police powers that will be necessary for this arrest warrant represents a dangerous threat to individual liberties.
8. See, for example, Kenichi Ohmae, *The End of the Nation-State: The Rise of Regional Economies* (New York: The Free Press, 1995); John Newhouse, "Europe's Rising Regionalism," *Foreign Affairs* 76 (January/February 1997), pp. 67–84.

References

Agnew, John. *Place and Politics: The Geographical Mediation of State and Society.* Boston: Allen & Unwin, 1987.
Allevi, Stefano. *Le parole della Lega.* Milan: Garzanti, 1992.
Allum, P.A. *Italy—Republic Without Government?* New York: W.W. Norton, 1973.
——. *Politics and Society in Postwar Naples.* Cambridge: Cambridge University Press, 1973.
—— and G. Amyot. "Regionalism in Italy: Old Wine in New Bottles?" *Parliamentary Affairs* 24 (Winter 1970/71): 53–78.
—— and Ilvo Diamanti. "The Autonomous Leagues in the Veneto." In *Italian Regionalism: History, Identity, and Politics,* edited by Carl Levy, 151–170. Oxford: Berg, 1996.
Amantia, Agostino. "Note sulla penetrazione della Liga Veneta in provincia di Belluno (distretto dell' 'Alta Piave'), 1979–1993." In *Lega e localismi in montagna: Il caso Belluno,* edited by Amantia Agostino and Ferruccio Vendramini, 9–52. Belluno: Istituto storico bellunese della resistenza e dell'eta contemporanea, 1994.
Bagnasco, Arnaldo. *L'Italia in tempi di cambiamento politico.* Bologna: Il Mulino, 1996.
——. "Introduction: An Unexpected and Controversial Return." In *Small and Medium-Size Enterprises,* edited by Arnaldo Bagnasco and Charles Sabel, 1–14. London: Pinter, 1995.
——. *Tre Italie: La problematica territoriale dello sviluppo italiano.* Bologna: Il Mulino, 1977.
Baldini, Gianfranco. "The Failed Renewal: The DC from 1982–1994." In *The Organization of Political Parties in Southern Europe,* edited by Piero Ignazi and Colette Ysmal, 110–133. Westport: Praeger, 1998.
Balducci, Massimo. "Italy and the Ratification of the Maastricht Treaty." In *The Ratification of the Maastricht Treaty. Issues, Debates, and Future Implications,* edited by Finn Laursen and Sophie Vanhoonacher, 195–201. Dordrecht: Martinus Nijhoff Publishers, 1994.

Bartolini, Stefano and Roberto D'Alimonte. "La competizione maggioritaria: le origini elettorali del parlamento diviso." In *Maggioritario ma non troppo*, edited by Stefano Bartolini and Roberto D'Alimonte, 317–372. Bologna: Il Mulino, 1993.

Becattini, Giacomo. "The Marshallian Industrial District as a Socio-Economic Notion." In *Industrial Districts and Inter-Firm Co-operation in Italy*, edited by Frank Pyke, Giacomo Becattini, and W. Sengenberger. Geneva: ILO, 1990.

Beirich, Heidi and Dwayne Woods. "Globalization, Workers and the Northern League." *West European Politics* 23 (2000): 130–142.

Bennett, Robert J. "Decentralization, Intergovernmental Relations and Markets: Towards a Post-Welfare Agenda?" In *Decentralization, Local Governments, and Markets*, edited by Robert J. Bennett, 1–28. Oxford: Clarendon, 1990.

Betz, Hans-Georg. *Radical Right-Wing Populism in Western Europe*. New York: St. Martin's Press, 1994.

—— and Stefan Immerfall, ed. *New Politics of the Right: Neo-Populist Parties and Movements in Established Democracies*. New York: Palgrave, 1998.

Biorcio, Roberto. *La Padania promessa*. Milan: Il Saggiatore, 1997.

——. "The Rebirth of Populism in Italy and France." *Telos* (Winter 1991–1992): 43–56.

——. "La Lega come attore politico: dal federalismo al populismo regionalista." In *La Lega Lombarda*, edited by Renato Mannheimer, 34–82. Milan: Feltrinelli, 1991.

Bossi, Umberto. *Processo alla Lega*. Milan: Sperling & Kupfer, 1998.

——. *Vento dal Nord: la mia Lega la mia vita*. Milan: Sperling & Kupfer, 1992.

—— and Daniele Vimercati. *La rivoluzione. La Lega: storia e idee*. Milan: Sperling & Kupfer, 1993.

Bozzo, Gianni Biaget. *Cattolici e Democristiani*. Milan: Rizzoli, 1994.

Brosio, G., G. Pola and D. Bondonio. *Una proposta di federalismo fiscale*. Turin: Fondazione Agnelli, 1994.

Brunello, Bruno. *Il pensiero di Carlo Cattaneo*. Turin, 1925.

Buchanan, James M. "Federalism as an Ideal Political Order and an Objective for Constitutional Reform." *Publius* 25 (Winter 1995): 19–28.

Caciagli, Mario. "Il resistibilie decline della Democrazia Cristiana." In *Il sistema politico italiano*, edited by Gianfranco Pasquino, 101–127. Rome: Laterza, 1985.

——. "The Movimento Sociale Italiano-Destra Nazionale and Neo-Fascism in Italy." *West European Politics* 11 (1988): 19–33.

Cafagna, Luciano. *Dualismo e sviluppo nella storia d'Italia*. Venezia: Marsilio, 1989.

Capecchi, Vittorio et al. *Il comportamento elettorale in Italia*. Bologna: Il Mulino, 1968.

Cappelin, Riccardo. "Regional Policy and Federalism in the Process of International Integration." In *Regional Growth and Regional Policy within the Framework of European Integration*. Heidelberg: Physica-Verlag, 1997.

La Carta di Chivasso, December 19, 1943. Reprinted in *Federalismo & Società* 2 (1995): 233–235.
Cartocci, Roberto. *Fra Lega e Chiesa*. Bologna: Il Mulino, 1994.
Cassese, Sabino. "Hypotheses on the Italian Administrative System." *West European Politics* 16 (July 1993): 316–328.
———. *Il sistema amministrativo Italiano*. Bologna: Il Mulino, 1983.
———. *Questione amministrativa e questione meridionale*. Milan: Giuffre, 1977.
———. *La formazione dello stato amministrativo*. Milan: Giuffre, 1974.
Istituto Cattaneo. www.cattaneo.it.
Cavorta, Francesco. "The Role of the Northern League in Transforming the Italian Political System: From Economic Federalism to Ethnic Politics and Back." *Contemporary Politics* 7 (2001): 27–40.
Ceccarini, Luigi and Fabio Turato. "Atlante geopolitico delle Leghe." *Limes* 3 (1996): 59–69.
CENSIS. *Rapporto sulla situazione sociale del paese*. Milan: Franco Angeli, 1995.
———. *Rapporto sul Nord-Est*. Milan: Franco Angeli, 1992.
Cento Bull, Anna. "Ethnicity, Racism and the Northern League." In *Italian Regionalism*, edited by Carl Levy, 171–188. Oxford: Berg, 1996.
———. "The Politics of Industrial Districts in Lombardy: Replacing Christian Democracy with the Northern League." *The Italianist* 13 (1993): 209–229.
——— and Mark Gilbert. *The Lega Nord and the Northern Question in Italian Politics*. New York: Palgrave, 2001.
——— and Paul Corner. *From Peasant to Entrepreneur: The Survival of the Family Economy in Italy*. Oxford: Berg, 1993.
Cheles, Luciano, Ronnie Ferguson, and Michalina Vaughan, eds. *The Far Right in Western and Eastern Europe*, 2nd ed. London: Longman, 1995.
Chiarini, Roberto. "The Italian Far Right: The Search for Legitimacy." In *The Far Right in Western and Eastern Europe*, edited by Luciano Cheles. England: Longman, 1995.
Chubb, Judith. *Patronage, Power and Poverty in Southern Italy*. Cambridge: Cambridge University Press, 1982.
Cippolina, Silvia. "Una nuova fiscalità per la piccola e media impresa: Ipotesi di breve periodo." In *La società della piccola impresa. Sfide e opportunità per la piccola e media industria*, edited by Paolo Feltrin, 227–240. Treviso: Unindustria, 1996.
Clark, Martin. *Modern Italy 1871–1995*, 2nd ed. London: Longman, 1996.
CNEL. *Laboratori territoriali: competizione e leadership nella questione settentrionale*. Rome: CNEL, 1996.
Coleman, William D. and Henry J. Jacek. "Capitalists, Collective Action and Regionalism: An Introduction." In *Regionalism, Business Interests and Public Policy*, edited by William Coleman and Henry J. Jacek, 1–12. London: Sage, 1989.
Colombo, Furio and Vittorio Foa. *Il sogno di una destra normale*. Rome: Donzelli, 1995.

Compagna, Francesco and Calogero Muscara. "Regionalism and Social Change in Italy." In *Center and Periphery: Spatial Variation in Politics*, edited by Jean Gottmann, 101–109. Beverly Hills: Sage, 1980.

Dardone, Maurizio and Pietro Trifone. *La lingua italiana*. Bologna: Zanichelli, 1985.

Desideri, Carlo and Vincenzo Santantonio. "Building a Third Level in Europe: Prospects and Difficulties in Italy." *Regional and Federal Studies* 6 (Summer 1996): 96–116.

De Luna, Giovanni, ed. *Figli di un benessere minore. La Lega, 1979–1993*. Florence: La Nuova Italia, 1994.

De Mauro, Tullio. *Storia linguistica dell'Italia unita*. Bari: Laterza, 1976.

Diamanti, Ilvo. *Il male del Nord*. Rome: Donzelli, 1996.

———. "Il Nord senza Italia?" *Limes* 1 (1996): 15–30.

———. "The Northern League: From Regional Party to Party of Government." In *The New Italian Republic*, edited by Steven Grundle and Simon Parker, 113–129. London: Routledge, 1995.

——— and Paolo Segatti. "Orgogliosi di essere Italiani." *Limes* 4 (1994): 15–36.

———. *La Lega. Geografia, storia, e sociologia di un nuovo soggetto politico*. Rome: Donzelli, 1993.

———. "La mia patria e il Veneto. I valori e la proposta politica delle leghe." *Polis* (August 1992): 225–255.

Diritto regionale, 8th ed. Naples: Esselibri-Simone, 1995.

Donovan, Mark. "A Party System in Transformation: The April 1992 Italian Election." *West European Politics* 15 (1992): 170–177.

Einaudi, Luigi. "Via il prefetto!" Originally printed in *La gazzetta ticinese*, July 17, 1944. Reprinted in *Federalismo & Società* 2 (1995): 228–232.

Elazar, Daniel J. "From Statism to Federalism: A Paradigm Shift." *Publius* 25 (Winter 1995): 5–18.

Ellwood, David W. "L'occupazione e la restaurazione istituzionale: Il problema delle regioni." *Italia contemporanea* 1 (1974): 23–41.

Farneti, Paolo. *The Italian Party System (1945–1980)*. New York: St. Martin's Press, 1985.

Feltrin, Paolo, ed. *La societa della piccola impresa. Sfide e opportunità per la piccola e media industria*. Treviso: Unindustria, 1996.

Fesler, James and Donald Khel. *The Politics of the Administrative Process*. Chatham: Chatham House, 1991.

Fondazione Agnelli. "Il nostro progetto geopolitico." *Limes* 4 (1994): 147–156.

Franchetti, Leopoldo and Sidney Sonnino. *Inchiesta in Sicilia*, vol. 1. Florence: Vallechi, 1974.

Franck, L. *Il corporativismo e l'economia dell'Italia fascista*. Turin: Einaudi, 1990.

Frankel, Paul H. *Mattei: Oil and Power Politics*. London: Faber, 1966.

Fried, Robert. *The Italian Prefects*. New Haven: Yale University Press, 1963.

Fumagalli, Andrea. "Il lavoro nero nella provincia di Bergamo." Istituto di Ricerche Economiche e Sociali. Milan: November 1995. Photocopy.

Fusaro, Carlo. *Le regole della transizione. La nuova legislazione elettorale italiana.* Bologna: Il Mulino, 1995.

Gallerano, N. "L'influenza dell'amministrazione italiana sulla riorganizzazione dello stato italiano, 1943–1945." *Italia contemporanea* 1 (1974): 4–22.

Galli, Giorgio. *Mezzo secolo di DC.* Milano: Rizzoli, 1993.

—— and Daniele Comero, eds. *Partiti storici e nuove formazioni: analisi del comportamento elettorale a Milano.* Milan: Franco Angeli, 1992.

Gilbert, Mark. "Transforming Italy's Institutions? The Bicameral Committee on Institutional Reform." *Modern Italy* 3 (1998): 49–66.

——. "Warriors of the New Pontida: The Challenge of the Lega Nord to the Italian Party System." *The Political Quarterly* 64 (1993): 99–106.

Ginsborg, Paul. *A History of Contemporary Italy: Society and Politics 1943–1988.* London: Penguin, 1990.

Giordano, Benito. "The Contrasting Geographies of 'Padania': The Case of the Lega Nord in Italy." *Institute of British Geographers* 33 (2001).

Giovagnoli, Agostino. *Il partito italiano. La Democrazia Cristiana dal 1942 al 1994.* Bari: Laterza, 1996.

Golden, Miriam. *Labor Divided: Austerity and Working-Class Politics in Contemporary Italy.* Ithaca: Cornell University Press, 1988.

Gourevitch, Peter. "Reforming the Napoleonic State: The Creation of Regional Governments in France and Italy." In *Territorial Politics in Industrialized Nations*, edited by Sidney Tarrow, Peter Katzenstein, and Luigi Graziano, 28–63. New York: Praeger, 1978.

Governo Provvisorio della Padania. *Manuale di resistenza fiscale.* Gallarate, 1996.

Gramsci, Antonio. *Prison Notebooks.* New York: International Publishers, 1971.

Graziano, Luigi. "Center–Periphery Relations and the Italian Crisis: The Problem of Clientelism." In *Territorial Politics in Industrialized Nations*, edited by Sidney Tarrow, Peter J. Katzenstein, and Luigi Graziano, 290–322. New York: Praeger Publishers, 1978.

Gremmo, Roberto. *Contro Roma: storie, idee e programmi delle leghe autonomiste del Nord.* Aosta: Il Gral, 1992.

Grew, Raymond. *A Sterner Plan for Italian Unity: The Italian National Society in the Risorgimento.* Princeton: Princeton University Press, 1963.

Grote, Jürgen R. "Small Firms in the European Community: Modes of Production, Governance and Territorial Interest Representation in Italy and Germany." In *Organized Interests and the European Community*, edited by Jürgen R. Grote, Justin Greenwood, and Karsten Ronit, 119–172. London: Sage, 1992.

Gruppo Lega Nord, Senato della Repubblica. *Revisione della costituzione in senso federale.* Treviso, 1995.

——. *Lo statuto della Lega Nord Italia Federale.* Treviso, 1995.

——. *Le ragioni della Lega.* Treviso, 1994.

Hainsworth, Paul, ed. *The Extreme Right in Europe and the USA.* New York: St. Martin's Press, 1992.

Hamel, Pasquale, ed. *La regione nella nazione*. Palermo: La Zisa. 1992.
Hine, David. "Federalism, Regionalism, and the Unitary State: Contemporary Regional Pressures in Historical Perspective." In *Italian Regionalism*, edited by Carl Levy, 109–130. Oxford: Berg, 1996.
———. *Governing Italy*. Oxford: Clarendon Press, 1993.
Hirst, Paul and Jonathan Zeitlin, eds. *Reversing Industrial Decline?* Oxford: Berg, 1989.
Hobsbawm, E.J. *Primitive Rebels*. New York: W.W. Norton, 1959.
Hooghe, Liesbet and Gary Marks. "'Europe with the Regions': Channels of Regional Representation in the European Union." *Publius* 26 (Winter 1996): 73–91.
Hooper, John. "A New Italian Renaissance?" *Washington Quarterly* (Spring 1998): 66–80.
Hueglin, Thomas O. "Regionalism in Western Europe. Conceptual Problems of a New Political Perspective." *Comparative Politics* 18 (July 1986): 439–458.
Iannello, Antonio. *L'inganno federalista e l'opposizione all'ordinamento regionale nel dibattito all'Assemblea Costituente*. Naples: Vivarium, 1998.
Ignazi, Piero. *Postfascisti?* Bologna: Il Mulino, 1994.
———. *Il polo escluso*. Bologna: Il Mulino, 1989.
Ilardi, Massimo. "Analisi dei dibattiti degli organi dirigenti dei partiti (1970–1985) sulla regionalizzazione del partito come organizzazione." In *Autonomia politica regionale e sistema dei partiti*, edited by Franco Cazzola, 47–71. Milan: Dott. A. Giuffre, 1988.
Immerfall, Stefan, ed. *Territoriality in the Globalizing Society*. New York: Springer, 1998.
ISTAT. "Lingua italiana e dialetti in Italia" (March 2002) www.istat.it.
———. *Rapporto sull'Italia*. Bologna: Il Mulino, 1996.
———. *Rapporto annuale*, 1994.
———. *45 anni di elezioni in Italia, 1946–1990*. Rome: Istat, 1992.
Keating, Michael. *The New Regionalism in Western Europe: Territorial Restructuring and Political Change*. Cheltenham, U.K.: E. Elgar, 1998.
———. "The Political Economy of Regionalism." In *The Political Economy of Regionalism*, edited by Michael Keating and John Loughlin, 18–40. London: Frank Cass, 1997.
———. "Regional Autonomy in the Changing State Order: A Framework of Analysis." *Regional Politics and Policy* 2 (Autumn 1992): 45–61.
Kitschelt, Herbert. *The Radical Right in Western Europe*. Ann Arbor: University of Michigan Press, 1995.
Kramer, Jane. "Dirty Hands." *The New Yorker*, March 28, 1994.
LaPalombara, Joseph. *Interest Groups in Italian Politics*. Princeton: Princeton University Press, 1963.
———. *Democracy Italian Style*. New Haven: Yale University Press, 1987.
Lega Nord. *Programma elettorale per la Padania*. Milan, 1996.
———. *Le ragioni della Padania*. Milan, 1996.

———. *Padania, le ragioni di una nazione.* Milan, 1996. Photocopy.
———. *Gazzetta Ufficiale della Padania.* Milan, 1996.
———. *Struttura federale.* Milan, 1993. Photocopy.
———. *Analisi e proposte per una riforma radicale del fisco,* supplement to *Lega Nord* 29 (May 1993).
———. *Un'Italia federale per l'Europa del 2000,* supplement to *Lega Nord* 9 (March 1993).
———. *Portiamo Milano in Europa. Programma Milano.* Milan, 1993.
———. "L'ideologia del movimento," 1993. Photocopy.
Leonardi, Robert, "The Regional Reform in Italy: From Centralized to Regionalized State." In *The Regions and the European Community,* edited by Robert Leonardi, 217–246. London: Frank Cass, 1992.
——— and Douglas A. Wertman. *Italian Christian Democracy. The Politics of Dominance.* New York: St. Martin's Press, 1989.
———, Rafaella Nanetti and Robert Putnam. "Devolution as a Political Process: The Case of Italy." *Publius* (Winter 1981): 95–117.
Lepschy, Anna Laura, Giulio Lepschy, and Miriam Voghera. "Linguistic Variety in Italy." In *Italian Regionalism,* edited by Carl Levy, 69–80. Oxford: Berg, 1996.
Levi, Margaret. *Of Rule and Revenue.* Berkeley: University of California Press, 1988.
Lipset, Seymour M. and Stein Rokkan. "Cleavage Structures, Party Systems, and Voter Alignments." In *Party Systems and Voter Alignments: Cross National Perspectives,* edited by Seymour M. Lipset and Stein Rokkan, 1–64. New York: The Free Press, 1967.
Loughlin, John. "'Europe of the Regions' and the Federalization of Europe." *Publius* 26 (Fall 1996): 141–162.
———. "State Traditions, Administrative Reform and Regionalization." In *The Political Economy of Regionalism,* edited by Michael Keating and John Loughlin, 41–62. London: Frank Cass, 1997.
Lovett, Clara. *The Democratic Movement in Italy 1830–1876.* Cambridge: Harvard University Press, 1982.
Luvera, Bruno. "L'internazionale regionalista tra mascera e volto." *Limes* 3 (1996): 35–58.
Lyttleton, Adrian. "Shifting Identities: Nation, Region and City." In *Italian Regionalism: History, Identity, Politics,* edited by Carl Levy, 33–52. Washington: Oxford-Berg, 1996.
Machin, Howard. *The Prefect in French Administration.* New York: St. Martin's Press, 1977.
Macioti, Maria. *Gli immigrati in Italia.* Rome: Laterza, 1991.
Mack Smith, Denis. *Modern Italy: A Political History.* Ann Arbor: The University of Michigan Press, 1997.
———. *The Making of Italy 1796–1870.* New York: Harper & Row, 1968.
Maier, Charles. "Democracy and Its Discontents." *Foreign Affairs* 73 (1994): 48–64.

Manifesto delle libere regioni del Nordest in un'Italia federale. Flyer handed out at a press conference Mestre (Veneto) Town Hall (February 15, 1997).
Mannheimer, Renato. "L'opinione pubblica del Nord Italia sul localismo e il federalismo." *Federalismo & Società* 1 (1994): 65–80.
———. "L'Elettorato della Lega Nord." *Polis* 2 (August 1993).
——— and Giacamo Sani. "Electoral Trends and Political Subcultures." In *Italian Politics: A Review* vol. 1, edited by Raffaella Nanetti and Robert Leonardi, 164–175. London: Pinter, 1986.
Marongiu, Gianni. *Storia del fisco in Italia* vol. 1. Turin: Einaudi, 1995.
Marshall, Alfred. *Industry and Trade.* London: Macmillan and Co., 1919.
Mazzonis, Daniele. "The Changing Role of ERVET in Emilia-Romagna." In *Local and Regional Responses to Global Pressure: The Case of Italy and Its Industrial Districts,* edited by Francesco Cossentino, 131–142. Geneva: International Labor Organization, 1996.
McCarthy, Patrick. *The Crisis of the Italian State.* New York: St. Martins Press, 1995.
Miglio, Gianfranco and Augusto Barbera. *Federalismo e secessione: un dialogo.* Milan: Arnoldo Mondadori, 1997.
Millan, Bruce. "The Committee of the Regions: In at the Birth." *Regional & Federal Studies* 7 (Spring 1997): 5–10.
Moioli, Vittorio. *Il tarlo delle leghe.* Milan: Comedit2000, 1991.
———. *I nuovi razzismi.* Rome: Edizioni Associate, 1990.
Morlino, Leonardo. "The Changing Relationship between Parties and Society in Italy." *West European Politics* 7 (1984): 46–66.
———. "Crisis of Parties and Change of Party System in Italy." *Party Politics* 2 (January 1996): 5–30.
Morra, Gianfranco. *Breve storia del pensiero federalista.* Turin: Oscar Mondadori, 1993.
Natale, Paolo. "La nuova mappa geopolitica." In *Milano a Roma: guida all'Italia elettorale del 1994,* edited by Ilvo Diamanti and Renato Mannheimer, 85–98. Rome: Donzelli, 1994.
———. "La Lega Lombarda e insediamento territoriale." In *La Lega Lombarda,* edited by Renato Mannheimer, 83–121. Milan: Feltrinelli, 1991.
———. "Le elezioni europee del 1989 in Lombardia. Un'analisi dei flussi eletorali." *Notiziario statistico regionale* supplement to no. 59 (March 1990).
———. "Le elezioni regionali del 1990 in Lombardia. Un'analisi dei flussi elettorali." *Notiziario statistico regionale* supplement to no. 60 (April 1990).
Newhouse, John. "Europe's Rising Regionalism." *Foreign Affairs* 76 (January/February 1997): 67–84.
Norton, Alan. *International Handbook of Local and Regional Government: Comparative Analysis of Advanced Democracies.* Aldershot: Gower House, 1994.
Notter, Harley A. *Postwar Foreign Policy Preparations* (Washington, 1949).
OECD. *Territorial Reviews, Italy.* Paris: OECD, 2001.
———. *Economic Surveys, Italy.* Paris: OECD, 1999.

———. *Economic Surveys, Italy 1995–1996.* Paris: OECD, 1997.
Ohmae, Kenichi. *The End of the Nation-State: The Rise of Regional Economies.* New York: The Free Press, 1995.
———. "The Rise of the Region State." *Foreign Affairs* (Spring 1993).
Oneto, Gilberto. *L'invenzione della Padania.* Bergamo: Foedus Editore, 1997.
Parker, Simon. "Electoral Reform and Political Change in Italy, 1991–1994." In *The New Italian Republic,* edited by Stephan Grundle and Simon Parker, 40–56. London: Routledge, 1996.
Parlamento Italiano. Legge costituzionale no. 3, October 18, 2001. "Modifiche al titolo V della parte seconda della Costituzione."
Pasquino, Gianfranco. "No Longer a Party State? Institutions, Power and Problems of Italian Reform." *West European Politics* 20 (1997): 34–53.
———. "Sources of Stability and Instability in the Italian Party System." *West European Politics* 6 (1983): 93–110.
Pivetti, Irene. "Immigrazione e cooperazione." *Quaderni della consulta Cattolica.* Lega Nord, 1993.
Piore, Michael and Charles Sabel. *The Second Industrial Divide.* New York: Basic Books, 1984.
Poggi, Gianfranco. *Catholic Action in Italy: The Sociology of a Sponsored Organization.* Stanford: Stanford University Press, 1967.
Przeworski, Adam and John Sprague. *Paper Stones.* Chicago: University of Chicago Press, 1988.
Putnam, Robert. *Making Democracy Work: Civic Traditions in Modern Italy.* Princeton: Princeton University Press, 1993.
———, Robert Leonardi, and Rafaella Nanetti. *La pianta e le radici: il radicamento dell'istituto regionale nel sistema politico italiano.* Bologna: il Mulino, 1985.
Rhodes, Martin, ed. *The Regions and the New Europe.* Manchester: Manchester University Press, 1995.
Rhodes, R.A.W. and Vincent Wright. "Introduction." *West European Politics* 10 (October 1987): 1–20.
Riall, Lucy. *Sicily and the Unification of Italy: Liberal Policy and Local Power, 1859–1866.* Oxford: Clarendon Press, 1998.
Riccaboni, Angelo and Rosana Ghirri. *European Financial Reporting: Italy.* London: Routledge, 1994.
Riker, William. "Two Party Systems and Duverger's Law." *American Political Science Review* 76 (December 1982): 753–766.
Rokkan, Stein and Derek Urwin. *Economy, Territory, Identity.* London: Sage, 1983.
Romanelli, R. *Il comando impossibile: stato e soceitá nell'Italia liberale.* Bologna: Il Mulino, 1988.
———. *L'Italia liberale.* Bologna: Il Mulino, 1979.
Romeo, R. *Il Risorgimento in Sicilia.* Bari: Laterza, 1950.
Rugge, Fabio. "Le leggi Bassanini: Continuità e innovazioni del riformismo Amministrativo." *Il Mulino* 4 (1997): 717–726.
Rusconi, Gian Enrico. *Se cessiamo di essere una nazione. Tra etnodemocrazie regionali e cittadinanza europea.* Bologna: Il Mulino, 1993.

Rusinow, Dennison I. *Italy's Austrian Heritage 1919–1946.* Oxford: Clarendon Press, 1969.
Ruzza, Carlo and Oliver Schmidtke. "The Making of the Lombard League." *Telos* (Winter 1991): 57–70.
———. "Roots of Success of the Lega Lombarda: Mobilization Dynamics and the Media." *West European Politics* 16 (1993): 1–23.
Sabbatacci, Giovanni and Vittorio Vidotto. *Storia d'Italia* vol. 2, *1861–1887.* Rome: Laterza, 1994.
Sabel, Charles. "Flexible Specialization and the Re-emergence of Regional Economies." In *Reversing Industrial Decline? Industrial Structure and Policy in Britain and Her Competitors,* edited by P. Hirst and J. Zeitlin, 17–70. London: Oxford, 1989.
———. *Work and Politics.* New York: Cambridge University Press, 1982.
Sabetti, Filippo. *The Search for Good Government: Understanding the Paradox of Italian Democracy* (Montreal: McGill-Queens University Press, 2000).
Sanantonio, Enzo. "Italy." In *Central and Local Government Relations,* edited by Edward Page and Michael Goldsmith, 107–129. London: Sage, 1987.
Sartori, Giovanni. "European Political Parties: The Case of Polarized Pluralism." In *Political Parties and Political Development,* edited by Joseph LaPalombara and Myron Weiner, 137–176. Princeton: Princeton University Press, 1966.
———. *Parties and Party System.* Cambridge: Cambridge University Press, 1976.
Schain, Martin. "The National Front in France and the Construction of Political Legitimacy." *West European Politics* 10 (April 1987): 229–252.
———, Aristide Zolberg, and Patrick Hossay, ed. *Shadows Over Europe: The Development and Impact of the Extreme Right in Western Europe.* New York: Palgrave, 2002.
Schmitter, Phillippe. "Still the Century of Corporatism?" In *Trends Towards Corporatist Intermediation,* edited by Phillippe Schmitter and B. Lehmbruch. Beverly Hills: Sage, 1979.
——— and Luca Lanzalaco. "Regions and the Organization of Business Interests." In *Regionalism, Business Interests and Public Policy,* edited by William Coleman and Henry J. Jacek, 201–229. London: Sage, 1989.
Sema, Antonio. "Leghismo di confine e secessionismo nel Friuli-Venezia Giulia." *Limes* 3 (1996): 71–88.
Sharpe, L.J. "The West European State: The Territorial Dimension." *West European Politics* 10 (October 1987): 148–167.
———. *The Rise of the Meso Government in Europe.* London: Sage Publications, 1993.
Smith, B.C. *Decentralization: The Territorial Dimension of the State.* London: George Allen & Unwin, 1985.
Spotts, Frederic and Theodor Wiser. *Italy, a Difficult Democracy: A Survey of Italian Politics.* Cambridge: Cambridge University Press, 1986.
Stella, Gian Antonio. *Schei. Dal boom alla rivolta: il mitico Nordest.* Milan: Baldini & Castoldi, 1996.
———. *Dio Po: gli uomini che fecero la Padania.* Milan: Baldini & Castoldi, 1996.

Stille, Alexander. "Italy's Bribery Scandals." *Italian Journal* 6 (1992): 19–20.
Taguieff, Pierre-Andrè. "From Race to Culture. The New Right's View of European Identity." *Telos* (Winter/Fall 1993–1994): 99–125.
Tarchi, Marco. "The Lega Nord." In *Regionalist Parties in Western Europe*, edited by Lieven de Winter and Hüri Tursan. London: Routledge, 1998.
Tarrow, Sidney. "Introduction." In *Territorial Politics in Industrial Nations*, edited by Sidney Tarrow, Peter Katzenstein, and Luigi Graziano, 1–27. New York: Praeger, 1978.
——. "Local Constraints on Regional Reform: A Comparison of Italy and France." *Comparative Politics* 7 (October 1974): 1–36.
Tattara, Giuseppe and Fabio Occari. "Struttura e organizzazione del sistema produttivo Veneto nell'ultimo quindicennio." In *La società della piccola impresa*, edited by Paolo Feltrin, 97–142. Treviso: Unindustria Treviso, 1996.
Trigilia, Carlo. "Italy: The Political Economy of a Regionalized Capitalism." *South European Society & Politics* 2 (Winter 1997): 52–79.
——. "A Tale of Two Districts: Work and Politics in the Third Italy." In *Small and Medium Sized Enterprises*, edited by Arnoldo Bagnasco and Charles Sabel, 31–50. London: Pinter, 1995.
——. *Sviluppo senza autonomia*. Bologna: Il Mulino, 1994.
——. "The Paradox of the Region: Economic Regulation and the Representation of Interests." *Economy and Society* 20 (August 1991): 306–327.
——. *Grandi partiti e piccole imprese*. Bologna: Il Mulino, 1986.
Turani, Giuseppe. *Il secondo miracolo economico Italiano*. Milan: Sperling and Kupfer, 1986.
Urwin, Derek W. and Stein Rokkan. *Economy Territory Identity*. London: Sage, 1983.
——. *The Politics of Territorial Identity*. London: Sage, 1982.
Valiani, Leo. Interviewed by Paolo Bertaccini. In *Federalismo & Società* 2 (1995): 83–88.
Veneziani, Marcello. *La rivoluzione conservatrice in Italia*. Varese: Sugarco Edizioni, 1994.
Venturini, Umberto. "Political and Economic Turmoil." *Italian Journal* 6 (1992): 8–11.
Veugelers, John W.P. "Recent Immigration Politics in Italy: A Short Story." In *The Politics of Immigration in Western Europe*, edited by Martin Baldwin-Edwards and Martin Schain. Portland: Frank Cass, 1994.
Vimercati, Daniele. *I lombardi alla nuova crociata: La Lega dall' esordio al trionfo*. Milan: Mursia, 1990.
Vitale, Alessandro. "Il federalismo di 'Giustizia e Libertà.'" *Federalismo & Società* 2 (1995): 89–94.
——. "Il federalismo de 'Il Cisalpino.'" *Federalismo & Società* 2 (1995): 95–98.
Walston, James. *The Mafia and Clientelism*. London: Routledge, 1988.
Waters, Sarah. "'Tangentopoli' and the Emergence of a New Political Order in Italy." *West European Politics* 17 (January 1994): 169–182.

Wild, Sarah. "The Northern League: The Self-Representation of Industrial Districts in Their Search for Regional Power." *Politics* 17 (1997): 95–100.

Weiss, Linda. *Creating Capitalism: The State and Small Business Since 1945*. London: Basil Blackwell, 1988.

Wilensky, Harold. "Leftism, Catholicism, and Democratic Corporatism: The Role of Political Parties in Recent Welfare State Development." In *The Development of Welfare States in Europe and America*, edited by Peter Flora and Arnold Heidenheimer. New Brunswick, N.J.: Transaction Publishers, 1984.

Woods, Dwayne. "The Crisis of Center–Periphery Integration in Italy and the Rise of Regional Populism." *Comparative Politics* 27 (January 1995): 187–203.

———. "The Center No Longer Holds: The Rise of the Regional Leagues in Italian Politics." *West European Politics* 15 (April 1992): 56–76.

Zarisky, Raphael. *Italy: The Politics of Uneven Development*. Hinsdale: The Dryden Press, 1972.

Index

8 of Venice, 1–2, 114

ACLI, 56, 61
Action party, 42–3, 46, 116
administrative system; centralization of, 7–8, 15–22, 28–36; crisis of, 8–9, 116; laws of, 33–4, 118; Napoleonic origins of, 8, 11, 17, 20, 35, 37; piedmontization of, 23–5; reform of, 116–21, 124; southernization of, 34–6, 64–5, 72
Albanian immigrants, 83, 85, 126
ALIA, 82–3, 94, 111
Alleanza Nazionale (AN); and devolution, 116, 121; formation of, 99; and immigration, 127; and the Lega, 101–2, 107, 109
Alleanza Nord, 86, 134
Allum, P.A., 50
Almirante, Giorgio, 61
ANCI (National Association of Italian Communes), 116
Andreotti, Giulio, 89
antiparty sentiment, 87–8, 90–1, 97–8, 125
anti-southern sentiment, 41, 83, 93
artisans, 65, 73–5, 94–5; and the Lega, 82, 110–11
assistenzialismo, 93
Austria, 13–14, 125–6, 130; and Alto Adige conflict, 32, 40, 49
avviso di garanzia, 89, 90, 102

Baden-Württemberg, 7, 67–8
Bank of Italy, 21, 33

Barbarossa, Federico I, 81
Basque region, 6, 103
Bassanini I law, 117–21
Bassolino, Antonio, 116
Bergamo, 56, 67, 86, 89, 121
Berlin Wall, 99
Berlusconi, Silvio, 99–104, 126, 152(n.1)
Bianco, Enzo, 116
bicameral committee for reform, 114–16, 121
Bologna, 48, 62
Boso, Ermino, 85
Bossi, Umberto; corruption accusations, 103; and the economy, 83; and globalization, 128; judicial scrutiny of, 109; leadership of, 2, 86–7, 108; xenophobia of, 4, 84, 127
Bourbons, 13–14, 22–4, 27, 29–30, 138(n. 48)
Bovezzo, 85
Brescia, 56

Cacciari, Massimo, 105, 113–14
Camicie Verdi, see Green Shirts
Camorra, 29
Campania, 63, 66, 69
Carta di Chivasso, 38
Casa delle Libertà, 125–7, 133
Cassa per il Mezzogiorno (fund for the South), 53, 57–8, 67
Catalonia, 7, 67, 103
Catholic Action, 28, 55–7, 62
Catholic movement, 55, 57

Catholic subculture, 56–7, 59, 74, 144(n. 19); demobilization of, 61–2, 77, 100, 124; and the Lega, 80, 100
Cattaneo, Carlo, 25
Cattaneo Institute, 56, 149(n. 38)
Cavour, Count Camillo, 14, 16–17, 22, 25–7, 29, 35
CCD–CDU (Christian Democratic Center/Union), 92, 132–3
CGIA, 94
CGIL, 62, 76, 89
Chamber of Deputies, 20, 86, 91, 100–2, 109, 131–2
Charles, King, 15
Chiesa, Mario, 89–90
Christian Democratic party (DC); anti-communism of, 45–6; and the Catholic movement, 55–7; clientelist networks of, 9–10, 57–60, 63–6, 72, 89, 123; and the Constituent Assembly, 42–5; decline of, 91–2, 99, 113, 124; electoral support for, 46, 131; hegemony of, 2, 46, 100; and the Lega, 80, 82, 86, 97–8; membership of, 59, 144(n. 19); and regional reform, 49, 51–2; and small–medium enterprises, 74–8, 92, 124; southernization of, 62–3, 80; and state centralization, 37, 46–7, 51–2
Cipolletta, Innocenzo, 73
CISL, 56, 61–2
civil servants, 33, 117–18; and regional reform, 48; southern origins of, 34, 64–5
Clean Hands, *see Mani Pulite* trials
clientelism; and the economy (North), 75–7, 124; and the economy (South), 9, 57–9, 64–7; origins of, 31, 35; and party organization, 52, 59–60, 63–4; and regional divisions, 10, 78, 123

CLNs (Committees for National Liberation), 38
Coldiretti, 59
Commencini, Fabrizio, 125
Committee of the Regions, 5, 96–7
Communist party (PCI); and the Constituent Assembly, 42–4; electoral support for, 46, 131; local governance of, 48, 98; and regional reform, 47–9; and small–medium enterprises, 75–8; *see also* Democratic Left (DS)
Como, 56, 86, 121
Confcommercio, 104
Confederation of Industry, 73, 76
Conference of Regional Presidents, 115
Conference on State and Communes, 117
Conference on State and Regions, 117
Confindustria, *see* Confederation of Industry
Constituent Assembly, 39, 42–5, 116
constitution, 3, 8, 16, 26, 38–40, 42, 109, 115; reform bill, 120–1; and the regions, 44–5, 47–51; *see also* Constituent Assembly
Constitution of the North, 103
corporatist policies (postwar), 76–8, 83, 124
corporatist state, 8, 32, 38
corruption, political 59, 64, 89–90, 103
Corsica, 6, 80
Craxi, Bettino, 46, 63, 81, 88–91
crime, 4, 85, 95, 102, 110
Crispi, Francesco, 30–2
Croatia, 6
Czechoslovakia, 6, 104

da Giussano, Alberto, 81
dalla Chiesa, Nando, 109, 151(n. 20)
De Benoist, Alain, 4

decentralization; definition of, 17–18; Europe, 5–6; *see also* reforms, devolutionary
deficit, 8, 20, 116
De Gaspari, Alcide, 39
delegislation decrees, 118
Democratic Left (DS), 92, 149(n. 49); constitutional reform bill, 120–1; electoral support for, 132–3; and small–medium enterprises, 77–8, 98; and Ulivo coalition, 101
Depretis, Agostino, 31
Destra, *see* Right party
dialects, linguistic, 14, 81–2, 87, 147(n. 7); in the Veneto, 80–1, 128
Di Pietro, Antonio, 89–90, 152(n. 1)

economic and industrial conditions; North, 23, 40, 66–9, 70–4, 113; Northeast vs. Northwest, 69–70; South, 64–7
Economist magazine, 73
education, 8, 71, 117; of Lega voters, 110–12
Einaudi, Luigi, 37–8, 43
elections, recent, 99–102, 104–5, 125–6, 131–4
electoral system, reform of, 88, 100–1, 113, 126
electoral turnout, 148(n. 31)
Emanuelle II, Vittorio, 15–16
Emilia-Romagna; economic conditions in, 66, 68–70, 78; Lega Emiliano-Romagnola, 86; local governance in, 48, 142(n. 42)
enti pubblici (special agencies), 33, 89
entrepreneurs; and industrial districts, 68; and the Lega, 82–3, 92, 94, 110–11, 127; and the Northern Question, 9, 70, 72–4, 113, 129; and the North–South divide, 23, 65; political orientation of, 75, 124; and recent reforms, 117–18; *see also* industrialists
Eritrea, 32
Euro, 8, 96
Eurobarometer polls, 87, 96
European Economic Community (EEC), 8, 96
European Federalist Movement, 38
European integration, *see* European Union
European Parliament, elections for, 79, 86, 102, 125, 134, 148(n. 24)
European Union (EU); convergence criteria of, 8, 116; and federalism, 39; opposition to, 128–9; and regional divisions, 96–7; and regional mobilization, 5–7; sanctions, 125–6
Exchange Rate Mechanism, Italy's exit from, 96
exports, northeastern, 70, 96

Fasci Siciliani, 39
fascism; and regional divisions, 35–6, 41–2; and state centralization, 32–4; transition from, 37–8, 43
federalism; and the Lega, 5, 83, 92–3, 125; nineteenth century debates, 8, 25–6; postwar debates, 38–9, 42–4
Federation of Industry (Federindustria), 72
Ferrari, Giuseppe, 25
Fiat, 23, 40, 75
Fini, Gianfranco, 99
First World War, 40
fiscal federalism, 51–2, 113, 118–20
fiscal system; centralized nature of, 11, 20–2, 24, 28–9, 51–2, 73–4; complexity of, 72–3, 78; recent reform of, 116, 118–20; regional imbalance of, 3, 9–10, 71–2
Florence, 21, 24, 62

Forza Italia (FI); electoral support for, 132; emergence of, 99; and the Lega, 100–2, 104, 125, 128
Four Motors of Europe, 7, 67
Freedom Party (Austria), 4, 125, 130
French Revolution, 14
Friuli-Venezia Giulia, 40, 48, 56, 62, 142(n. 43); economic conditions in, 66–70, 74; support for the Lega in, 105, 125, 134

Gardini, Raul, 90, 103
Garibaldi, Giuseppe, 13, 29, 30, 36
Gava, Antonio, 77
GDP, regional, 66
gender, 112
Genoa, economic conditions in, 40, 67, 69–70
genocide, 44
Gentilini, Giancarlo, 126
Germany, 15, 45, 104, 119; and small–medium enterprises, 67–8, 75
Ginsborg, Paul, 58
Giustizia e Libertà, 38, 43
globalization; economic impact of, 70, 111; opposition to, 127–8, 152(n. 5); and regional divisions, 6–7, 129, 136(n. 9); and xenophobic parties, 129–30
Governo Provvisorio per L'Indipendenza della Padania, 108
Gramsci, Antonio, 32, 138(n. 48)
Green party formations, 101, 131–3
Green Shirts, 108–9, 114
Guardia Nazionale Padana, see Green Shirts
Guidi, Guidalberto, 72

Haider, Jörge, 2, 125–6

L'Idea Nazionale, 32
illiteracy, 14
immigration; in Europe, 4–5, 130; and the Lega, 83–5, 95, 97, 126–8; legislation, 84, 126–7; and the MSI, 84, 147(n. 18); of southern Italians, 41
INAIL, 58
industrial districts; and the Lega, 91–2, 97; regional concentration of, 9–10, 68–70, 123; *see also* small–medium enterprises
industrialists, 22–3, 82, 103, 113, 127, 138(n. 48); *see also* entrepreneurs
INEA, 33
INPS, 58
Institutional Reform and Devolution, ministry of, 126
International Association for the Defense of Threatened Languages and Cultures, 80
IRAP (*Imposta regionale sulle attività produttive*), 118–20
IRER, 74
IRI, 33
Iron Curtain, 45
Irpinia, 59
irredentism, 32, 38, 40
Islam, 127
Italian Social Movement (MSI); electoral support for, 57, 60–1, 131; and immigration, 84, 147(n. 18); and the regions, 47; transformation of, 99; *see also* Alleanza Nazionale (AN)

Jutland (Denmark), 68

kickbacks, 5, 58, 89, 91, 103
Kingdom of Italy; formation of, 13–15; financial situation of, 20–2
Kingdom of the Two Sicilies, 24

labor legislation, 41
Lateran Treaty (Concordat), 15
Left party, 20, 30–2
Lega Lombarda, 81–5

Lega Nord; coalition partners, 101–2, 125–6; decline of, 125–6; and European integration, 96–7, 128; and federalism, 5, 83, 92–3; formation of, 86–7; and globalization, 127–9; and immigration, 83–5, 95, 97, 126–8; leadership of, 87; and the local economy, 82–3, 91–2, 94–5, 97–8, 105, 113, 127; membership of, 88–9; organizations of, 89; and secession, 82, 87, 92, 103–5, 106–8; social base of, 110–12; tax revolts of, 93–5; and vigilante groups (*ronde*), 85

Legnano, 81

Le Pen, Jean-Marie, 2, 4

liberalism, 16, 19, 20, 22

Liberal party (PLI), 42–4, 46, 92, 131

Libya, 32

LIFE (*Liberi imprenditori federalisti europei*), 73, 114, 146(n. 56)

Liga Fronte Veneto, 125

Liga Veneta, 79–82, 85–6, 125, 148(n. 24); electoral support for, 131, 134

Liguria, 23–4, 134; economic conditions in, 66, 68–9; Union Ligure, 86

Lira, 21; devaluation of, 70, 96

local government, *see* regions, Italian

Lombardy; Catholic subculture in, 55–6, 62–3; *convocato degli estimati*, 18; economic conditions in, 7, 66–9; and the Lega, 2, 81–2, 85–6, 89, 91–2, 105, 107, 125, 134; *Movimento Autonomista Padano*, 41; during the Risorgimento, 13, 18, 23–4, 26, 28; secessionist tendencies in, 106

Lussu, Emilio, 38–9, 43

Maastricht Treaty, 96–7, 116
macinato (Gristmill tax), 21

Mack Smith, Denis, 29

Mafia, 29, 34, 59, 77, 83, 93, 109

Mani Pulite trials, 89–92, 102, 125; failure of, 152(n. 1)

March on the Po, 106–8

Marcos, subcommander, 114

Maroni, Roberto, 102

Marshall aid, 46

Miglio, Gianfranco, 93

Milan; corruption in, 89–90, 103; electoral campaigns in, 95–7, 100, 109

Minghetti, Marco, 26–7, 35

Minimum Tax, 93–5, 111, 149(n. 55)

Modena, 13, 48

Monarchists, 42, 47, 57, 60, 131

Montedison Group, 75, 90

Movement of the Mayors, 112–13, 116

MSI, *see* Italian Social Movement

multiculturalism, 4, 84, 128, 130

Mussolini, Benito, 32–5, 37–8, 41

Naples, 21, 29, 60, 62, 77, 116

Napoleonic administrative system, *see* administrative system

National Front, French, 4, 129

NATO, 120

Nazi-Fascist regime, 41, 44

'Ndrangheta, 29

Negri, Toni, 148(n. 32)

neo-fascists, *see* Italian Social Movement (MSI)

New Right, *see* Nouvelle Droite

North Africa, 4, 83

Northern Question, 9, 71–4, 97, 113, 124

Nouvelle Droite, 4

OECD, 51, 71, 117, 119

Olivetti, 23, 75

Osservatore Romano, 108

Padania, 103, 106, 127; referendum for, 107–8

Padani Imprenditori Uniti (PIU), 111; see also ALIA
Palermo, 39, 62
Papal States, 14–5, 25
Parlamento del Nord, 108
Parma, 13, 48
partitocrazia, 91, 93, 124
party cartels, 101, 133, 150(n. 6)
Party of the Northeast, 113–14
Patelli, Alessandro, 103
patronage, see clientelism
peasants, 18, 29–30, 36, 83
pensions, 34; disability, abuse of, 58–9
Pica Law, 29
Piedmont; economic conditions in, 41, 55, 66–9; and the Lega, 81, 134; *Movimento Autonomista Regionale Piemontese* (MARP), 41, 83; Piemont Autonomista, 86; during the Risorgimento, 13–18, 21–4, 26, 29, 35
Piedmontization, 23
Pillitteri, Paolo, 90
Pirelli, 23, 75
Pivetti, Irene, 102–3
Polo coalitions, 101–4, 133
Pontida, 103
Popular Front, 46, 49, 131
Popular party; pre-war, 43, 63; since 1994 (PPI), 92, 132
populist Right parties, 2, 4–5, 11, 84–5, 111, 125–6, 129–30
Poujade, Pierre, 60
prefect; piedmontization of, 23–4; powers of, 17–20, 30–3, 46–7; southernization of, 34
preference votes, 60, 88
Processo alla Lega, 128, 152(n. 5)
Prodi, Romano, 104
proportional representation (PR), 100–1, 132, 150(n. 6)
prostitution, 95
Provincial Administrative Junta, 30
Prussia, 14–15

public administration, see administrative system
public debt; during the Risorgimento, 20–1, 24; during the 1990s, 124
Puglia, 63, 66, 69
Putnam, Robert, 10, 50, 142(n. 42)

Quebec, 104, 107

racism, 4, 5, 84
Radical party, 87–8, 131, 148(n. 32)
Rattazi, Urbano, 19
Red Belt, 48, 56, 63
Red Brigades, 1, 148(n. 32)
referendums; constitutional (devolution), 3, 120–1; electoral law, 101; independence of Padania, 107–8; preference votes, 88; public funding of political parties, 90–1; republican, 42
reforms, devolutionary, 116–21, 124–5
Reggio di Calabria, 61
Reggio Emilia, 48
regionalism; in Europe, 5–7, 79, 103–4, 129–30; in wealthy regions, 6–7
regional states, 136(n. 9)
regions, Italian; control committees, 47; formation of, 44–5; and local identity, 27; nineteenth century debates on, 26–8; opposition to, 45–7; and party organization, 52; reform of (1970s), 49–50; reform of (1990s), 116–21; weakness of, 50–2; *see also under individual names*
regions with special statutes, 48–50, 52, 74, 80, 143(n. 53)
Repubblica del Nord, 86
Repubblica Partigiana, 38
Republic of Venice, 1
Republican party (PRI), 46, 131

Resistance, anti-fascist, 38, 41–4, 93, 140(n. 5)
Rhône Alpes, 7, 67
Rifondazione communista (RC), 92, 101, 121, 131–3, 149(n. 38)
Right party, 16–17, 20, 30–1, 37; fiscal policies of, 21–2
Risorgimento; legacies of, 11, 35–6; and national identity, 14–15; origins of, 13–14; see also unification of Italy
Rocchetta, Franco, 79–81
Rossano (Veneto), 70
Rosselli, Carlo, 38

Salò, Republic of, 41, 60
Salvemini, Gaetano, 141(n. 30)
San Marco Square, 1, 114
Sardinia, 13, 48, 59, 66, 80; Partito Sardo d'Azione (PSd'A), 39, 80
Savoy Dynasty, 14, 17
Schei, 70
Schelba Law, 47, 49
Scotland, 5
secession; postwar movements, 39–40, 44, 48; public opinion, 105–6; threats by the Lega, 82, 87, 92, 103–5, 106–8
Second World War, 40
Segato, Giuseppe, 1
Segni, Mario, 88
senate, 49, 86, 101
September 11th, 120, 128
Seveso, 85
Sicily; autonomy of, 48, 143(n. 53), 149(n. 51); economic conditions in, 66; and the Lega, 93; *Movimento per L'indipendenza della Sicilia* (Sicilian Independence Movement), 39; during the Risorgimento, 13, 22, 24, 29
Silicon Valley, 68
Sindacato Padano, 89, 111
Sinistra, see Left party
Slovenia, 6, 39

small–medium enterprises; challenges to, 9, 71–3, 94, 118, 146(n. 56); and the Christian Democrats (DC), 74–7; and the Communist party (PCI/DS), 77–8; growth and success of, 67–70; and the Lega, 82–3, 103, 124; see also industrial districts
SMEs, see small–medium enterprises
Social Democratic party (PSDI), 46, 92, 131
Socialist party (PSI), 42, 75; and the Christian Democrats (DC), 49, 76; decline of, 92; southernization of, 63–4
Somalia, 32
South-Tyrol, see Trentino-Alto Adige
Southern Question, 22, 66
Soviet Union, 46
Spadolini, Giovanni, 46
Spain, 6–7, 67, 103
Staller, Iona ("Ciccolina"), 148(n. 32)
state, see administrative system
state holding companies, 8, 58, 64; see also under individual names
state infrastructure, problems of, 73–4, 113
Statuto Albertino (Albertine Statute), 15–16
Stella, Gian Antonio, 70
Stille, Alexander, 90
Sturzo, Luigi, 43, 141(n. 30)
subsidiary, principle of, 117
Südtiroler Volkspartei (SVP), 80, 131, 143(n. 7)
Sweden, 68

tangenti, see kickbacks
tariffs, 23, 129
Tarrow, Sidney, 50
Tatarstan, 6
taxation, see fiscal system
Tax Day, 104
tax evasion, 75
terrorism, 1, 102, 128

Third Italy, 68–70, 77–8, 98
Thousands volunteer army, 13, 29
Togliatti, Palmiro, 44
Tognoli, Carlo, 90
Torchiani, Alberto, 38
trasformismo, 31
Treaty of St. Germaine, 40
Trentino-Alto Adige, 3, 48, 56, 80, 106, 134; conflict over, 32, 40, 49; economic conditions in, 66–70, 74
Treviso, 79, 121, 126
Trieste, 32, 40, 49
tripartite agreements, 76–7
Truman Doctrine, 45
Turin, 40–1, 62, 67
Tuscany; Alleanza Toscana, 86; economic conditions in, 66, 69; during the Risorgimento, 13, 18, 23

UIL, 62, 76
Ulivo, 101, 104, 108, 115, 125, 133; reforms of, 116–21
unemployment; in the South, 22, 29, 34, 60–1, 65–6; in the North, 69–70
unification of Italy; northern bias of, 22–5; southern revolts during, 29–30; and state centralization, 8, 15–17, 20–2, 25–8; top-down nature of, 14–16; *see also* Risorgimento
Union Valdôtaine, 79–80, 131
Unione Nord Occidentale dei Laghi Prealpini (UNOLPA), 81
Unione per L'Europa Federalista, 148(n. 24)

United Conference on State-Regions-Communes, 117
United Kingdom, 5, 101
United States, 46
L'Uomo Qualunque party, 60

Valle d'Aosta, 3, 38, 48, 79–80, 121, 134; economic conditions in, 66, 68
Varese, 81, 86, 149(n. 49)
Vatican, 15, 56; and the Lega, 107–8, 127–8
Veneta Serenissima Repubblica, *see* 8 of Venice
Venetian dialect, 70, 79, 80–1, 128
Veneto, the; Catholic subculture in, 55–6, 62; economic conditions in, 66–70, 73–4, 78, 105, 113; and the Lega, 86, 100, 105–6, 114, 121, 125–8, 134; and the Liga Veneta, 79–82; and regional identity, 27, 80, 128–9; during the Risorgimento, 13, 15, 28; secessionist tendencies in, 1–2, 105
Venice, 1, 25, 62, 105–6, 113–14
Vento dal Nord, 84
Verona, 121
Via il prefetto, 38, 43
Vicenza, 79, 121

Wales, 5
welfare, 8, 33, 58, 74, 84, 101
WTO, 129

Young Industrialists, organization of, 127
Yugoslavia, 6, 40, 49, 104